SO-AUR-142

IRS Mileage Rates for 2005 & 2006:

Business rate: 2005 - **40½¢** until August 31, increased to **48½¢** Sept. 1 through Dec. 31, 2005. Rate for 2006 - **44½¢**.

Medical & moving mileage rate: 2005 - **14¢**, increased to **22¢** Sept. 1 through Dec. 31, 2005. The rate for 2006 - **15¢**.

Contribution rate: 2005 & 2006 - **14¢**. Volunteers can be reimbursed at the business rate if they adequately account to the organization, however, the IRS is proposing to discontinue this in the future.

We Encourage you to Utilize the Internal Revenue Services's Web Site. At **www.irs.gov**, click on "IRS Publications and Forms". Choose "Publications or Forms," click on it. **Find** the form or publication that you need, click on "Retrieve Selected Files," one more click on the PDF file and it shows on the screen, click on the printer and you have a hard copy! **Any time you see a web site in the text, you can access more in depth forms and information.**

Health Savings Accounts: Health Savings Accounts (HSAs), beginning January 1, 2004, allow deductible contributions to be set aside to cover medical expenses that are not covered by a high deductible medical policy. A custodial account can be established with any institution qualified to be the custodian of an IRA.

Parsonage Allowance FRV Limitation Codified: Congress passed the "Clergy Housing Allowance Clarification Act of 2002", and the fair rental value computation is now codified in Sec. 107. (See Chapter Two for a more complete discussion.)

Sale of principal residence exclusion for sales after May 6, 1997: Allows homeowners to exclude tax on gain of up to $250,000 if single and up to $500,000 if married and filing jointly. (See Chapter Two for more complete discussion.)

Earned Income Credit Increased for some taxpayers. Since 2002, "earnings" for earned income credit does not include Sec. 403(b) contributions, Sec. 401(k) contributions, Sec. 125 Cafeteria plans, etc. Tax-free parsonage allowance will be included as earnings for some ministers and not for others. Be sure and study Chapter 3, page 73.

Child Tax Credit: In addition to the 2005 exemption of $3,200 for each dependent child, the Child Tax Credit is a non-refundable credit against federal taxes. The **2005** credit is **$1,000** per child. (2006 to 2010 - $1,000) An eligible child must be **under the age of 17 by the close of the year** in which the credit is claimed. The child must also be your dependent child, grandchild, stepchild, or foster child. The phaseout threshold of modified adjusted gross income for joint filers is $110,000; single or head of household filers is $75,000; married separate filers is $55,000. Taxpayers with unused child tax credit may qualify for the refundable Additional Child Tax Credit under some rather complex rules.

IRA Contributions: Total **individual** contributions to all IRAs (regular & Roth) for **2005** cannot exceed **$4,000**, or **$4,500** if you are 50 or older by the end of the year. (2006 - $4,000, plus $1,000 catch up) IRA contributions limits will increase to $5,000, plus $1,000 catch up by year 2008. For active participants in employer's plans the phaseout threshold of income increases annually until 2007. The **2005** range for single taxpayers is $50,000 to $60,000, for married taxpayers filing joint is $75,000 to $85,000. An active participant spouse does not keep the non-active participant spouse from making a deductible contribution. Distributions from an IRA for up to $10,000 of first time home buyer expenses and for higher education costs will not be subject to the 10% early withdrawal penalty.

Roth IRAs: Contributions to a Roth IRA are not deductible, but distributions of money held in the account for five years or longer, in addition to other requirements, are tax free when distributed.

Paying For Education: Education tax planning is very important. Several provisions are available to help offset the cost for you, your spouse or your children's college education. Among the provisions are the HOPE and Lifetime Learning credits that allow a credit for tuition and related expenses, Coverdell Education Savings Accounts, rules for qualified tuition programs, penalty-free withdrawals from regular IRAs for education expenses, exclusion for employer-provided assistance, deductions for interest on education loans, and an above-the-line deduction for qualified higher education expenses. (See "Education," in Chapter Three for a more complete discussion.)

Contribution Substantiation: Since 1993, any donor who makes a cash contribution of **$250** or more must obtain substantiation of the contribution from the donee to obtain a deduction. Each contribution is viewed separately. All contributions made on the same date, however, should be combined for purposes of determining if the donor has exceeded the $250 level. The taxpayer donor must be given the statement by the donee the **earlier** of the date his tax return is filed or the due date of the return (including extensions).

Include on the statement: (1) Date gift was given, (2) Name of donor, (3) Name and address of donee organization, (4) The $ amount if cash or a simple description if property (5) One of these statements: "Only intangible religious benefits were received by the donor."**or** "Value of tangible benefit donor received was $_____."

IRS Publication 526, "Charitable Contributions" and **IRS Publication 1771**, "Charitable Contributions Substantation and Disclosure Requirements," have complete details. Treasurers and members of an organization's financial board **must download and read** these IRS Pubs from **www.irs.gov** every year.

Contribution Substantiation for Vehicles Donated to Charity - Effective January 1, 2005: A charitable deduction under Sec. 170(a) will be denied to any taxpayer who donates a vehicle, boat, or airplane and fails to obtain a written acknowledgement from the donee, unless the claimed value is $500 or less.

The amount deductible will be the gross sales price when the **organization sells** the donated vehicle. Within 30 days of sale, the donee must furnish an acknowledgement statement to the IRS and to the donor. Include on the statement: (1) the name and taxpayer identification number of the donor , (2) the vehicle identification number. (3) a certification that the vehicle was sold in an arm's length transaction between unrelated parties, (4) The gross proceeds from the sale, and (5) a statement that the deductible amount may not exceed the amount of such gross proceeds.

The amount deductible will be the blue book value (determined by the donor) when the **organization retains** the vehicle for its usage. Within 30 days of the transfer, the donee must furnish an acknowledgement statement to the IRS and to the donor. Include on the statement: (1), (2) and (3) a certification of the intended use and the intended duration of such use and, (4) a certification that the vehicle would not be transferred in exchange for money, other property, or services before completion of such use or improvement.

IRS has released now Form 1098-C, Contributions of Motor Vehicles, Boats, and Airplanes. The form is used by donee organizations to report the contribution of qualified vehicles to the IRS under new IRC section 170(f)(12). The form may also be used to provide the donor with a contemporaneous written acknowledgment of the contribution.

Worth's Income Tax Guide

for

Ministers

2006 Edition

(For Preparing 2005 Tax Returns)

B.J. Worth

Evangel Publishing House

Nappanee, Indiana 46550

Evangel Publishing House
P.O. Box 189
Nappanee, Indiana 46550-0189

Toll-Free Order Line: (800) 253-9315
www.evangelpublishing.com

ISBN 1-928915-68-X
ISSN 1528-1353

NOTICE

This book is also available in digital format on CD-ROM disk (ISBN 1-928915-69-8). For more information, please contact Evangel Publishing House.

This publication is designed to provide accurate and authoritative information in regard to the subject matter covered. If legal advice or other expert assistance is required, the services of a competent professional person should be sought. It will be most important to check for any changes in interpretations, rulings, or technical corrections made by Congress and the IRS.

Printed in the United States of America

9 8 7 6 5 4 3 2 1

Foreword

My name is B.J. Worth, founder and owner of Worth Tax & Financial Service. My staff and I are excited to be celebrating the **33ⁿᵈ anniversary** of doing taxes in Winona Lake/Warsaw, IN area this spring of 2006!

I am blessed with a very experienced staff of tax consultants and customer service specialists. One of the most sought after designations for a tax consultant is that of becoming an EA. To become "enrolled to practice before the IRS" one must sit for a two-day exam administered annually by the IRS and meet continuing education requirements. Worth Tax & Financial Service is privileged to have four tax accountants who have the designation of EA.

Having published **"Worth's Income Tax Guide for Ministers"** since 1973 and the **"Professional Tax Record Book"** since 1982, we have a large clientele of ministers from all over the world! Many of you use more than one auto for business and needed a smaller log book for each auto. Our **"Auto Log"** book is shown on page 141 for $5.99. It contains the two auto sections from the "Professional Tax Record Book."

Taxpayers need us and we need taxpayers. Our two-fold goal is to keep our clients' taxes to a minimum and to maximize their earning power. When congress passes new tax legislation in complex language, it is imperative that you as a taxpayer let our professional preparers help you through the maze.

You will find references to Internal Revenue Code Sections, Revenue Rulings, court cases, IRS Publications, etc. throughout this publication. Quotations of important portions of tax law and regulations are included to give you confidence in what you read and learn.

It is necessary for us to update **"Worth's Income Tax Guide for Ministers"** each year. So we must strongly encourage you to READ EACH NEW EDITION carefully in order for you to be able to apply the law changes to your situation.

A minister quite often has difficulty teaching and communicating to the church officials how they, the employer, can assist him in paying the least amount of tax legally possible. A one hour tape presentation of **"Minister's Compensation Package, Tax & Financial Planning,"** is available to share the basic information with your financial committee. We encourage you to take advantage of our "Tax Preparation by Mail" service and our comprehensive payroll service. Detailed information is given at the end of the book.

We want to be your tax professional! We would love to meet you in person at one of our seminars.

- B.J. Worth, EA, ATA, CTP

The National Republican Congressional Committee's

Business Advisory Council

2004 Businesswoman of the Year

presented to

Beverly Worth

In recognition of meritorious service as an Honorary Chairman of the Business Advisory Council and for outstanding support of President Bush and the Republican Party.

Tom Reynolds
Chairman, NRCC

On March 14-15, 2005, I was privileged to attend 2005 Tax Reform Workshop in Washington DC!

It was an exciting day on the 15th. During the day many from all of the States were presented certificates as "2004 Businesswoman of the Year". Of course the men were presented certificates as "2004 Businessman of the Year".

In the evening we had dinner with President Bush. He was the keynote speaker. The meal was awesome and the music was great. There was a lot of good energy in the room.

Thanks for letting me share it with you. As a client or as a person who has been helped by the information of "Worth's Income Tax Guide for Ministers" you have helped us grow. To serve you is our ministry. God Bless You and God Bless America!

Table of Contents

TABLE OF CONTENTS

## CHAPTER ONE

Income and Fringe Benefits

Employees of churches and integral agencies of churches are divided into two classifications: the dual-status minister and the lay employee. It is important to determine the proper status of each employee when they are employed. To qualify for the unique **dual-status** tax treatment an employee of a church or an integral agency of a church must be performing ministerial duties. These duties include preaching, teaching, evangelism, conduct of worship, administration, baptisms, weddings, funerals, and communions. In J.M. Ballinger, U.S. Court of Appeals, 10th Circuit, No. 82-1928, 3/7/84, it was stated, "We interpret Congress' language providing for an exemption for any individual who is 'a duly ordained, commissioned, or licensed minister of a church' to mean that **the triggering event** is the assumption of the duties and functions of a minister." Therefore, with or without formal credentials, the date of hire becomes an important date at which the unique dual-status tax treatment begins.

Dual-status tax treatment means that the minister is an **employee** for income reporting, fringe benefit and expense deducting purposes, and **self-employed** for social security purposes. There is an opportunity to make a decision to become exempt from paying Social Security on ministerial earnings. Parsonage allowance can be designated in advance and to the extent used, it is free from income tax. The employer of a dual-status minister does not have to withhold federal income tax, it is optional.

Employees of churches and integral agencies of churches who are not performing ministerial duties are **lay** employees. Employees of non-integral agencies are lay employees, even if they are formally credentialed, unless their church or denomination "assigned or designated" them to the position.

There are definite tax advantages to being a dual-status minister. A close examination of court cases and letter rulings reflect a very friendly definition of who is entitled to the unique dual-status tax treatment. A full discussion with quotations and citations is in Chapter Two.

Where to Report Income

Dual-Status Minister

Ministers employed by churches and integral agencies of churches have a dual-status treatment in the Internal Revenue Code. They are to be treated as employees for income tax reporting according to "common law rules" in Reg.31.3401(c)-1; and as self-employed for social security reporting Sec. 1402(a)(8). A dual-status minister's Form W-2, Wage and Tax Statement, Box 3, for social security wages and Box 5, for medicare wages should be left blank. The **chart shown in Chapter Six, page 105,** is a good guide indicating what is considered taxable income to be entered on Form W-2, Box 1.

Withholding of income tax for the dual-status minister is not required according to Sec. 3401(a)(9); it is optional. If the dual-status minister did not file Form 4361, it is necessary for social security to be computed on Schedule SE of his personal tax return. If a minister has filed Form 4361, "Application for Exemption from Self-Employment Tax for Ministers," and has received an approved copy, he is exempt from social security on earnings from the ministry and needs to indicate that by writing "Exempt---Form 4361" on the self-employment line of Form 1040, page 2.

Ministers are considered employees for income reporting, expense deducting, and fringe benefit eligibility. Unreimbursed or reimbursed without "an accountable plan," automobile, travel, and professional expenses are allowed only as miscellaneous itemized deductions on Schedule A. They are also subject to limitations: (1) meals & entertainment are reduced by 50%, then combined with other miscellaneous deductions, (2) only the percentage of unreimbursed expenses spent in earning the taxable salary are allowable, and (3) they are further reduced by 2% of the Adjusted Gross Income.

Lay Employees

Lay Employees are employees for both income and social security purposes. A lay employee's Form W-2, Box 1 will show his salary, Box 3 will show the social security wage, and Box 5 will show the medicare wage. Until the end of 1983, a nonprofit organization or church was exempt from withholding and matching social security on their lay employees, unless they chose to cover them by filing Form SS-15. As a part of the Social Security Amendments Act of 1983, social security coverage was extended on a **mandatory** basis to all lay employees of nonprofit organizations as of January 1, 1984. The Tax Reform Act of 1984 provided for an election by a church or qualified church-controlled organization that is opposed for religious reasons to the payment of social security taxes, not to be subject to such taxes. By filing Form 8274 lay employees of churches that make the election **are liable for paying social security** on their personal returns on Schedule SE, Section B. Electing church employers have the responsiblity of withholding income tax, filing quarterly reports, and preparing a W-2 for each employee. It is very important that the employer educate the staff of their responsibilty to pay their Social Security on Schedule SE and include it with their Form 1040. (See complete discussion in Chapter Four and the examples of the W-2 in Chapter Six.)

Unreimbursed or reimbursed without "an accountable plan," automobile, travel, and professional expenses are allowed only as miscellaneous itemized deductions on Schedule A. They are also subject to limitations: (1) meals & entertainment are reduced by 50%, then combined with other miscellaneous deductions, and (2) they are further reduced by 2% of the Adjusted Gross Income.

Employed Ministers Are Not to Use Schedule C For Reporting Salary

Employed ministers are definitely self-employed for social security purposes. However, for income reporting, expense deducting, and fringe benefit provision purposes, the Internal Revenue Code speaks clearly about their status being that of an employee. IRS publications on the issue have historically presented the dual-status treatment for ministers performing services for a church or an integral agency of a church. To ignore the historic IRS position and report a minister's salary and deduct their professional expenses on Schedule C will often cause an audit and an assessment of additional tax liability by moving expenses from Schedule C to Schedule A. Thousands of ministers, have been audited and have experienced additional tax liability, because they used Schedule C.

"Worth's Income Tax Guide for Ministers" is happy to have clearly focused our efforts on educating church employers and their ministers on how to establish an accountable reimbursement plan for employee business expenses to produce the **desired lower tax liability without conflicting with existing IRS code and regulations.** Ministers who have prepared their returns or permitted our service to prepare their returns as dual-status ministers have experienced a much lower audit risk. If their return is audited they will not be assessed an additional tax liability because of how they reported their ministry income and expenses.

● *Historic IRS Position*

The IRS's position that an employed minister is an employee for income reporting purposes is well defined in the following quote from IRS Publication 517, page 3:

"EMPLOYMENT STATUS FOR OTHER TAX PURPOSES

Even though you are considered a self-employed individual in performing your ministerial services for social security tax purposes, you may be considered an employee for income tax or retirement plan tax purposes. For income tax or retirement plan tax purposes, some of your income may be considered self-employment income and other income may be considered wages.

Common-law employee. Under common law rules, you are considered either an employee or a self-employed person depending on all the facts and circumstances. Generally, you are an employee if your employer has the legal right to control both what you do and how you do it, even if you have considerable discretion and freedom of action. For more information about the common-law rules, see Publication 15-A, Employer's Supplemental Tax Guide.

If you are employed by a congregation for a salary, you are generally a common-law employee and income from the exercise of your ministry is considered wages for income tax purposes. However, amounts received directly from members of the congregation, such as fees for performing marriages, baptisms, or other personal services, are considered self-employment income.

Example. A church hires and pays you a salary to perform ministerial services subject to its control. Under the common law rules, you are an employee of the church while performing those services.

If you are not certain whether you are an employee or a self-employed person, you can get a determination from the IRS by filing Form SS-8."

Before requesting a determination from the IRS, study a copy of the full text of Revenue Ruling 87-41. It states, "If the relationship of employer and employee exists, the designation or description of the relationship by the parties as anything other than that of employer and employee **is immaterial**." To draft a contract or an agreement to state that an independent contractor relationship exists when facts and circumstances indicate an employer/employee relationship actually exists would be an exercise of futility. It also does not matter how payments are measured or paid, what they are called, or whether the employee works full or part time.

Wages earned as an employed minister are to be reported on Form W-2 for income tax purposes, but no social security taxes are withheld. This is because you are treated as self-employed for social security purposes. You must pay self-employment tax on those wages yourself unless you request and receive an exemption from self-employment tax. Your **Form W-2, Box 3** for social security wages and **Box 5** for medicare wages **should be left blank.**

● *The 20 Common Law Rules*

As an aid to determining whether an individual is an employee under the common law rules, twenty factors have been developed based on an examination of cases and rulings. In applying the IRS twenty-factor test, there is no set number of factors that make the payee an employee. Each case is evaluated on its own merits. Some of the factors that indicate the presence of **"the right to control"** weigh more in importance on the scale of determining if an employer/employee relationship exists. The threshold level of control necessary to find employee status is generally lower when applied to professional services than when applied to nonprofessional services. Ministers are professionals. If enough of the factors indicate there is an employer/employee relationship and the employer does not treat the employee correctly, the IRS penalties are substantial.

In Revenue Ruling 87-41,CB 1987-1, 296, we find a list of **THE TWENTY COMMON LAW FACTORS.** This list, along with our explanations, is as follows:

(1) *Compliance with instructions;* A payee who MUST OBEY the payor's instructions about when, where and how he is to do the work is apt to be an employee. Even if no instructions are given, the control factor is present if the employer has the right to control how the work results are achieved. A minister paid by a church or organization is generally required to hold a certain theological position and maintain an honorable lifestyle and hold worship services at set times, teach classes, etc.

(2) *Training required;* The use of an employee handbook or staff meetings would be a factor of control and indicative of employee status. A payee who is an independent contractor ordinarily receives no training from the payor.

(3) *Integration of services into business operations;* How closely related to the work of the payor is the work of the payee? It would seem rather difficult to prove a church or organization's purpose and ministry is not closely integrated with the purpose and ministry of the minister hired to perform ministerial duties. A minister has the responsibility to lead a local church in conformance with the beliefs of the church. This is another factor that indicates control. A payee who is an independent contractor would have a separate line of business from the payor.

(4) *Services rendered personally;* If the payor requires a payee to physically perform the services himself, this shows control by the payor over the payee. An independent contractor would have the right to hire a substitute without getting the payor's consent.

(5) *Hiring, supervising, and paying assistants;* When the payor hires, trains and pays the staff working with the payee it indicates control by the payor and employee status. Independent contractors must have the right to hire staff or assistants at their own discretion, regardless of payor's wishes.

(6) **Continuing relationship;** An ongoing long term relationship between the payor and the payee indicates an employee status. A continuing relationship may exist even if work is performed at recurring, although irregular, intervals. An independent contractor will finish an assignment project and work for several payors.

(7) *Set hours of work;* A payee's ability to schedule his activities according to his own desire merely demonstrates that less supervision is necessary in connection with a professional. When the payor sets regular hours of work it is a definite indication of control and an

employee status. An independent contractor will schedule a job and have the right to change the date and time and give scheduling priority to other jobs.

(8)   _Full time required;_ When a payee must work full time for one payor, it indicates control and employee status. An independent contractor is free to work when and for whom he wishes.

(9)   _Work done on premises;_ When the payor provides the premises for a payee to perform the work to be done it indicates an employee status. When the employing church or organization owns the worship location or office in which the professional minister performs most of his duties it indicates the factor of control.

(10) _Services performed in order or sequence set;_ When the payor has the right to establish the schedule and routines of the payee, an employer/employee relationship exists. A church employer has regular worship services, committee meetings, etc., that a minister must plan for and lead as scheduled. A minister does not have the ability to unilaterally discontinue the regular services of a local church. An independent contractor evangelist schedules meetings any day or evening of the week he may choose.

(11) _Oral or written reports;_ An employee is usually required to give reports or an accounting of his time and accomplishments. An independent contractor submits invoices to the payor.

(12) _Payment by hour, week, month;_ When a payee is paid by the hour, week, month, mile, etc., this is an indication of employee status. An independent contractor estimates his cost of labor and materials and invoices the payor by the job.

(13) _Payment of business and/or traveling expenses;_ This factor weighs as light as a feather. It is good tax planning for either an employee or an independent contractor to "adequately account" to the employer or payor and be reimbursed for job related expenses. An employee who does not establish an accountable plan with his employer can only deduct the expenses on Schedule A if he itemizes his deductions. An independent contractor is able to deduct his job related expenses on Schedule C.

(14) _Furnishing of tools and materials;_ When the payor provides the necessary tools and materials for a payee to carry out his duties, an employer/employee relationship is indicated. An independent contractor owns, repairs and takes with him from job to job the tools necessary for his trade.

(15) _Significant investment;_ When the payor provides the work facilities and the payee performing the services is not required to make an investment, an employer/employee relationship is indicated. A church provides the church building for holding services and an office in which to perform administrative services and often buys religious materials for the minister. To voluntarily purchase books, tapes, computer equipment, furnishings for a home office, etc., does not count as required significant investment.

(16) **_Realization of profit or loss;_** An employee is shielded from risk of loss. If a payee is subject to a real risk of economic loss due to significant investments and bonafide liabilities it indicates an independent contractor status. An independent contractor evangelist could incur travel and advertising expenses and experience economic loss if he failed to secure adequate engagements.

(17) _Working for more than one firm at a time;_ A payee who performs services for more than one firm at a time could be a part-time employee of each firm. However, if a payee works or consults with many clients and customers simultaneously, it would be a strong indicator of an independent contractor status.

(18) _Making service available to general public;_ To the extent of honorariums received from individuals for ministerial services (weddings, funerals, etc.), outside speaking engagements, writing, etc., a minister receives independent contractor income to be reported on Schedule C. There are many ways of holding one's self out to the public such as: business cards, a business name at the top of an invoice, a business listing in a phone book, distribution of a brochure, advertisements in a newspaper or trade journal, placement of business name on key chains or jackets, etc.

(19) **_Right to discharge;_** An employer has the ability to fire an employee. An employer exercises control through the threat of dismissal, which causes the worker to obey the employer's instructions. A payee serving as a minister of a church or organization is accountable to the payor to maintain certain theological positions, an acceptable lifestyle and an acceptable performance of his duties. This is true in a denominational connectional

church polity as well as in an independent autonomous church polity. That in connectional church polity a bishop or overseer appoints the minister to a church and the church usually pays the minister for services rendered indicates more control and is a substantial indication of a co-employer/employee relationship. While the congregation of a connectional church cannot fire a minister, they can certainly seek dismissal for just cause through the bishop or overseer. An independent contractor, on the other hand, can not be fired so long as the independent contractor produces a result that meets the contract specifications.

(20) ***Right to terminate relationship without incurring liability.*** When a payee has the right to terminate his relationship with the payor at any time he wishes without incurring liability, indicates an employer/employee relationship. An independent contractor agrees to complete a specific job and is responsible for its satisfactory completion or is legally obligated to make good for failure to complete the job.

• *Additional Factors to Consider*

To be eligible for "Tax Free" fringe benefits such as group medical insurance, group term life insurance, etc., an individual must be a common law employee. Hypothetically, if a minister could be considered as an independent contractor and use Schedule C for reporting salary and expenses, **he would have to report as taxable income** the value of any fringe benefits provided by a payor.

To be eligible to make contributions to a Sec. 403(b) Tax Sheltered Account, prior to 1997, an individual had to be a common law employee of a nonprofit organization according to Revenue Ruling 66-274. A provision in the Small Business Job Protection Act of 1996 permits participation in tax-sheltered accounts by a minister, evangelist, or chaplain, who in connection with the exercise of his ministry is a self-employed individual or is working for an employer that is not a qualified nonprofit organization.

When the source of income is from a nonprofit organization: Payment for services performed on a regular and continuous basis is to be treated as salary, not independent contractor income. To be a nonprofit corporation, it is important that individuals do not personally benefit or inure from funds and assets acquired. **If a minister actually had complete control of funds and assets of a church, it would no longer be a nonprofit organization or church.**

A business owner who creates a for-profit corporation becomes its employee when paid for services rendered. Revenue Ruling 71-86 states that a president, sole shareholder, who sets his own hours, duties, salary and was not responsible to anyone else, was an employee for income tax withholding, social security and federal unemployment tax purposes. Similarly, Revenue Ruling 73-361 treats an officer performing substantial services as an employee.

When the source of income is from individuals for whom a service was performed, reporting the income on Schedule C is correct. Honorariums received for performing weddings, funerals, baptisms and counseling are correctly reported as self-employment income on Schedule C.

Preparer penalties: Tax preparers are subject to negligence penalties if they knowingly prepare a return incorrectly. After a careful study of the citations just presented, a tax preparer who disregards the position of the IRS by not preparing an employed minister's tax return as dual-status would be guilty of negligently understating the minister's tax liability. Sec. 6694 provides for a substantial penalty per return prepared with an intentional disregard of rules or regulations.

Churches who fail to prepare W-2's for their employees are subject to many penalties. Providing a Form 1099 to an employed minister rather than a W-2 can result in a $50 penalty as it is **necessary to prepare "correct" informational returns to avoid penalties**. It is very important to learn what the law requires and carefully meet those obligations. Chapter Six discusses the rules and shows examples of payroll reporting and informational returns.

Statutory employee status cannot be used by ministers: It is a status **limited to four occupational groups**. Generally, statutory employees receive a W-2 and are able to deduct their business expenses on Schedule C. Because of this ability, some ministers have attempted to claim this status.

The four specific occupational groups deemed to be statutory employees regardless of whether they are employees under the usual common law guidelines are: (1) agent-drivers and commission drivers engaged in the distribution of various products; (2) full-time life insurance salespersons; (3) home workers performing work according to specifications furnished by the person for whom the work is performed, on materials or goods provided by such person that are required to be returned to such person or a person designated by him; and (4) traveling or city salespersons other than those acting as agent-drivers or commission drivers.

● *WHY all the Confusion over Status and Contention with the IRS?*

Often a church treasurer or board will ask their minister what tax status they prefer as if it is an optional decision. Our theological colleges and seminaries do a very poor job teaching ministerial students about tax law and how it applies to them. Due to inadequate knowledge of tax law, many wrong decisions have been made.

Many clergy tax advisors, accountants, and publications have continued to recommend or show examples of using Schedule C for **employed ministers**. The "fight for the right to use Schedule C" that has caused thousands of ministers to be audited and assessed additional tax liabilities is unfortunate.

If you call the IRS "800" number six times and ask for information concerning the correct status of a minister, you may get six different answers. It is unfortunate that some of the confusion concerning the minister's correct status has been caused by uninformed IRS employees and the courts. Going against the historic position stated in IRS publications results in taxable fringe benefits and **increases the IRS audit exposure.** Most ministers claiming to be independent contractors cannot afford legal representation to pursue their case through the courts.

● *An Important District Court Case - Weber v. Commissioner, 103 T.C. 378, 386 (1994)*

In North Carolina, IRS audited several hundred United Methodist ministers' tax returns that reported their salary income and professional expenses spent to earn that income on Schedule C. A tax liability was assessed when the professional expenses were changed from Schedule C to Schedule A, Itemized Deductions. These audits resulted in a District Court Case in North Carolina, Weber v. Commissioner, in January, 1993. The case was well represented by Rev. Weber's denomination and the written result was released on August 25, 1994. An appeal was filed and the final decision was received on July 31, 1995. The IRS position stands. This case was a test case for the United Methodist ministers as to the issues it contains. Petitioners in many of the pending cases agreed to be bound by the final decision in this case.

Special Trial Judge John J. Pajak, seemed to have carefully read the Book of Discipline of the United Methodist Church. He decided that the "right to control" test was of primary importance and found that Weber was subject to significant control. The court stated, "generally a lower level of control applies to professionals. Petitioner is a professional minister." He was required to work at the church to which he was assigned and was required to attend meetings. He had to explain the position of the Discipline on any topic he chose to present in his sermons. He did not have the authority to unilaterally discontinue the regular services of a local church. Though the church did not give him a Form W-2, the court gave that factor little weight. The Court found that Reverend Weber's position was intended to be permanent as opposed to transitory and that the benefits provided by the Church indicated an employment relationship.

Methodist ministers, spouses, and dependents are covered by life insurance and contributions are made to the General Board of Pensions of the United Methodist Church which provides payments upon retirement. Ministers are expected to make voluntary contributions to the pension plan equal to 3 percent of their salary. As an employee, Rev. Weber is entitled to tax free treatment of these fringe benefits.

A more recent U.S. Tax Court decision in Radde v. Commissioner, T.C. Memo 1997-490 upholds the Weber decision that as a minister Rev. Radde was an employee. In Private Letter Ruling 9825002, a United Methodist minister, who served as a presiding elder, **was denied his request** to be considered an independent contractor.

● *Other Tax Court Cases have Resulted in Conflicting Decisions.*

The tax courts have added to the confusion by giving conflicting decisions. On the same day that Rev. Weber's District Court Case was released, another judge in Florida gave a conflicting opinion in Shelley v. Commissioner, T.C. Memo 1994-432. The church Rev. Shelley pastored was a member of the International Pentecostal Holiness Church. The judge's opinion that Rev. Shelley was an independent contractor is a decision by a small Tax Court that the IRS will not follow. However, Weber v. Commissioner was a decision of a District Court that was agreed to be a precedent setting case.

On December 2, 1996, in Greene v. Commissioner, T.C. Memo 1996-531, it was determined that an Assembly of God missionary to Bangladesh was an independent contractor rather than an employee. On June 20, 1997, Alford v. United States, U.S. Court of Appeals for the eighth circuit, No. 96-3287 also determined that an Assembly of God minister was an independent contractor rather than an employee. Both IRS and the District Court determined that Alford was an employee. The District Court concluded that Alford was an employee of not only the local church but also of the district and national organizations. If this decision had not been appealed it would have exposed the district and national organizations to unnecessary liability. The U.S. Court of Appeals correctly determined that there was no employer/employee relationship with the district or national organizations and also determined that there was no employer/employee relationship with the local church.

NOTE: The Assembly of God national organization's recommendation is to disregard the Alford decision and to accept the employer/employee relationship when the facts and circumstances support it.

● *What to do if your employer gives you Form 1099 instead of Form W-2?*

After gathering all the facts and circumstances of the relationship between a payor and a payee, based on the common-law guidelines, determine what the payee's correct status is. If an incorrect informational return has been issued by the payor, **it is important** to educate the payor why an employer/employee relationship exists. Making the corrections according to step #1 below will reduce the audit exposure for the employee and result in the correct returns being prepared in the future.

1. Have the payor prepare a corrected Form 1099 with -0- income shown. Then prepare a Form W-2 correctly reporting the taxable salary in Box 1.

2. When an employed dual-status minister receives Form 1099 rather than a Form W-2 **and the payor will not prepare corrected forms,** we recommend the following procedure for preparing Form 1040:

   a. Enter the amount shown as income on the Form 1099 on Schedule C as gross income because IRS computers will scan the informational return and expect it to be there.

   b. Subtract the same amount as "wages taken to Form 1040, line 7" in the expense section of Schedule C to have a net result of zero on Schedule C to the extent of the salary. Any honorariums received will remain as taxable on the Schedule C.

   c. Then enter the amount as income on Form 1040, line 7 as though it were wages on a W-2. IRS computers will accept an amount on line 7 that is greater than the total wages reported on W-2s attached to the return.

   d. Use Form 2106 and Schedule A to deduct any unreimbursed employee business expenses.

There will be a higher audit exposure if the return is prepared according to Step 2 because Schedule C income from one Form 1099 appears to the IRS computers as a potential misclassification of status. However, if audited, there will be no additional tax assessed for an incorrectly prepared Form 1040.

Taxable Sources Of Income

Important Definition of Income: Gross income, according to Sec. 61, includes all income (cash, value of property, or value of services) from whatever source, unless it is specifically excluded by a section in the Internal Revenue Code. It is important to understand that regardless of what a payor or payee calls a sum of money, property or value of service; facts and circumstances will determine whether it is taxable or not. **Any income that is received because of services performed is taxable**. Generally, the employee will be taxed on all remuneration from a payor that is not a qualified fringe benefit (Chapter One), housing allowance (Chapter Two), or reimbursement for professional expenses under an accountable plan (Chapter Three).

According to Revenue Ruling 68-67, whether a religious worker receives support from an organization or from individuals directly, the dominant reason for such payments is that the religious worker performs ministry services. Voluntary contributions, irrespective of their designation as "gifts," made directly to religious workers are includible in gross income. Furthermore, voluntary contributions, which are designated for a specific missionary, made by individuals or groups and transmitted directly to the mission, should be included in the mission's receipts and included on the missionary's Form W-2, Box 1.

It is wrong to conclude that if a donor cannot deduct the gift to a minister or missionary's support, that it is not necessary for the recipient to report the gift as taxable income. The payee receiving taxable support and the payor deducting a Schedule A contribution are two separate acts. According to Commissioner v. Duberstein, 363 U.S. 278, 285 (1960), the Supreme Court holds that **when the contribution is for services rendered it is irrelevant that the payor derives no economic benefit**. Contributions must be paid directly to a qualifying organization in order for the donor to be able to deduct them on Schedule A. Contributions paid directly to an individual are never allowable as Schedule A deductions.

Professional Income

Fees, offerings, or gifts for speaking, performing weddings, funerals or baptisms are considered professional income. An independent contractor, evangelist, or missionary receives professional income from the churches to which he ministers as well as from individual supporters. When as a minister you have provided a service and the person receiving the benefit of your ministry gives you money, it should be considered as earned professional income according to Reg 1.61-2(a)(1).

When as an independent religious worker you personally receive your support from individual contributions, it becomes necessary to show these amounts on Schedule C and to deduct the expenses of doing ministry to arrive at net income. If large amounts of money for work projects are received, it becomes difficult to prove they are legitimate ordinary and necessary ministry expenses to the IRS in an audit. **The ideal solution for this Schedule C problem is for the independent religious worker to establish an employer/employee relationship with a church.** (See complete discussion of this recommendation in Chapter Six.)

Income received from writing, lecturing, radio or television appearances, etc., are additional types of professional income. The income or royalties and expenses of selling religious tapes and books are to be shown on Schedule C as professional income, according to Revenue Ruling 59-50. For ministers not exempt from social security, the net profit will be considered social security earnings.

If honorariums and fees for weddings, funerals, etc., are paid directly to the employer and not personally received by the minister, they would not be taxable to him.

Salary From Employer

Compensation or salary, for services rendered, received from an employing church is to be reported in the W-2, Box 1. When an employer gives a **bonus or "love gift"** to an employee it is simply additional salary and should also be included in the W-2, Box 1. Honorariums or gifts that are received by the minister from individuals to whom he ministers or from whom he receives support are to be included on Schedule C. Two court cases, Banks v. Commissioner, T.C. Memo 1991-641 and Goodwin v. United States Court of Appeals, KTC 1995-479 (8th Cir. 1995), involved ministers who had received three or four large special occasion offerings each year on a regular basis and had not included them on their tax returns. Both ministers were assessed large sums of income tax and Social Security tax for three years plus many penalties and several years of interest by the time the court decisions were final.

Gifts of other than cash should be considered at their fair market value (FMV) and, if from the employer, included in the W-2. A common occurrence involves a donor giving an auto to the church. The church gives a contribution receipt with the auto's description and the date of the gift to the donor. The donor is to determine the FMV and deduct it as a contribution on Schedule A. If the church then "pays" or transfers the auto to their minister, they must include the FMV of the auto in the minister's Form W-2.

Congregations who own the parsonage and decide to **sell it at a bargain price or transfer the ownership** of the parsonage outright to their minister are actually paying him a considerable amount of "extra" compensation. The difference between the amount paid and the amount of its fair market value at the time of the transfer is taxable according to Reg. 1.61-2(d)(2). To avoid an excessive tax burden in the year of transfer we suggest the following: The employer should loan the employee the amount of the difference between the FMV and the amount paid by the employee and, over a period of time, forgive a portion of the loan each year. The annual income would be the amount of forgiveness and if the loan is secured by the home, it would be principal payment that can be parsonage allowance. (See discussion of "Loans from employers" in Chapter Two)

Benevolence to an employee or a family member: When an employer helps an employee or a member of an employee's family with crisis needs it will result in taxable compensation to the employee. **To avoid this, we recommend** that a local non-employer, nonprofit organization (such as Red Cross) be utilized to raise funds for the crisis needs of an employee.

Only small gifts of merchandise are non-taxable: According to Revenue Ruling 59-58, "The value of a turkey, ham or other item of merchandise purchased by an employer and distributed generally to each of the employees engaged in his business at Christmas, or a comparable holiday, as a means of promoting their good will, does not constitute wages." The ruling also states **that this rule "will not apply** to distributions of cash, gift certificates, and similar items of readily convertible cash value, regardless of the amount involved." This tax-free provision of giving small non-cash gifts of merchandise to your minister might include T-bone steaks, a neat tie, or a package of golf balls.

Social Security Paid By the Employer

When an employer agrees to provide extra payment to a dual-status minister to pay all or part of his social security tax, **it must be shown as taxable salary** according to Revenue Ruling 68-507. Dual-status ministers are treated as self-employed taxpayers when computing their social security on Schedule SE. Their combined rate of social security tax and medicare tax is 15.3% less adjustments. It may be convenient to have the employer pay this amount to the minister on a quarterly basis, to coincide with the due dates of his estimated tax payments.

On Schedule SE the gross social security base is adjusted to allow one half of social security as a deduction. On Form 1040, page 1, an adjustment for one half of the social security paid by the self-employed taxpayer is allowed.

The wage base for the two parts of the social security tax (social security and medicare) are different. **The 7.65% combined rate** is made up of 6.2% rate for social security and 1.45% rate for medicare.

Here is the schedule of what has happened since 1995:

YEAR	SOCIAL SECURITY WAGE BASE	MEDICARE WAGE BASE	EMPLOYEE RATE FICA	Medicare	SELF-EMPLOYED RATE
1995	$61,200	No limit	6.20%	1.45%	15.30%
1996	$62,700	No limit	6.20%	1.45%	15.30%
1997	$65,400	No limit	6.20%	1.45%	15.30%
1998	$68,400	No limit	6.20%	1.45%	15.30%
1999	$72,600	No limit	6.20%	1.45%	15.30%
2000	$76,200	No limit	6.20%	1.45%	15.30%
2001	$80,400	No limit	6.20%	1.45%	15.30%
2002	$84,900	No limit	6.20%	1.45%	15.30%
2003	$87,000	No limit	6.20%	1.45%	15.30%
2004	$87,900	No limit	6.20%	1.45%	15.30%
2005	$90,000	No limit	6.20%	1.45%	15.30%
2006	$94,200	No limit	6.20%	1.45%	15.30%

Insurance

The cost of regular term and permanent life insurance (whole, universal, etc.), paid by the employer is a taxable fringe benefit if the minister names the beneficiary of his choosing. Any premium paid for group term life insurance **over $50,000** coverage is also taxable. The Table from Reg. 1.79-3(d)(2), shown on page 23, is to be used to compute the amount to be included in an employee's income, even though the employer's actual premium may be more or less.

Housing

We recommend that the dual-status minister "over estimate" his parsonage allowance that is required to be designated in advance by his employer. When filing the tax return, any unused parsonage allowance becomes taxable income and is to be entered on Form 1040, line 7, as "excess parsonage allowance."

The lay employee who is provided living quarters that are not on the premises of the employer, nor for the convenience of the employer, nor a requirement of the job, must show as taxable income the value of the living quarters provided. This value is also subject to social security tax. (Sec. 119 qualifications are not met.)

Non-Accountable Allowances

If you are paid a non-accountable expense allowance or reimbursement and are not required to submit your records and receipts to your employer, the income has to be shown on your Form W-2. For example: when an employee receives $400 a month for his auto expenses and is not required by a written accountable plan to submit a mileage log to his employer as substantiation, the auto allowance must be reported on Form W-2, Box 1.

It is very important to establish a written accountable reimbursement plan and "adequately account" to your employer in order not to lose some or all of the deduction for your professional expenses. A complete discussion of how to establish an accountable reimbursement plan is in Chapter Three.

Personal Use of Auto Provided by Employer

Strict regulations require the **value of personal use** of an employer owned auto to be included in the W-2 as a taxable fringe benefit. The amount to be included in income is to be reduced by any amount the employee pays the employer for the taxable fringe benefit. (See complete discussion in Chapter Three.)

Non-Taxable Sources of Income—Exclusions

Fringe Benefits

Gross income, for tax purposes, includes all income from whatever source unless specifically excluded by an Internal Revenue Code Section. Many code sections provide rules on how to establish **qualified tax-free** fringe benefits. Any **non-qualified** fringe benefits provided by an employer are taxable fringes that must be included as wages on Form W-2, box 1. Before establishing employee fringe benefits that are **subject to nondiscrimination rules**, seek the assistance of an attorney and/or benefits consultant. With congressional changes happening often, existing plans must be continually examined and revised to meet new requirements.

Fringe benefits are available for either dual-status or lay employees of nonprofit employers and employees of for-profit employers. Providing qualified fringe benefits in an employee's "pay package" reduces the base upon which both income tax and social security tax are paid.

To be qualified, most fringe benefit options must meet nondiscrimination tests. **There are two fringe benefits that are free from the nondiscrimination tests** and if provided for some of the staff but not everyone on staff, they are still a tax-free fringe benefit for the recipient: (1) accident & health insurance provided to an employee and family and (2) certain church plans providing **group term** life insurance to employees.

Qualified Retirement Plan Contributions

For retirement plans, the Internal Revenue Code considers the salaried minister as an "employee." It would be wrong for an "employee" to set up a plan designed for self-employed taxpayers.

Distributions from qualified retirement plans to which contributions were based on wages earned while performing ministerial duties can be designated 100% as "housing allowance". To the extent the minister incurs housing expenses, the distribution is tax-free. (See Suggested Wordings in Chapter Two.)

● *Sec. 401(a) - Employer Qualified Retirement Plan*

A qualified pension, profit-sharing, or stock bonus plan is a definite written program and arrangement which is communicated to the employees and which is established and maintained by an employer. It has a vesting schedule and is expensive to establish and maintain. Many large corporations are abandoning their Sec. 401(a) plans and setting up Sec. 401(k) plans. Annual contributions by an employer to a qualified retirement plan on the behalf of an employee cannot exceed the lesser of (1) $42,000, or an additional $4,000 if age 50 or older by end of the year, or (2) 25% of the employee's compensation for the year. (2006 - $44,000 annually with an additional $5,000 available if age 50 or over by end of year.)

● *Sec. 401(k) - Salary Reduction*

Beginning in 1997, nonprofit organizations are allowed to establish 401(k) or CODA plans. Between July 2, 1986 and December 31,1996, nonprofit employers generally could not establish 401(k) or CODA plans. 401(k) plans that existed before July 2, 1986 were allowed to continue. The maximum amount that an employee can defer under all 401(k) plans is 100% of compensation limited to **$14,000** annually, with an additional **$4,000** available if age 50 or over by end of year. (2006 - $15,000, with an additional $5,000 available if age 50 or over by end of year.)

● *Sec. 403(b) - Tax Sheltered Account (TSA)*

Tax Sheltered Accounts are available to public school employees and employees of nonprofit organizations. Ministers employed by a nonprofit organization are eligible for making contributions to a Sec. 403(b) retirement account. Since January 1, 1997, a minister, evangelist, or chaplain, who in connection with the exercise of his ministry is a self-employed individual or is working for an employer that is not a qualified nonprofit organization, can also contribute to a TSA. TSAs are the most popular retirement plans to be established by nonprofit employers.

This code section provides **two methods of funding.** An employer can provide a 403(b) plan that includes **both** forfeitable contributions by the employer and non-forfeitable voluntary contributions made by the employee through a salary reduction plan. Or an employer can provide a 403(b) plan that includes either method of funding without the other. An employer can provide a Sec. 403(b)(7), voluntary salary reduction plan **without** the complexities and cost of a 403(b)(9) plan.

Employer Contributions - Forfeitable (employee loses if not vested) can be made by the **employer** to a Sec. 403(b)(9) account on behalf of its employees. The maximum limit for a defined contribution plan applies (lesser of $42,000 or 100% of pay). The cost to establish and administer this type of Sec. 403(b)(9) employer plan that must meet discrimination testing causes it to not be cost effective for an employer with a small staff.

Salary Reduction Contributions - Non-Forfeitable (employee is always 100% vested) can be made for the **employee** to a Sec. 403(b) account established by the employer for voluntary salary reduction contributions. For 2005, an employee can contribute up to 100% of compensation limited to **$14,000** annually, with an additional **$4,000** available if age 50 or over by end of year. (2006 - $15,000, with an additional $5,000 available if age 50 or over by end of year.)

Contributions to a TSA account by a dual-status minister **are not** subject to social security and medicare tax according to **Revenue Ruling 68-395**. However, contributions to a TSA account by a lay employee **are** subject to social security and medicare tax withholding according to **Revenue Ruling 65-208**.

A Sec. 403(b) retirement annuity or a Sec. 403(b)(7) mutual fund account can be established to accept only **non-forfeitable** voluntary salary reduction contributions. The employer is required to **notify all** of the employees that they have the opportunity to make voluntary salary reduction contributions to the 403(b) plan. It is not necessary that they all choose to participate. Many employers provide Sec. 403(b)(7) plans that only allow salary reduction non-forfeitable voluntary contributions because **they are quick to establish and involve very little cost of administration.** Plans established with a mutual fund family as custodian typically cost a nominal **$5 to $25**, regardless of how many employees participate. Employees of nonprofit organizations who change employers from time to time like the "portability" of a Sec. 403(b) non-forfeitable type of plan. A change of employers requires a new custodial agreement to be established. (See additional discussion of non-forfeitable TSA plans under "Voluntary Tax Shelter Retirement Plans".)

● *Sec. 408(k) - Simplified Employee Pension (SEP)*

Only an **employer** may establish a SEP. The employer makes contributions directly to a SEP-IRA account or annuity that has been set up for each employee with a broker, bank, or insurance company qualified to sponsor an IRA under Sec. 408(k). Providing the plan was amended to include the 2001 Tax Act new law limits, contributions are limited to 25% on first $200,000 of compensation, with maximum of $42,000. Employer contributions must be made to a SEP for each employee age 21 or over who has worked for the employer for at least 3 of the last 5 years and received annual compensation of $450 or more. Contributions to SEPs must not discriminate in favor of highly compensated employees. Employer contributions must be determined under a definite written allocation formula and withdrawals must be allowed. Because the SEP-IRA is established in the employee's name it is 100% vested and portable.

Employees of tax-exempt organizations and state or local governments **may not** make additional voluntary salary reduction contributions to a Sec. 408(k) SEP. They are eligible for Sec. 403(b)(7) salary reduction plans instead.

● *Sec. 408(p) - Savings Incentive Match Plan for Employees (SIMPLE)*

For years beginning after December 31, 1996, a SIMPLE retirement plan is a written salary reduction arrangement that allows a **small employer** (an employer with 100 or fewer employees) to make elective contributions to a simple retirement account (IRA) on behalf of each eligible employee. The plan document is provided by the IRS and is *"really"* **simple** to establish and administer by an employer.

For 2005, an employee can contribute up to 100% of compensation limited to **$10,000** annually, with an additional **$2,000** available if age 50 or over by end of year. (2006 - $10,000, with an additional $2,500 available if age 50 or over by end of year.) The employer is required to match the employees' contributions on a dollar for dollar basis, up to 3% of compensation, or elect to make 2% nonelective contributions on behalf of all eligible employees. Eligible employees are those who earned at least $5,000 in compensation from the employer during any two prior years and who are reasonably expected to receive at least $5,000 in compensation during the year. The plan document allows an employer to choose between $0 and $5,000 for the compensation requirement and to choose between zero to two prior years for the time requirement.

If the employer desires to allow the employees to designate their own investment and financial institution, Form 5304-SIMPLE should be used to establish the plan. If the employer desires to designate one financial institution, Form 5305-SIMPLE should be used to establish the plan. Both the employee contributions and the employer contributions are **non-forfeitable** (employee is always 100% vested). A participating employer is not allowed to maintain another retirement plan.

Distributions from a SIMPLE retirement account are subject to IRA rules. However, withdrawals of contributions during the two-year period beginning on the date the employee first participated in the SIMPLE plan are subject to a 25% early withdrawal penalty rather than 10%.

● *Sec. 414(e) - Church plans*

A plan established and maintained for its employees by a church or by a convention or association of churches exempt from tax under Sec. 501 is excluded from minimum participation, vesting, and funding rules. These rules may be elected. A church plan may be administered by an independent organization, such as a retirement board or a bank. Amounts contributed are limited, according to Sec. 415(c), to $42,000 or 100% of the participant's compensation.

● *Distributions from Employer Qualified Retirement Plans (QRP)*

Upon retiring, resigning, or disability an employee usually has choices to make as to how he wants the distribution from a Qualified Retirement Plan to be paid out. The choices are provided for in the employer's plan document. **Tax Planning Is Important.** Information about the rate of return, survivor benefits, etc., are going to enter into the decision you must make at retirement time. Each taxpayer's tax situation will differ. **Ask your tax advisor** which choice of distribution provided by your plan will have the least tax liability.

When a minister has a choice of receiving a lump-sum distribution, **it is important to "roll over"** or transfer trustee to trustee **into a tax-sheltered Sec. 403(b)**. Penalties of early withdrawal and employer's requirement to withhold 20% of the distribution for income tax are avoided. It is important to make the transfer into a Sec. 403(b) account, **retain the proper identity of earnings from the ministry**, and preserve the opportunity for designated parsonage allowance. If you "roll-over" a lump-sum distribution into an IRA, you may not be able to designate the distributions from the IRA account as tax-free parsonage allowance.

Periodic income distribution: The choice of monthly income from a qualified plan or a Sec 403(b) rollover account is more attractive to dual-status ministers because of the ability to designate it as tax-free parsonage allowance.

The payor of a lump-sum distribution from an employer's Qualified Retirement Plan is required to withhold 20% of the distribution for income tax **unless** you ask for a transfer from trustee to trustee.

Lump-Sum Distributions have a special 10-year averaging available if you were born before 1936, receive the entire balance from all of the qualified plans in one year and do not "roll-over" any portion of the lump-sum distribution.

● *Penalties*

Early distributions are generally subject to 10% early withdrawal penalties if received before age 59° or disability. **Two ways to avoid the 10% penalty are**: (1) Early distributions can be rolled over to another qualified account or (2) distributions can be received as part of a series of substantially equal periodic payments received at least once a year for the life or life expectancy of the taxpayer or for joint lives of taxpayer and beneficiary. (Sec. 72(t)(2)(A)(iv)).

● *Retired Ministers & Parsonage Designation*

A **retired minister** receiving an otherwise taxable distribution from a qualified Sec. 401(a), Sec. 401(k), Sec. 403(b), Sec. 408(k), Sec. 408(p) or Sec. 414(e) plan may have a **"parsonage allowance"** designated by the former employer or denominational pension board according to Rev. Ruling 63-156. We recommend that a perpetually worded designation state that 100% of the retirement income be designated as parsonage allowance and be tax free to the extent spent for housing. **(See sample wording in Chapter Two)** Language found in the Department of Labor Regulations under ERISA indicate that both types of contributions to a Sec. 403(b) plan (forfeitable and non-forfeitable) are considered as contributions to an employer's plan and both types are eligible for parsonage allowance designation.

Distributions from an IRA or a Keogh retirement plan may not be eligible to be designated as non-taxable housing because their contributions are not identifiable as being based on earnings from the ministry.

According to Rev. Ruling 72-249, the parsonage allowance exclusion is not available to the surviving spouse who continues to receive retirement income as a beneficiary.

Third party payors of retirement plan distributions **will include** the gross distribution on Form 1099-R, Box 1. Not being able to determine the taxable amount, Box 2a could be left blank and Box 2b could be checked. As a retired minister receiving distributions from a retirement plan that has been designated as "parsonage allowance," you are to enter the gross amount on Form 1040, line 16a. It is the responsibility of the retired minister to show as taxable on Form 1040, line 16b any designated distributions not spent for parsonage expenses. If all of the distribution has been spent for parsonage expenses enter -0- on line 16b.

Group Term Life Insurance

An **exemption** from the **nondiscrimination rules** of Sec. 79 applies to certain church plans providing group term life insurance to employees. Premiums paid by an employer for group term life insurance on the first $50,000 coverage are not to be included in income according to Sec. 79. Any coverage for group term life insurance **over $50,000** is taxable. Use the Table from Reg. 1.79-3(d)(2) to compute the amount to be included in an employee's income, even though the employer's actual premium may be more or less.

The only time premiums paid by the employer for regular term or permanent life insurance are not taxable is when the employer is named as beneficiary.

Cost Per $1,000 of group term life insurance protection for 1-Month Period

[Reg. 1.79-3(d)(2)]

Age	Cost
Under 25	5¢
25 through 29	6¢
30 through 34	8¢
35 through 39	9¢
40 through 44	10¢
45 through 49	15¢
50 through 54	23¢
55 through 59	43¢
60 through 64	66¢
65 through 69	$1.27
70 and above	$2.06

Accident And Health Insurance

There are no **discrimination rules** that apply to **insured accident and health plans.** Premiums paid for group accident and health insurance by an employer for employees, their spouses, or their dependents are not taxable income according to Sec. 106. Premiums for group accident and health plans are able to be a "tax free" fringe benefit. A plan underwritten by an insurance policy or a prepaid health care plan must involve the shifting of risk to an unrelated third party to be considered an insured plan.

Whenever possible, an employer should pay the premium for accident and health insurance directly to the insurer. For an employee who pays his premium directly to the insurer, the employer can reimburse him and it qualifies as a "tax free" fringe benefit. It is recommended that the employee be given a separate check specifically for the purpose of accident and health premium reimbursement. The employee must account to the employer for the amount of the premium and provide proof that the insurance is in force. (Revenue Ruling 61-146)

An employer's continuation of health insurance coverage for an employee that is laid off or retired is tax free. Medical coverage provided to the family of a deceased employee is tax free since it is treated as a continuation of the employee's fringe-benefit package. If you are age 65 or older, Medicare premiums and supplemental policies paid or reimbursed to you by your employer qualifies as a "tax free" fringe benefit.

Tax qualified long-term care insurance contracts issued after 1996 will be treated the same for income tax purposes as accident and health insurance contracts. For those not able to use the cost as a deduction, non-tax qualified long-term care contracts are available.

● HSA - Health Savings Accounts (New in 2004)

Health Savings Accounts (HSAs) were created by the Medicare bill signed by President Bush on December 8, 2003 and are designed to help individuals save for future qualified medical and retiree health expenses on a tax-free basis. Sec. 223, permits eligible individuals to establish Health Savings Accounts for taxable years after December 31, 2003. Because of the short period of time between the enactment of HSAs and the effective date of Sec. 223, many taxpayers who are eligible to establish and contribute to HSAs were unable to do so in 2004 because trustees or custodians were not yet established.

Health Savings Accounts, new and innovative, will change the way millions can save to meet their health care needs. All 250 million non-elderly Americans will now have access to an HSA, and one that is far more attractive than the Archer MSAs that were enacted in 1996.

Any individual who is covered by a high-deductible health plan (HDHP) may establish an HSA. Contributions can be made in one or more payments at the convenience of the individual, at any time prior to the due date of the tax return without extensions, generally April 15th. Amounts contributed to a HSA belong to individuals and are completely portable. Every year the money not spent will stay in the account and gain earnings tax-free, just like an IRA. Unused amounts remain available for later years (unlike amounts in Flexible Spending Arrangements that are "use it or lose it" if not used by the end of the year). Tax-advantaged contributions can be made by individuals or employers: the individual and family members can make **tax deductible contributions** to the HSA even if the individual does not itemize deductions or the individual's employer can make contributions that are not taxed to either the employer or the employee. Funds distributed from the HSA are not taxed if they are used to pay qualifying medical expenses. HSA owners between age 55 and 65 are allowed to make additional catch-up contributions. Individuals eligible for Medicare, may not open an HSA.

Qualified medical expenses that HSAs can be used for are those defined in Sec. 213(d) and include non-prescription medicines and drugs. However, dietary supplements that are merely beneficial to general health are not reimbursable.

Funds in an HSA may be invested as the account holder sees fit (certificates of deposit, money market funds, mutual funds, etc.) except they may not be invested in life insurance contracts.

There are many resources for HSA information. Rev. Proc. 2004-50 explains HSAs in question and answer format as does IRS Publication 969. At the U.S. Department of the Treasury website, **www.treas.gov,** under Direct Links, Money management, click on Health Savings Accounts. By clicking on the Resources link, you will be redirected to additional websites including HSA and HDHP providers.

- *HIPAA - Health Insurance Portability and Accountability Act of 1996*

HIPAA provides for improved access, portability and renewability of health insurance coverage. **An unfortunate byproduct of HIPAA's very complex requirements affected the tax-free fringe benefit treatment of some individual policies.** Since June 30, 1997, HIPAA requires health insurance companies to offer group coverage to all employers with two or more employees. State governments had to adopt guidelines and had the option to require group policies to be offered to employers with one employee.

Some **individual** health policies were amended to prohibit tax-free fringe benefit treatment for their premiums. Some insurers require participants to sign statements indicating that their individual premiums are not being paid by their employer or reimbursed by their employer as a fringe benefit. Employers who were unable to obtain a group policy before HIPAA's changes **should seek group coverage** for their employees and replace such individual policies. Pre-existing condition exclusions are reduced by the employee's period of creditable coverage as of the enrollment date, so long as the person does not have more than a 63-day break in coverage. **To continue paying for an individual health policy, that requires the insured to sign a statement as described above, will cause the employee to be taxed on the premiums as a "taxable fringe benefit."**

- *MSAs - Archer Medical Savings Accounts*

Archer Medical Savings Accounts (MSAs) have been discontinued after December 31, 2005. An Archer MSA is a tax-exempt trust or custodial account with a bank or an insurance company in which you can save money for future medical expenses. This account must be used in conjunction with a high deductible health plan (HDHP). MSAs can be rolled over into HSAs. (IRS Publication 969)

- *Fraternal Medical Co-ops*

Fraternal form of non-insurance carriers, such as The Christian Care Ministry, Brotherhood Newsletter, Samaritan Ministries, etc, are not normally incorporated under state insurance laws as are insurance companies. Lutheran Brotherhood, Woodmen of the World and others have existed for a long time. The monthly payments to a fraternal form of medical non-insurance **qualifies** for "tax free" fringe benefit treatment. These co-op providers have group characteristics and will not require participants to sign any statement as described above.

- *WHY It Is Important to Establish Medical Risk Protection as a Fringe Benefit:*

If an employee were to receive taxable salary and pay their own medical insurance premiums, two costly things happen:

1. *Because of the 7.5% limitation on Schedule A or not having enough to itemize, the premium may not be deductible, and*
2. *Social security tax will be paid on that portion of the salary.*

NOTE: Employed ministers who pay their own health insurance premiums cannot deduct the cost on Form 1040, line 29, self-employed health insurance deduction.

Health Reimbursement Arrangements - (HRA)

During 2002, IRS Notice 2002-45 and Rev. Ruling 2002-41 gave employers guidelines on establishing Health Reimbursement Arrangements. The HRA **must be paid for by the employer;** employees can not make a salary reduction election to pay for an HRA. An HRA provides reimbursements up to a maximum dollar amount for a coverage period and any unused portion of the maximum dollar amount at the end of a coverage period is carried forward to increase the maximum reimbursement amount in subsequent coverage periods. Employees, their spouses, and their dependents can be reimbursed for out-of-pocket medical costs that would otherwise be Schedule A medical deductions. **Nondiscrimination rules of Sec. 105(h) apply to HRAs.**

The complex interaction between HRAs and Sec. 125 health flexible spending arrangements is explained in IRS Notice 2002-45. Revenue Ruling 2004-45 addresses the interaction between Health Savings Accounts (HSAs), Sec. 125 health flexible spending arrangements, and health reimbursement arrangements (HRAs).

Self-Insured Medical Reimbursement Plans

A qualified medical expense reimbursement plan is a plan or arrangement under which an employer pays the medical expenses incurred by its eligible employees, their spouses and dependents and is non-taxable according to Sec. 105(b). **Strict nondiscrimination rules in Sec. 105(h)** do apply to self-insured plans. The employer may make payments directly to the provider of the service (the physician, hospital, or insurer) or it may reimburse the employees. The upper limit or cap, for example, $500 or $1,000, must be uniform for all employees eligible for the plan. **When funded by a salary reduction**, it becomes a **"use it or lose it"** fringe benefit. Available amounts not used for medical expenses cannot be paid as additional compensation or carried over to the next year.

Caution: Reimbursing an employee for the extra medical expenses typically not covered by an insurance policy **without** an established qualified medical reimbursement plan in place results in taxable income for the employee. **It is wise to seek the assistance** of an attorney and/or benefits consultant to draft a qualified self-insured plan.

When an employer has a qualified Sec. 125 Cafeteria Plan, it can include a self-insured medical reimbursement option. As a non-taxable option in a Sec. 125 Cafeteria Plan, each employee would be allowed to choose the "cap" that would best fit their family.

Disability Insurance

Premiums for disability insurance paid by the employer are not taxable income according to Sec. 105(e). The income from a disability plan provided by the employer is taxable as sick pay. Either the employer or the third party payor must report benefits as salary on Form W-2, subject to the appropriate withholding requirements. Benefits received by a dual-status minister will be subject to social security, unless he is exempt as an individual.

However, if the **employee** pays the premium for a private disability insurance policy, the cost of the premium is not deductible, and the income from the plan is **not taxable**.

Cafeteria Plans

A cafeteria plan is a separate written benefit plan maintained by an employer or a third party administrator under which all participants are employees and each participant has the opportunity to select the particular benefits that he desires according to Sec. 125. A plan must offer both a cash benefit and at least one statutory nontaxable benefit. Nontaxable benefits include group term life insurance up to $50,000 coverage, dependent care assistance, disability benefits, accident and health benefits, self-insured medical reimbursement benefits, and group legal services. There has been a reduction in the cost of adopting a prototype plan from a third party administrator and the annual cost of maintaining the plan. IRS Notice 2002-24 suspended the requirement to file Form 5500 for Sec. 125 plans.

Salary reduction agreements under which participants elect to reduce their compensation or to forgo increases in compensation can be utilized to begin a cafeteria plan. Benefits are of the **"use it or lose it"** nature and therefore should be set conservatively.

Qualified Moving Reimbursement

Unreimbursed qualified moving expenses to move the family when there is a change of job location is an above-the-line deduction subtracted from gross income in arriving at adjusted gross income under Sec. 62(a). Reimbursed qualified moving expenses from an employer **with** an accountable plan are excludable from an employee's gross income as a qualified fringe benefit under Sec. 132(a)(6). Reimbursed qualified moving expenses from an employer **without** an accountable plan are to be included in an employee's gross income. The employee can then deduct the qualified moving expenses as an adjustment. Having an accountable plan for moving reimbursement requires the same three rules that are discussed fully in Chapter Three for reimbursed professional expenses.

Qualified moving expenses are limited to the reasonable cost of:
1. Moving household goods and personal effects from the former residence to the new residence; (includes cost of packing, crating, transporting your goods; also includes the cost of storing and insuring your goods for any period of 30 consecutive days after the day your things are moved from your former home), and
2. Traveling, including lodging during the period of travel from the former residence to the new place of residence. Auto travel can be the actual gas and oil expenses for the trip or the IRS mileage allowance for moving **Jan 1 to Aug 31 15¢** and **Sept 1 to Dec 31 22¢** a mile in **2005**. (2006 - 18¢) (Use travel expenses for only one trip for yourself and members of your household. However, all of you do not have to travel together or at the same time.)

The following costs of moving are unqualified and **nondeductible**: meals, temporary living expenses, pre-move house hunting trips, expenses of sale or lease of a home, and expenses of purchase or lease of a home. An employer reimbursement to an employee for costs of moving that are not allowable is taxable salary and must be reported on Form W-2.

Two requirements of **Sec. 217** must be met for moving expenses to be allowable. The new place of work must be at least **50 miles** farther from the former home than was the former place of work. Employment in the new area must be full-time for **39 weeks** during the 12 month period immediately following the move. Self-employed persons must be working 78 weeks during a 24-month period immediately following the move. **Employed ministers** are subject to the 39 week work requirement.

If the employer expects the employee to satisfy the 50 mile and 39 weeks of work requirements for deduction, the allowable moving reimbursement is not subject to income tax withholding or social security. Dual-status ministers and lay employees do not pay social security on allowable moving reimbursements.

If the employer knows that the requirements of Sec. 217 **will not be met**, the nonqualifying moving reimbursement is subject to both income tax and social security tax withholding for the lay employee. Nonqualifying moving expense reimbursement paid to a dual-status minister is subject to income tax and social security tax and the additional tax liability should be included in his estimate or optional withholding.

Educational Assistance Programs

An educational assistance program is a plan established and maintained by an employer under which the employer provides educational assistance to employees. Education expenses that improve or develop the capabilities of an individual, not limited to courses that are job related or part of a degree program, qualify under Sec. 127. The annual excludable amount for educational assistance is **$5,250**.

Public Law 107-16 eliminated the termination provision from Sec. 127 and gave it a permanent status. **Graduate level courses qualify** for the exclusion effective for courses that began after December 31, 2001.

Notice in **Chapter Three that educational expenses that are job related** can be reimbursed by an employer as business expenses or deductible on Schedule A if unreimbursed.

Qualified Tuition Reduction

Employees of qualified educational organizations described in **Sec. 170(b)(1)(A)(ii)** can exclude from gross income qualified tuition reduction, including cash grants. An educational organization is described in Sec. 170(b)(1)(A)(ii) has as its primary function the presentation of formal instruction, and it normally maintains a regular faculty and curriculum and normally has a regularly enrolled body of pupils or students in attendance at the place where its educational activities are regularly carried on.

This fringe benefit is **not available** for any other type of nonprofit organizations according to Revenue Ruling 78-184. A church that provides tuition payments for employee's children must treat the payments as a **taxable fringe benefit**, as payment for services. (Private Letter Ruling 9226008)

According to Sec. 117(d)(2), the exclusion applies to tuition for education provided at the employer's school as well as at any educational institution. The exclusion is limited to education below graduate level. A special rule applies to graduate students at eligible educational institutions who are engaged in teaching or research activities for the institution.

Qualified tuition reduction applies to: (1) an individual currently employed by the educational institution; (2) a person separated from service with the institution due to retirement or disability; (3) a widow or widower of an employee who died while employed by the institution, (4) spouses and dependent children of the above.

The nondiscrimination rules under Sec. 414(q) apply to a qualified tuition reduction plan.

Qualified Scholarships

While scholarships are typically provided to non-employees, we felt it important to include the following "non-fringe benefit" discussion, following the educational topics we have just discussed.

Sec. 117(a) provides for qualified scholarships given to degree candidates to be excluded from income to the extent amounts are used for "qualified tuition and related expenses." Related expenses include fees, books, supplies, and equipment required for courses of instruction. Additional amounts for room, board, or incidental expenses are not excludable. So that recipients understand their tax liabilities, they should be formally advised in writing that amounts granted for expenses incurred are taxable income if the total amount exceeds tuition and fees required for enrollment and related expenses according to IRS Notice 87-31. Add the taxable amount to any other amounts on Form 1040, line 7. Then write "SCH" and the taxable amount in the space to the left of line 7.

To establish a private foundation that can grant qualified scholarships requires legal assistance. Revenue Procedure 76-47 (clarified by 85-51, amplified by 94-78) establishes seven conditions and a percentage test or a facts and circumstances test for a qualified scholarship program. The program must impose minimum eligibility requirements that limit the independent selection committee's consideration to those children of employees who meet the minimum standards for admission to an educational institution. No more than 10% of the program's recipients can be employee's children.

Voluntary Tax Shelter Retirement Plans

The following "sheltered" retirement plans are those to which a taxpayer can contribute on a voluntary basis and reduce their taxable earnings by the amount of the contribution. When a taxpayer has an income tax liability, it is good tax planning to consider making contributions to a "sheltered" retirement plan. Even when a minister has **no income tax** liability, he may wish to contribute to a Sec. 403(b) Tax Sheltered Account and **reduce his social security base.**

When an employer establishes a voluntary salary reduction 403(b) account for one employee, it is required that all of the employees on staff be notified that they have the opportunity to make voluntary salary reduction contributions to a 403(b) account. It is not necessary that they choose to participate.

Employees of nonprofit organizations contributing to a Sec. 403(b) voluntary salary reduction plan can also make contributions to an individual IRA account or annuity. Between July 2, 1986, and January 1, 1997, a nonprofit organization could not establish a Sec. 401(k). Since 1997, tax exempt organizations can set up 401(k) plans. Contributions to a Sec. 408(p) Simple Retirement Plan can only be made to the extent of Schedule C honorariums and professional income.

● *Retirement Savings Contributions Credit*

For tax years after 2001 and before 2007, low income taxpayers are allowed a tax credit for a portion of contributions made to Traditional IRAs, Roth IRAs, elective deferrals made to a Simple IRA, 401(k), 403(b), or 457(b) plan. The maximum credit is 50% of the individual's first $2,000 contributed; thus the maximum credit per each individual is $1,000. However, contributions are reduced by any distributions taken during a 2 year lookback period. Compute the credit on Form 8880 and enter the credit on Form 1040, line 51.

● *Effect of Sec. 911 Foreign Earned Income Exclusion*

According to Reg. 1.403(b)-1(e)(2), foreign earned income counts as includible compensation if an employee wishes to make contributions to a TSA.

According to Reg. 1.219-1(c)(1), for IRA purposes compensation does not include foreign earned income and/or housing that is excluded from income and contributions to an IRA are not allowed.

● *Distributions and Penalties*

Early distributions of voluntary plans before age 59$\frac{1}{2}$ or disability are subject to the 10% early withdrawal penalty. To transfer or "roll-over" distributions within 60 days to another qualified tax shelter plan will prevent tax in the year of distribution and the 10% penalty. According to Sec. 72(T)(2)(A)(iv), early distributions which are part of a series of substantially equal periodic payments received at least once a year for the life or life expectancy of the taxpayer or for joint lives of taxpayer and beneficiary will not be subject to the 10% penalty regardless of taxpayer's age..

Required minimum distributions from most qualified plans must begin by April 1 of the calendar year following the calendar year in which you reach 70$\frac{1}{2}$. No contributions can be made after reaching 70$\frac{1}{2}$ for all plans except the Sec. 403(b) and Simple Plan.

If taxpayer continues to work after 70$\frac{1}{2}$, a Sec. 403(b) can receive contributions and is not required to begin distributions until after retirement.

Tax Sheltered Accounts - (TSA)

TSAs are available for employees of nonprofit organizations or public schools according to Sec. 403(b). IRS Publication 571 contains additional information on TSAs. An employee of a qualified organization can make an election to reduce their taxable salary and request that the employer make **non-forfeitable** (employee is always 100% vested) contributions to a Sec. 403(b) plan. For an employee who continues to work past age 70$\frac{1}{2}$, contributions can still be made.

Salary reduction contributions to a TSA are not to be shown on the W-2 as income in Box 1. The amount of the contribution is required to be shown with the appropriate code in Box 12, Form W-2.

Contributions **are subject** to social security tax and medicare tax for the lay employee, according to **Revenue Ruling 65-208**, and must be included on the W-2, Box 3 and Box 5.

Contributions to a TSA by a dual-status minister **are not subject** to social security according to **Revenue Ruling 68-395**. If you have paid social security on contributions to a TSA as a dual-status minister you should file amended returns for the open years and request a refund.

Beginning in years after December 31, 1996, a self-employed minister will be treated as his own employer that is presumed to be an exempt organization eligible to participate on his behalf in a Sec. 403(b) plan. Ministers employed by non-exempt organizations can participate in Sec. 403(b) plans so long as their duties consist of the exercise of ministry. With the absence of a W-2, the amount of the contribution must be deducted on Form 1040, line 28.

In **2005**, an employee can exclude up to 100% of includible compensation for the employee's most recent year of service or **$14,000** with an additional **$4,000** catch up if age 50 or over by the end of the year, whichever is the smallest amount. (2006 - $15,000 with an additional $5,000 catch up if age 50 or over by end of year) If a taxpayer can participate in a Sec. 401(k) plan with another for-profit employer, the combined limit for both plans will be $14,000.

A special election allows a certain long-term employee to "catch up" on the funding of their retirement benefit by increasing their elective deferrals over the **$14,000 limit**. An employee who has completed **15 years of service** with a qualified organization can make an additional contribution. If during your church career, you transfer from one organization to another or to an associated organization, treat all this service as service with a single employer. Under the election, the annual limitation is increased by the **smallest of**: (1) **$3,000**; (2) $15,000 minus any elective deferrals made by the organization and previously excluded under the catch-up election; or (3) $5,000 times the employee's years of service minus the elective deferrals made to plans of the organization in earlier taxable years. In effect, elective deferrals for an employee (under 50) who qualifies for the 15 year rule is **$17,000** for 2005, (over 50 - **$21,000**)

● *Includible Compensation*

Includible compensation for the employee's most recent year of service is a combination of income and benefits received in exchange for services provided to the employer that maintains the employee's 403(b) account, and that the employee must include in income. Beginning in 1998, Sec. 403(b)'s definition of includible compensation was expanded to include (1) elective deferrals (your employer's contributions made on your behalf under a salary reduction agreement), (2) amounts contributed or deferred by your employer under a Sec. 125 cafeteria plan, (3) amounts contributed or deferred by your employer under a Sec. 457 plan, and (4) income otherwise excluded under the foreign earned income exclusion.

An employee's most recent year of service is the employee's last full year (ending no later than the close of the taxable year for which the limit on annual additions is being determined) that the employee worked for the employer that maintains a 403(b) account on the employee's behalf. (Sec. 403(b)(4)). The most recent year of service may precede the taxable year by up to five years; thus, contributions may be made for an employee for up to five years after retirement, based on the last year of service before retirement. (Sec. 403(b)(3)).

Beginning in 1997, compensation for a self-employed minister who is treated as if employed by a nonprofit organization is his **net earnings from self-employment** reduced by contributions to retirement plans and the deduction for one-half of the self-employment tax. This definition for includible compensation for an evangelist clearly takes the combination of **salary and parsonage allowance** from Schedule SE.

In Private Letter Ruling 200135045, the IRS concluded that Sec. 107 housing allowance **was not** includible compensation for the employee because it was not required to be reported anywhere on an informational return by the employer. **However**, in a footnote, the IRS stated, "ministerial services are covered by social security provisions under the Self-Employment Contributions Act (SECA)." Under Sec. 1402(a)(8), Sec. 107 housing allowance **is included** in determining net earnings from self-employment for purposes of SECA. Now an employee can contribute up to 100% of includible compensation, subject to the annual limitations; the question of whether housing allowance is considered as "includible compensation" or not, affects fewer ministers.

A private letter ruling is directed only to the taxpayer who requested it. Section 6110(k)(3) of the Code provides that it may not be used or cited by others as precedent.

Individual Retirement Accounts - (IRA)

You may also contribute annually to an IRA. IRS Publication 590 contains detailed information on IRAs. The maximum spousal IRA limit for a married couple filing jointly is $8,000 for 2005, or $8,500 if only one of you is 50 or older, or $9,000 if both of you are 50 or older, as long as your combined compensation is at least that much. Contributions for 2005 must be made by April 17th, 2006. You can set up and make contributions to an IRA if you received taxable compensation during the year and have not reached age 70° by the end of the year.

Total **individual** contributions to all IRAs (regular & Roth) for a tax year cannot exceed **$4,000**, or **$4,500** if you are 50 or older by the end of the year. (2006 - $4,000, plus $1,000 catch up) IRA contributions limits will increase to $5,000, plus $1,000 catch up by year 2008.

According to Reg. 1.219-1(c)(1), for IRA purposes, compensation **does not include Sec. 911**, foreign earned income and/or housing that is excluded from income and contributions to an IRA are not allowed.

• *Sec. 408(a) - Traditional Individual Retirement Accounts*

Payments to a regular Individual Retirement Account (IRA), if paid by an employer, must be shown as salary, subject to social security, and subtracted as an adjustment on Form 1040, line 32, if allowed as deductible contributions.

You will receive a Form 5498 by May 31, from the trustee of your account, each year stating the amount you have contributed for the current year and the value of your account. The earnings of an IRA accrue tax-free as long as you do not withdraw them.

For those who are active participants in an employer retirement plan, SEP, TSA, or a Keogh; contributions to an IRA can still be made but may not be deductible contributions. Since 1998, active participation in an employer-sponsored plan by one spouse does not prevent the non-participating spouse from making a deductible contribution to an IRA unless their combined AGI reaches the phaseout level between $150,000 and $160,000. For active participants in 2005, the AGI phaseout range for making deductible IRA contributions for single persons is **$50,000 to $60,000**. For married persons filing jointly the range is **$75,000 to $85,000**. For married persons filing separately, if they lived together for any part of the year, the phaseout range is **$0 to $10,000**. For active participants in 2006, the AGI phaseout range for making deductible IRA contributions for single persons is $50,000 to $60,000. For married persons filing jointly the range is $75,000 to $85,000. The phase-out range reaches $80,000-$100,000 in 2007 for married persons filing jointly.

There is a provision that allows you to designate contributions as non-deductible, even if they qualify as deductible. **This prevents "wasted" deductions when there is no tax liability.** It allows the combination of "sheltered" and "non-sheltered" contributions to the same plan. Contributions that you choose to designate as non-deductible can be changed to deductible on an amended return for three open years.

Recordkeeping for non-deductible contributions to an IRA is the **responsibility of the taxpayer!!** Form 8606 is necessary to be completed and attached to your Form 1040. The non-deductible basis or contributions will be returned to you in retirement as non-taxable. If a taxpayer fails to keep record of the basis of his IRA account, the IRS can treat it as fully taxable upon withdrawal. Keeping copies of your tax returns in a safe place for your total working lifetime is your responsibility. The earnings of non-deductible or designated contributions are sheltered from tax until withdrawal.

Since 1998, **penalty free** withdrawals from IRAs can be used for qualified higher education expenses and up to $10,000 (lifetime cap) of qualifying "first time" home-buyer expenses. You are a "first time" home buyer if you did not have a present ownership interest in a principal residence in the two year period before the acquisition of a new home. Such distributions would be subject to regular tax.

● *Sec. 408A - Roth Individual Retirement Accounts*

Contributions to a Roth IRA are non-deductible in the year of the contribution. As with regular IRAs, **earnings accumulate within a Roth IRA tax free**. Qualified **distributions** from a Roth IRA **are also tax free** and not subject to a 10% penalty. Qualified distributions are those made after a 5 year period, and in addition, made after age 59½, after death to a beneficiary, after becoming disabled or distributed to pay for "qualified first time home buyer expenses." Nonqualified distributions are includible in income to the extent they exceed total contributions and are subject to a 10% penalty unless an exception applies. **Total individual** contributions to all IRAs (regular & Roth) for a tax year cannot exceed **$4,000**, or **$4,500** if you are 50 or older by the end of the year. (2006 - $4,000, plus $1,000 catch up) IRA contributions limits will increase to $5,000, plus $1,000 catch up by year 2008. For single persons the phaseout range is **$95,000 to $110,000**. For married taxpayers filing a joint return the phaseout range is **$150,000 to $160,000**. For married persons filing separately, if they lived together for any part of the year, the phaseout range is **$0 to $10,000**.

Roth IRAs are a wonderful choice for the non-tax paying minister's retirement planning. A Roth IRA invested in a mutual fund will capture the long term growth of the capital market.

Existing IRAs may be converted to Roth IRAs if your modified adjusted gross income is $100,000 or less. The conversion of a regular IRA to a Roth IRA is treated as a taxable distribution. A conversion from a regular IRA to a Roth IRA is taxable in the year it is done.

If you have contributed to or converted to a Roth IRA during the year and later become ineligible because your income is too high or because you are filing a married separate return, there are provisions for recharacterizing or unconverting back to a regular IRA. Timely recharacterizing can be chosen because you or your tax advisor discover that it was unwise to convert to a Roth IRA and pay tax. Treasury Decision 9056 is the final regulation for conversions and Reg. 1.408A-5 provides rules regarding the recharacterizing of IRA contributions.

Self-Employed Keogh Plans (H.R. 10)

Salaries received as "employees" are not eligible for making contributions to self-employed Keogh plans. Only income from honorariums or true independent contractor status qualify as income from which Keogh contributions can be made under Sec. 401(c). Contributions and other additions to a defined contribution plan on one's own account or on account of another employee cannot exceed the lesser of $42,000, or 100 percent of the participant's compensation.

Housing Exclusion

Two separate types of housing are provided in the tax law. Dual-status employees **must use** Sec. 107 housing. Lay employees that meet the requirements must use Sec. 119 housing.

Lay Employees - Sec. 119

For the lay employee (janitor, dorm parents, managers, caretakers, etc.), the value of employer furnished lodging and utilities is not taxable if:

1. Furnished on your employer's business premises;
2. For your employer's convenience;
3. And as a condition of your employment. Regular and emergency duties must be continuous, on constant 24-hour call.

All three conditions must be met or the value of housing provided is taxable. The exclusion does not apply if an employee can take cash instead of the housing.

"In the case of an individual who is furnished lodging in a camp located in a foreign country by or on behalf of his employer, such camp shall be considered to be the business premises of the employer," according to Sec. 119(c).

Employees of colleges, universities, and other educational institutions described in Sec. 170(b)(1)(A)(ii), can exclude the value of qualified campus lodging, provided they satisfy an adequate rent requirement. The rent must be at least equal to the lesser of:

1. *5% of the appraised value of the lodging, or*
2. *the average of rentals paid by individuals (other than employees or students) for comparable lodging held for rent by the educational institution.*

If the rent paid is less than the lesser of these amounts, you must include the difference in your income. The lodging must be appraised by an independent appraiser and the appraisal must be reviewed on an annual basis. If the rent paid is more, the employee gets to exclude the entire lodging's value according to Sec. 119(d) and IRS Pub 525, pages 6 & 7.

Originally, Sec. 119 housing had been subject to social security. A Supreme Court Decision (Rowan Companies, Inc. v. United States) and Revenue Ruling 81-222 stated that the IRS cannot have a different definition for wages for the lay employee for income and social security purposes. Therefore, the value of the meals and lodging that had been subject to social security in the past became exempt retroactively.

Dual-Status Minister - Sec. 107

Dual-status ministers are not taxed on the parsonage provided them and/or the parsonage allowance paid to them as a part of their compensation. Chapter Two gives full detailed discussion on how to designate in advance and compute tax-free parsonage allowance.

Unfortunately, the Rowan court case has no effect on the Sec. 107 for the dual-status minister. According to Flowers v. Commissioner, TC Memo 1991-542, parsonage provided and/or parsonage allowance paid **are still subject to social security** unless Form 4361 has been timely filed. Some tax advisors have applied the Rowan case to Sec. 107, **out of context**, and the IRS has assessed the preparer the negligence penalty for each return filed in error. If you have failed to pay social security on your housing under Sec. 107, we would advise you to amend your returns and pay the correct amount of social security.

NonTaxable Gifts & Benevolence

According to Sec. 102, gifts received directly from relatives and personal friends for personal reasons are not taxable income. When you **have not performed a service** and someone gives you a gift **and it does not come from an employer**, the gift can be considered non-taxable.

Deacon's Fund or Benevolence Fund: Churches should never hesitate to help people in the community who are unemployed, have a catastrophic illness, been an accident victim, or aged. Benevolent gifts to non-employees that are based on their needs are **non-taxable and are never** to be reported on an information return (Form 1099). Churches should be actively meeting the benevolent needs of their community.

Often a church is asked to "funnel" a designated contribution to a specific individual. If that individual **is involved** in a ministry or missionary endeavor and the church finance committee is given control of the gift and chooses to honor the request, it should be treated as compensation to the individual receiving it, and included in the church's payroll reports. When the gift can be forwarded to a mission organization with which the individual is employed, that organization can include the amount in their payroll reports. If the individual to whom the gift is designated **is not involved** in a ministry, extreme caution must be exercised by the church. When a designated recipient is a relative of the donor and not involved in a ministry, deductible contribution receipts should not be issued. **Deductible contribution receipts should not be issued when the church does not have the right to control the monies.**

Caution: When an employer helps an employee or a member of an employee's family with crisis needs it will result in taxable compensation to the employee, according to Sec. 61. **We recommend** that a local non-employer, nonprofit organization (such as Red Cross) be utilized to raise funds for the crisis needs.

Accountable Reimbursement Plan for Professional Expenses

Auto, travel, and professional expenses that are reimbursed by an employer who has adopted an accountable reimbursement plan according to Sec. 62(2)(A), are not required to be shown on the employee's W-2. The employee must "adequately account" to his employer. Chapter Three contains tax savings and audit reduction reasons for establishing an accountable reimbursement plan with your employer.

Sec. 457 Deferred Compensation Plans

Employees who have fully funded qualified tax shelter retirement plans may be able to defer additional taxable income through a Sec. 457 "non-qualified deferred compensation plan." These plans, which frequently use a trust arrangement known as a "rabbi trust," may be adopted with a model rabbi trust published by the IRS in Rev. Proc. 92-64.

To successfully defer taxes under a "non-qualified plan," the compensation deferred must, until actual payment, continue to be owned by the employer and be available to the employer's creditors if the employer becomes bankrupt or insolvent. The annual limitation for Sec. 457 deferrals is 100% of includible compensation up to **$14,000** for **2005**. (2006 - $15,000)

Distributions from a Sec. 457 plan are wages subject to income tax withholding and are to be reported on **Form W-2**. Social security and medicare taxes should be withheld and matched for a lay employee participant. A dual-status minister participant will be subject to social security and medicare tax unless he has become exempt by filing Form 4361. Distributions to a beneficiary of a deceased participant under a Sec. 457 plan are reported on Form 1099-R. (IRS Notice 2003-20)

Prizes and Awards

Prizes and awards received in recognition of past accomplishments, even if you are selected without action on your part and you are not expected to render any future services, are taxable according to Sec. 102(c). They can be non-taxable if you "designate" the prize to charity according to Sec. 74.

Gratuity Payments to a Retired Minister

Payments made by a congregation to a retired minister (because of age or disability), if he is not expected to perform any further services, are non-taxable. Such non-taxable gifts based on gratitude and appreciation can be given after a minister retires in addition to his receiving taxable pension from an established plan. It is also necessary that the payments not be required by an established plan or **agreement entered into before retirement** and that they are determined in the light of the financial position of the congregation and the needs of the recipient, who had been adequately compensated for his past services.

A statement in Osborne v. Commissioner, T.C. Memo 1995-71: "In Revenue Ruling 55-422, the Service indicated that a payment by a congregation to a retiring clergyman would qualify as an excludable gift where, among other circumstances, there was a closer personal relationship between the recipient and the congregation than is found in secular employment situations."

This is a unique special provision for retired clergy. In all other careers all payments after retirement are taxable to the retiree because of past services. (Sec. 102(c)(1)) In Goodwin v. United States, KTC 1995-479, the judge said, "...the legislative history suggests that section 102(c)(1) was enacted to address other fact situations..."

## CHAPTER TWO

Parsonage Allowance

The understanding of this chapter will result in tremendous income tax savings. Some dual-status ministers have spent many years in the ministry and have not been aware of how to "designate" their expenses of providing a home as non-taxable parsonage allowance. Internal Revenue Code Sec. 107 says:

"In the case of a minister of the Gospel, gross income does not include—-

1. **The rental value of a home furnished to him as part of his compensation; or**

2. **The rental allowance paid to him as part of his compensation, to the extent used by him to rent or provide a home and to the extent such allowance does not exceed the fair rental value of the home, including furnishings and appurtenances such as a garage, plus the cost of utilities."**

Are You Entitled to the Parsonage Allowance Exclusion?

The answer to the question, "Are you entitled to parsonage allowance?" is also going to answer another question, "Are you considered self-employed for social security purposes?" **Sec. 107's** regulations refers us to **Sec. 1402(c)'s** regulations for the definition of some important terms. When we determine that you are entitled to tax-free parsonage allowance, we will have also determined that you are to be considered self-employed for social security purposes. **Dual-status means** that you are an **employee** for income reporting, fringe benefit, and expense deducting purposes and **self-employed** for social security purposes.

When we determine that you are not entitled to tax-free parsonage allowance, we will have also determined that you are to be considered as a lay employee for income tax and social security withholding purposes.

Generally, there are three circumstances to be considered. (1) Are you employed by a church or an integral agency of a church? (2) Are you performing ministerial services? and (3) Are you ordained by a church or "the equivalent thereof?" While all three tests must be satisfied for you to be treated as a dual-status minister for tax purposes, recent court cases and letter rulings reflect a very friendly definition of circumstance #3.

Are You Employed by a Church or An Integral Agency of a Church?

To qualify for minister's tax treatment and tax-free parsonage allowance your employer must be a church or an integral agency of a church. (See "Two Exceptions")

Churches (or a convention or association of churches) are exempt from federal income tax under Sec. 501(a) as a religious organization described in Sec. 501(c)(3) and further described in Sec. 170(b)(1)(A)**(i)**. Churches and their integrated auxiliaries receive an **"automatic"** exemption recognition. A church **is not required to file Form 1023** to be exempt from federal income tax or to receive tax deductible contributions. In many states a church is not required to become incorporated. We feel it is wise for a church to protect themselves legally by incorporating at the state level. When a congregation has a membership, separate accounting, and meets regularly for worship services, they are a church. **Many churches do not have and do not need** a determination letter from the IRS. When a church voluntarily files Form 1023 to obtain formal recognition of their exemption they will receive a determination letter. Form 8718 must accompany the Form 1023 and requires either a $150 or a $500 fee to the IRS. Two IRS Publications, **1828** "Tax Guide for Churches and Religious Organizations" and **557** "Tax Exempt Status for Your Organization" are recommended resources.

Religious organizations that are not churches can be under the control of a church or group of churches by drafting their bylaws to meet most of the requirements of **Revenue Ruling 72-606** and be an integral agency of a church.

Organizations that are not integral agencies of a church, must file Form 1023. They will receive a determination letter stating that they are an organization described in Sec. 501(c)(3) and further described in Sec. 170(b)(1)(A)**(vi)**. Two well known national non-denominational, non-integral agency organizations are Youth for Christ and Child Evangelism Fellowship.

● *Two Exceptions Available For Those Not Employed by a Church*

Only a church or an integral agency can give authority to a minister to perform the duties of the ministry. Therefore it would be important for a minister to have been formally ordained, licensed or commissioned by their church before utilizing either of the following exceptions.

First exception to the requirement that your employer must be a church or an integral agency is provided if you are **assigned or appointed** to perform services at an organization that is not a church by your denomination or church. When you are considering employment by an organization that is not a church or an integral agency, have your church or denomination assign you to the position during the hiring process **before** you accept the position. (See "Qualifying Service Includes" from Reg. 1.1402(c)-5(b), item #7, on page 36.)

The Second exception is provided when the services you are performing is that of conducting religious worship or ministering sacerdotal functions. This exception makes it possible for a **chaplain**, even though he may be employed by a secular organization or an **evangelist**, who holds engagements in rented auditoriums or stadiums, to qualify for minister's tax treatment. A chaplain or evangelist can have their housing allowance designated by their home church or their denomination.

Definition of Church

The following definitions will help you determine the correct status of your organization. Regulations for Sec. 107 state:

> *"The term, religious organization, has the same meaning and application as is given to the term for income tax purposes."*

The scope of what organizations are included in the definition of "churches" is found in the instructions of **IRS Pub. 557, page 25.** *"Because beliefs and practices vary so widely, there is no single definition of the term "church" for tax purposes. The Internal Revenue Service considers the facts and circumstances of each organization applying for church status."* A separate organization affiliated with a church will be considered an integrated auxiliary if the principal activity of the organization is exclusively religious. Examples of organizations considered to be integrated auxiliaries of a church are a men's or women's organization, a religious school (such as a seminary), a mission society, or a youth group.

A church or organization may be liable for tax on its unrelated business income. Unrelated business income is income from a trade or business, regularly carried on, that is not substantially related to the charitable, educational or other purpose constituting the basis for the organization's exemption. An organization must file Form 990T if it has $1,000 or more gross income from an unrelated business.

The following partial list of organizations that are not required to file an annual information return (Form 990) gives us an **"expanded definition"** of what the IRS deems to be a church to satisfy Sec. 107 and Sec. 1402(c). *(Summary from Pub. 557, page 8:)*

1. A church, an interchurch organization of local units of a church, a convention or association of churches, an integrated auxiliary of a church.
2. A school below college level affiliated with a church or operated by a religious order, even though it is not an integrated auxiliary of a church.
3. A mission society sponsored by or affiliated with one or more churches or church denominations, more than half of the society's activities are conducted in, or directed at, persons in foreign countries.
4. An exclusively religious activity of any religious order. (See discussion of "Religious Orders" in Chapter Five.)

No part of an organization's net income may inure to the benefit of any individual.

Integral Agency of a Church

A nonprofit organization with a determination letter showing it is not a church but is described as an organization for charitable, educational, or other purposes in Sec. 170(b)(1)(A)**(vi)**, would be able to treat an employee performing ministerial duties as a dual-status minister for tax purposes and designate parsonage allowance if it meets **most of the requirements** of Revenue Ruling 72-606 to be an integral agency of a church.

Revenue Ruling 70-549 and Revenue Ruling 72-606 clearly state what is required for a school, mission, or other religious organization to be under the control of a church and qualify as an integral agency of a church. The eight criteria listed in **Revenue Ruling 72-606** are:

1. whether the religious organization incorporated the institution;
2. whether the corporate name of the institution indicates a church relationship;
3. whether the religious organization continuously controls, manages, and maintains the institution;
4. whether the trustees or directors of the institution are approved by or must be approved by the religious organization or church;
5. whether trustees or directors may be removed by the religious organization or church;
6. whether annual reports of finances and general operations are required to be made to the religious organization or church;
7. whether the religious organization or church contributes to the support of the institution; and
8. whether, in the event of dissolution of the institution, its assets would be turned over to the religious organization or church.

The only time a nonprofit organization that is neither a church nor an integral agency of a church can treat an employee as a dual-status minister is when he has been assigned or appointed by a church or when his duties are conducting worship or ministering sacerdotal functions. All other employees will be lay employees regardless of their duties.

In the court case, Flowers v. U.S. CA 4-79-376-E, 11/25/81, it was found that Texas Christian University only met two of the possible eight tests of Revenue Ruling 72-606. Therefore, an ordained employee could not have a parsonage allowance as allowed by Sec. 107. Though Texas Christian University has a close relationship with the Disciples of Christ they did not evidence direct or indirect control by the church. TCU had been an integral agency of the Disciples of Christ and had changed their bylaws to become a non-integral agency. Doing so qualified them for favorable financing and bond issues for growth and expansion.

In Private Letter Ruling, 9144047, the teaching staff of a college was allowed to be dual status, because their employing college was deemed to be an integral agency of a church.

We advise any organization that is unsure of their standing to examine their determination letter from the IRS and their bylaws. If it is determined that your organization is a non-integral agency, consider obtaining legal assistance to amend your bylaws to comply with those areas of control and to become an integral agency of a church.

Are You Performing Ministerial Services?

The salary or honorarium you receive for services which are ordinarily the duties of a minister of the gospel is eligible for minister's tax treatment and tax-free parsonage allowance. There is no parsonage allowance exclusion for a minister who volunteers and receives no ministerial income.

As a minister you are not required to be performing all of the duties or even able to perform all of the duties to be a dual-status minister for tax purposes. Since 1978, according to Revenue Ruling 78-301, it is only necessary that a minister be able to perform **"substantially all"** of the duties of the ministry to be a minister for tax purposes.

Regulations describe the following types of services that a minister in the exercise of his ministry performs:

1. the ministration of sacerdotal functions, (*includes baptism, communion, marriage and funerals*)
2. the conduct of religious worship, (*includes preaching, bible study, evangelism, and music*)
3. service in the administration, control, conduct, and maintenance of religious organizations, including integral agencies, under the authority of a church or church denomination, and
4. the performance of teaching and administrative duties at theological seminaries. (*Includes parochial schools, colleges, and universities which are integral agencies of a church or church denomination according to* Revenue Ruling 62-171.)

● **Qualifying Services Include (*Summary from Reg. 1.1402(c)-5(b).*)**

1. A minister employed as minister of a church is eligible for parsonage allowance. If more than one minister is on the staff, they may all exclude their parsonage allowance as long as their duties are those of ministers of the gospel.
2. Conducting religious worship services or ministering sacerdotal functions are ministerial services whether or not performed for a church or integral agency of a church. This provision makes it possible for a **chaplain** to qualify for dual-status treatment, even though he may be employed by a secular organization.

3. Service performed by a chaplain at either a church-related hospital or health and welfare institution, or a private nonprofit hospital is considered to be in the exercise of his ministry according to Revenue Ruling 71-258.

4. A minister engaged in the control, conduct, and maintenance of an integral agency of a religious organization or church. Members of the executive staff and those serving as departmental managers are performing qualifying ministerial services according to Revenue Ruling 57-129. Duties can include **supervising** all aspects of an organization's finances, fund raising, plant and equipment, kitchen operations and housekeeping according to Private Letter Ruling 8142076.

5. A minister serving on the faculty as a teacher or administrator of a college or seminary which is operated as an integral agency of a church according to Revenue Ruling 71-7.

6. A minister serving on the faculty as a teacher or administrator of an undergraduate or parochial school that is affiliated with a church. (Included in the "expanded definition" of a church)

7. A minister **assigned or designated by a church to perform services for an organization that is not a church,** even though such service may not involve the conduct of religious worship or the ministration of sacerdotal functions, is in the exercise of his ministry. **Example:** A minister assigned to perform advisory service to a printing company in connection with the publication of a book dealing with the history of his church denomination. (Reg. 1.1402(c)-5(b)(v)) Your services are ordinarily not considered to have been assigned or designated by your church if any of the following are true:

    a. The organization for which you perform the services did not arrange with your church for your services.

    b. You perform the same services for the organization as those performed by its other employees who were not designated as you were.

    c. You perform the same services before and after the designation.

8. A rabbi is a minister of the gospel and qualifies for the parsonage allowance. Cantors also qualify according to Revenue Ruling 78-301.

9. A minister who performs evangelistic services at churches away from his permanent home may exclude parsonage allowance paid to him by the churches according to Revenue Ruling 64-326.

10. Writing or producing religious books, articles, audio or video tapes is considered to be in the exercise of your ministry. Royalty income from their sale is self-employment income.

11. Though not able to be treated as self-employed when an employee of a government entity, Sec. 107 parsonage designation was allowed in C.T. Boyd, Jr. v. Commissioner, T.C. Memo 1981-528, by the Church Federation of Greater Indianapolis, Inc., even though Boyd was employed by the Indianapolis Police Department as Senior Chaplain. As a police chaplain he was under the direct supervision of the Chief of Police. However, the Federation retained supervision over Boyd's ecclesiastical performance and maintained day to day contact with him. He was not able to be treated as self-employed when an employee of a government entity. This is **an exception** to Sec. 107 and Sec. 1402(e) qualification being simultaneous.

● **Non-Qualifying Duties Include** *(Summary from Reg. 1.1402(c)-5(c).)*

1. Ministers who were administrators of nonprofit nursing homes. The nursing homes were not religious organizations nor integral agencies of a church. The services performed by the ministers were not the type of services that qualified. (Jesse A. Toavs et al., 67 TC 897)

2. If a minister is performing a service for an organization which is neither a religious organization nor operated as an integral agency of a religious organization and the service is not performed following an assignment or designation by his ecclesiastical superiors, then the service performed is not in the exercise of his ministry. **Example:** A minister is employed by a university to teach mathematics and history. The university is not a church nor an integral agency of a church. He receives honorariums from time to time performing wedding and funerals for friends. The honorariums are his only ministerial income.

3. Routine services performed by secretaries, stenographers, mail clerks, file clerks, janitors, etc., are not in the exercise of ministry according to Revenue Ruling 57-129. Usually the services performed by doctors, nurses, auto mechanics, pilots, carpenters, cooks, etc., are not in the exercise of ministry.

4. A chaplain in the armed forces is specifically denied this exclusion since he is considered to be a commissioned officer, and as such is not a minister in the exercise of his ministry. Military officers are given tax-free housing, therefore, Sec. 107 is not needed.

5. Similarly, service performed by an employee of a State as a chaplain in a State prison or a government owned hospital is considered to be performed by a civil servant of the State and not by a minister in the exercise of his ministry. In Private Letter Ruling 9052001, the chaplain's employment, supervision, evaluation, and termination were strictly the responsibility of the warden. The chaplain's church had designated a housing allowance. However, since written reports or contacts between the chaplain and his church were voluntary, he was not entitled to exclude a housing allowance as a civil servant of the State.

Are You Ordained By A Church Or "The Equivalent Thereof?"

If you are employed by a church or an integral agency of a church and are performing ministerial services, you are considered to be "the equivalent of" ordained at the time you begin your employment. When a church calls or hires you to be their minister, they have informally given you the authority to conduct religious worship and to administer ordinances at the time of employment. You satisfy the "ability to perform services in control, conduct and maintenance of the church" merely by being employed by a church as their minister. In Salkov v. Commissioner, supra, 46 TC at 190 (1966) it was concluded that the congregation's formal selection of the taxpayer as their cantor constituted commissioning him as their minister.

Here is a very important court definition of a "duly ordained, commissioned, or licensed" minister. In J.M. Ballinger, U.S. Court of Appeals, 10th Circuit, No. 82-1928, 3/7/84, it was stated:

*"Not all churches or religions have a formally ordained ministry, whether because of the nature of their beliefs, the lack of a denominational structure or a variety of other reasons. Courts are not in a position to determine the merits of various churches... We interpret Congress' language providing an exemption for any individual who is `a duly ordained, commissioned, or licensed minister of a church' to mean that the **triggering event** is the assumption of the duties and functions of a minister."*

It is very important for a minister who wishes to become exempt from social security to be aware of the date his/her ministry begins. Parsonage allowance must be designated in advance and to the extent used, it is free from income tax. The deadline for a timely filed "Application for Exemption from Self-Employment Tax for Ministers," Form 4361, is the due date of the tax return (including extensions) for the second year in which he/she earns more than $400 from the ministry. The minister who is formally ordained, licensed, or commissioned by his church or denomination experiences a very important and meaningful event. However, when he receives formal credentials **after the date of being hired by a church**, it is not an important event for tax purposes. On the **date of being hired** by a church, he was **entitled to ministerial tax status**.

Adversely, Private Letter Ruling 200318002 ignored both the 1966 Salkov case and Ballinger case cited above. The IRS stated as their opinion that the formality of credentials was a necessary fact. In the Technical Advice Memorandum, they rejected the "date of hire" as the beginning of ministry.

Only a church or an integral agency can give authority to a minister to perform the duties of the ministry. **When a minister is not employed by a church or an integral agency,** it is important for him to have been formally ordained, licensed or commissioned as a minister by a church before being "assigned or designated" to a position with a non-church. When a minister, as **an independent evangelist or a chaplain,** performs worship and/or ministers sacerdotal functions at locations outside of a church, it is also important for him to have been formally ordained, licensed, or commissioned as a minister by a church.

Prior to 1978, Revenue Ruling 65-124 was very strict in stating that a minister had to be able to perform **"all"** the religious functions of the church to be defined as "ordained" for tax purposes.

Since 1978, Revenue Ruling 78-301 added the word **"substantially"** to the definition in order to allow Jewish cantors to qualify for parsonage allowance. Exactly what was meant by "substantially all" was unclear until 1989. Two tax court cases involving ministers with limited authority who waited until formal ordination to file Form 4361 to become exempt from social security were decided. IRS denied both applications as being untimely filed. In Private Letter Ruling 9221025 the teaching staff of a school below college level were deemed to be ministers for tax purposes even though they were unable to conduct public adult worship or any of the sacerdotal functions. In Private Letter Ruling 199910055 it was determined that the Minister of Education, Minister of Music and Minister of Stewardship, all ordained deacons, were ministers for tax purposes. Performing ministerial duties and being **recognized as a religious leader** by his church qualifies a minister, administrator or teacher for ministerial tax status.

James S. Wingo, 89 TC No. 64, Docket No. 8613-85: Taxpayer was an ordained "deacon" and licensed as a probationary minister of the United Methodist Church beginning in 1980. He became an ordained "elder" in 1984 and wished to become exempt from social security. The United Methodist Church considers both "deacons" and "elders" as ordained ministers of the Church, and as an appointed full-time minister Rev. Wingo was permitted to administer the sacraments, provide for the organizational concerns of the local church, conduct divine worship, preach the Word, perform marriage ceremonies, and bury the dead. IRS determined that for purposes of applying for the exemption from self-employment tax **under Sec. 1402** or for obtaining the parsonage exclusion **under Sec. 107**, Rev. Wingo was a minister.

John G. Knight, 92 TC No. 12, Docket Nos. 45505-86, 27182-87: Taxpayer was a licentiate of the Cumberland Presbyterian Church and served as a supply minister. He preached, conducted the worship service, visited the sick, performed funerals, and ministered to the needy. Because he was not ordained, he could not moderate the session, administer sacraments, or solemnize marriages. Duties and functions were considered by the court to be appropriate for a "duly ordained, commissioned or licensed minister."

Private Letter Ruling 199910055: A local church requested rulings for three "ordained deacons" whose duties were to assist the senior minister. The Minister of Education's duties included planning and supervising youth, adult, and family activities. He selected the curriculum, scheduled activities, and coordinated lay volunteers. The Minister of Music coordinated all choir and music activities. The Minister of Stewardship performed financial and managerial functions. He encouraged members of the congregation to give their time, talent, and money to the church. They met with the elder to plan the worship services, assist with the sacraments, and officiate at weddings and funerals. All three positions were deemed to be eligible for ministerial tax treatment.

Haimowitz v. Commissioner, T.C. Memo 1997-40: Mr. Haimowitz served for 30 years as an executive director of a temple. He never claimed ministerial tax status or housing allowance during his working years. He eventually performed more religious duties, such as helping students with memorization of blessings, Torah readings, and elocution. He frequently helped plan weddings and participated in the wedding ceremony as a witness to the contract, but he never officiated. After he retired, **never having shown himself to have been recognized as a religious leader** by the temple, he claimed that his pension should be tax-free parsonage allowance. He provided no evidence that a housing allowance had been designated in advance, so it was not allowed and was not appealable.

Private Letter Ruling 9221025: Because some churches allow both genders to be given full authority in the ministry and others extend full authority only to the men, an unequal tax advantage resulted for some women in the ministry. On February 20, 1992, Private Letter Ruling 9221025, gave a positive answer to a major denomination concerning their "commissioned" female teachers being eligible for dual-status treatment. The female staff performed full-time public ministry functions including: classroom teaching; evangelizing; counseling individuals; leading Bible study groups, devotions, worship services for youth, and a congregation's music ministry; giving the children's sermon at the regular Sunday worship service, coordinating lay church workers; caring spiritually for the sick and imprisoned and their families; etc., The female staff could not perform adult worship for both genders and could not perform any sacerdotal functions.

After this decision, the female teaching staff was changed to dual-status tax treatment and parsonage allowance was designated for them.

Private Letter Ruling 200318002: In a Technical Advice Memorandum it was determined that the "date of hire" did not constitute an adequate equivalent of a "duly ordained, commissioned or licensed" minister for the administrators and teachers of a christian school, affiliated with a church.

Cases of Kirk v. Commissioner, 51 T.C. 66 (1968) AFFIRMED, 425 F.2d 492 (D.C. Cir 1970) and Lawrence v. Commissioner, 50 T.C. 494 (1968) were cited. Cases before 1978 reflect the historic IRS position that to be a minister of the gospel one had to be able to perform all of the duties of the ministry. The TAM states that "at a minimum, the person is required to be duly ordained, licensed, or commissioned."

That Rev. Ruling 62-171, Rev. Ruling 78-301, J.M. Ballinger, U.S. Court of Appeals, 10th Circuit, No 82-1928, 3/7/84, and John G. Knight, 92 TC No.12, Docket Nos. 45505-86, 27182-87 were all ignored in the TAM is unfortunate. Though it reflects the attitude of the IRS drafter, it is disappointing that case history and a very important court definition from the J.M. Ballinger court case were ignored. As a result, we have Private Letter Ruling 9221025 and Private Letter Ruling 200318002, both addressing the administators and teaching staff of christian schools, giving us very diverse guidance.

• *Summary Comments*

Making a determination of the correct tax status of an employee at the time he is hired is important. An employee that **qualifies** for dual-status minister tax treatment needs to have his housing allowance designated in advance. If he wishes to consider whether to become exempt from paying social security on his earnings from the ministry, he needs to understand when his ministry begins and file before the due date of the second return in which he earns $400 or more. (See complete discussion in Chapter Four.) A lay employee that **does not qualify** for dual-status tax treatment is subject to withholding of payroll taxes on his wage and matching of social security and medicare taxes by the employer.

When you consider all facts and circumstances of each employer and employee relationship in light of the citations (various regulations, court cases, revenue rulings and private letter rulings), you may discover that your church has not properly classified some of your staff members.

Due to the adverse attitude reflected in **Private Letter Ruling 200318002**, discussed above, a parochial school who has not extended dual-status tax treatment to their administrators and teaching staff may want to first request their own private letter ruling. For a parochial school who has the practice of formally commissioning their administrators and teaching staff, stay on course, continue to treat them as dual-status ministers. There is much solid ground, regulations, rulings and case history to support your position.

The impact of a church, an integral agency of a church or a parochial school making a switch to dual-status tax treatment for their qualifying staff can cause confusion. It is important to inform them of the tax law provisions that apply to them and teach them to keep records for the new housing allowance for which they are entitled. An employer who has been matching social security and medicare tax should be willing to pay **an additional salary factor** equal to the matching portion to each staff member affected. Otherwise, an employee with little or no parsonage expense would experience an economic loss. Federal income tax savings for $10,000 of parsonage expenses will be $1,000 for those in the 10% bracket, $1,500 for those in the 15% bracket, or $2,500 for those in the 25% bracket. There will be state income tax savings also.

Employees who have been accustomed to having their taxes withheld by their employer will appreciate an employer who will continue to withhold taxes under the optional withholding provisions. Withholding should be adequate to prepay the reduced income tax and social security and medicare tax at the self-employed rate of 15.3%

Whether or not an employee has an opportunity to elect to become exempt from social security will depend on the date they were hired or the date they began performing ministerial duties.

Parsonage Allowance Exclusion Rules

What Does the Parsonage Allowance Exclusion Include?

It includes anything spent to provide a home for the dual-status minister and his family. Regulations for Sec. 107 state that the parsonage allowance does not include food or a maid. Parsonage allowance is the tax-free treatment of a minister's **personal** home expenses on a **cash basis.** Do not use business capital asset rules. Do not depreciate home capital expenses. Parsonage allowance expenses include those for the house, its contents, the garage, and the yard. The following list shows typical expenses that are to be considered in computing the amount of parsonage allowance:

1. Rent or principal payments, cost of buying a home, and down payments.
2. Real estate taxes and mortgage interest for the home. These expenses are deductible again as itemized deductions. **A DOUBLE DEDUCTION**, but allowable by IRS!! (Revenue Ruling 62-212 and Sec. 265(a)(6)) **An amazing "tax shelter"!**
3. Insurance on the home and/or contents.
4. Improvements, repairs, and upkeep of the home and/or contents. Such as a new roof, room addition, carpet, garage, patio, fence, pool, appliance repair, etc.
5. Furnishings and appliances: dish washer, vacuum sweeper, TV, VCR, DVD, stereo, piano, computer (personal use), washer, dryer, beds, small kitchen appliances, cookware, dishes, sewing machine, garage door opener, lawnmower, hedge trimmer, etc.
6. Decorator items: drapes, throw rugs, pictures, knick knacks, painting, wallpapering, bedspreads, sheets, towels, etc.

7. Utilities - heat, electric, non-business telephone, water, sewer charge, garbage removal, cable TV, non-business internet access, etc. (Show long distance business telephone calls, the business percent of cellular phone and internet access usage as a professional expense. Both income tax and self-employment tax will be reduced.)

8. Miscellaneous - any thing that maintains the home and its contents that you have not included in repairs or decorator items: cleaning supplies for the home, brooms, light bulbs, dry cleaning of drapes, shampooing carpet, expense to run lawnmower, tools for landscaping, garden hose to water lawn, etc.

The expenses in item No. 8 are often purchased at the grocery or variety store. It is a good practice to buy a supply of household cleaning supplies separately and save the receipt. An easy way to keep record of them is to use the "Housing Expense" section of our **"Professional Tax Record Book."**

Do Not Include the following: Maid (or any labor hired for maintenance such as lawn care), groceries, personal toiletries such as toothpaste, shampoo, deodorant, laundry and dish soap, paper products; personal clothing, coats, shoes, jewelry; toys, bicycles, hobby items, cassette tapes, CD's, computer games, computer application software, VCR movies, etc. When a cellular phone is used outside of the home, do not use the personal portion as parsonage allowance.

Parsonage allowance is free from income tax, **but subject to social security and medicare tax.** Parsonage expense details, receipts, and records are **not to be submitted to the employer.** They are handled differently than the professional business expenses we will discuss in Chapter Three. The personal home expenses can remain confidential. If the designated amount is greater than the amount substantiated, it is the responsibility of the individual minister to show the "excess parsonage allowance" as income on Form 1040, line 7.

● *Double Deduction of Interest & Taxes*

Sec. 265(a)(6) provides for the deduction of home mortgage interest and property taxes on Schedule A even though all or part of the mortgage is paid with funds you get through a nontaxable parsonage allowance. In 1983 Congress attempted to end the "double deduction," but Revenue Ruling 83-3 was revoked by Sec. 265(a)(6). This "double deduction" has been available since 1962. Revenue Ruling 62-212 provided for this amazing "tax shelter" and it was strengthened with an addition to Sec. 265.

● *Interest Rules*

Interest from loans for the initial purchase of a home, improvements and furnishings can be used for parsonage allowance exclusion. However non-mortgage interest for home purchases will not be allowable on Schedule A as "personal interest." Mortgage and home equity loan interest will qualify as Schedule A "mortgage interest" deduction because the home is used as collateral. Mortgage and home equity loan interest for the purchase of and improvement of the parsonage can also be used for parsonage allowance exclusion. Mortgage and home equity loan interest for any other purpose will not be allowable as parsonage allowance exclusion. If a home equity loan is used for home improvements and the purchase of an auto, only the home improvement portion of the interest can be used as parsonage allowance exclusion.

● *Cash Basis*

Since capital expenditures for home principal, improvements, furniture, and appliances are on a cash basis, it is important to understand when to deduct them if the purchase involves borrowed funds. Any purchases with bank charge cards are treated the same as if you paid cash for the item. Any purchases for the home that involves a loan from a bank, store, or individual are treated as not paid for in full. Non-credit card loan payments for home, improvements, and furniture are to be deducted as they are paid.

● *Transition Periods*

Generally, a minister can use the expenses of one home for his parsonage allowance exclusion. When he owns a vacation or second home on a permanent basis, he can only use the expenses for the "main" home as parsonage allowance exclusion.

During a temporary period of changing employers, changing parsonages, or building a parsonage, expenses for two parsonages are allowable according to a tax court case, Fred B. Marine, 47 TC 609 (1967). The temporary period would continue as long as both homes remained personal use. If before a sale, the previous home is rented, the rental income and expenses will generally be reportable on Schedule E.

• Sale of Personal Residence

There is no requirement that the cost of purchasing and improving a residence be adjusted or reduced by the tax-free principal portion of parsonage allowance. Therefore, in reporting the sale of a personal residence, the whole cost basis is used to determine gain or loss. If the sale of a personal residence results in a loss, it is not deductible from other taxable income.

The Taxpayer Relief Act of 1997 provided for an exclusion of $250,000 of gains on the sale of a personal residence for a single owner and $500,000 for married owners. There are two tests:

1. "Once-in-two-years." You must not have used this rule for at least two years prior to the current sale.
2. "Used-as-your-home." In the 5 year period before the current sale, you must have used the property as your home for a total of at least two years.

If you meet the tests, you can exclude the gain. Ministers who have owned their home and relocate to a church that provides them a parsonage can sell without incurring tax on the gain if the two tests are met. If the two tests are not met, the gain is taxable. However, you can claim a reduced exclusion if you sold the home due to a change in health or job transfer by employer. **IRS Publication 523**, "Selling Your Home," explains all the details of selling a personal residence.

The above rules for the sale of a personal residence never apply to the sale of business or rental property. Business property sales will result in taxable gains or deductible losses.

How Much of a Minister's Salary Can Be Designated?

This question has experienced a lot of activity the past couple of years. **The fair rental value computation remains as the "top limit".** Congress codified and strengthened their intent and position by passing the "Clergy Housing Allowance Clarification Act of 2002" on May 20, 2002. The new text Congress added to Sec. 107 is quoted at the beginning of this Chapter. (See "Warren v. Commissioner Tax Court Case")

• IRS Position as Stated in Publication 517

Nothing in the Internal Revenue code or regulations establish a "flat" dollar limitation or a percentage of income limitation for the parsonage allowance exclusion. **The amount designated as parsonage allowance must be a specific dollar amount or a specific percentage of salary.** Employers can designate a blanket percentage of their staff's salaries as parsonage allowance. Individuals on their staff who anticipate incurring a greater amount for parsonage expenses should be allowed to ask for a higher amount to be designated.

Publication 517, page 8, gives the **historic** explanation of how much the parsonage allowance can be:

> *"If you own your home and you receive as part of your pay a housing or rental allowance, you may exclude from gross income the **smallest** of the following:*
> 1. The amount actually used to provide a home,
> 2. The amount officially designated as a rental allowance, or
> 3. The fair rental value of the home, including furnishings, utilities, garage, **etc**.
>
> *You must include in gross income any rental allowance that is more than the smallest of your reasonable pay, the fair rental value of the home plus utilities, or the amount actually used to provide a home."*

Reasonable pay means that a minister should not be over-compensated for the amount of time spent and amount of work accomplished. Usually the opposite is true, a minister is under-compensated. In Revenue Ruling 78-448, a tax protest minister was considered to have been over-compensated and was not allowed to have 100% of his compensation be tax-free housing allowance **because he did not perform any services to earn it**. The Revenue Ruling deals with a tax protest situation, and has no application to a legitimate church/minister employment relationship. Some IRS personnel have wrongly claimed that Revenue Ruling 78-448 prevents a minister from using 100% housing designation. In the recent tax court case, Warren v. Commissioner 114 T.C. 23, fourteen judges agreed that a minister's parsonage allowance **can be 100%** of his compensation.

Fair Rental Value: The **"top limit"** that can be claimed by a minister as parsonage allowance exclusion is based on his furnished home's fair rental value, cost of utilities, etc. Actual expenses incurred up to this "top limit" can be used as parsonage allowance exclusion. In the year of purchase, or a year in which a major payment of principal or a large outlay for improvements or furniture is made, it is important to carefully compute the "top limit" as follows:

FRV of house + FRV of furniture + decorator items + utilities + miscellaneous

To support the computation of your housing allowance in a year of major expenditures we recommend you obtain a professional appraisal of your home's fair rental value. Fair rental value is what it would cost to rent a comparable home in your neighborhood. A "rule of thumb" among realtors nationwide is that the fair rental value of a home (without furnishings) amounts to **1% of the appraised fair market value** per month. This formula is fairly accurate. However, **the condition, location, local market demand, and local economic conditions** of your home will need to be considered.

Example: If your home is appraised at $150,000, the monthly FRV could be $1,500. Annual FRV could be $18,000 ($1,500 X 12).

The fair rental value of furniture is more difficult to compute. Based on the amount, age, and condition, we recommend that you estimate your furniture FRV conservatively.

We have included space on the "Worksheet for Form 2106" to compute the limitation in a year of major expense. FRV of the home would take the place of down payment, closing costs, principal, interest, taxes, insurance and major repairs (line 4 through line 9). FRV of the furniture would take the place of actual furniture purchases (line 10). Actual costs of decorator items (line 11), utilities (line 12), and miscellaneous items (line 13) are to be used. We have **included an example** of the computation of the "top limit" in Rev. Snodgrass's return in Chapter 7.

When actual expenses exceed the fair rental value limitation they are lost. There are no provisions for carryover of unused portions. Rather than lose the ability to exclude your down payment or major home expenses, it has been wise to consider obtaining a second mortgage and spreading the cost over a few years and keep within the "top limit" each year. (See "Tax Plan")

• *Warren v. Commissioner Tax Court Case*

In Warren v. Commissioner, 114 T.C. 23, decided on May 16, 2000, it was determined that a minister's parsonage allowance should not be limited by the fair rental value computation. Of the seventeen judges considering the case, fourteen agreed and three dissented. The majority stated that Sec. 107(2) was limited to the amount **used** to provide a home, not the fair market rental value of the home. They stated that the burden of obtaining valuation estimates could become troublesome where rental value is in dispute. It is their opinion that neither the statues nor the legislative history requires the imposing of potentially burdensome valuation obligations. The parsonage allowance provided for in Sec. 107(2) simply requires that the source of the funds be the minister's compensation. Thus, fourteen judges agreed that a minister's parsonage allowance should not be limited by the fair rental value computation. The case also clearly stated that a minister's parsonage allowance could be 100% of his compensation.

The IRS appealed the decision in September, 2000. A serious new issue of the constitutionality of parsonage allowance was raised when Professor Erwin Chemerinsky filed a motion to intervene in the appeal.

Congress **acted quickly** with Public Law 107-181, on May 20, 2002. **Congress reinstated the fair rental value limitation as their intent.** The "Clergy Housing Allowance Clarification Act of 2002" added new text to Sec. 107, and it is quoted at the beginning of this Chapter. The Warren v. Commissioner, Tax Court No. 14924-98, August 26, 2002, was dismissed.

Therefore, parsonage allowance really has not changed, just strengthened, and still limited by the Fair Rental Value computation.

• *Tax Plan*

Loans from employers can be used to spread principle payments over a period of time and avoid losing the benefit of parsonage allowance expenses. It is important that interest be charged if the loan exceeds $3,000 and that the loan be secured by the home and recorded at the courthouse. Sec. 483 rules concerning "below market" interest loans require that the **Applicable Federal Rate** (published monthly by the IRS) be charged for loans over $3,000. Based on the date of the loan, apply that month's rate for the duration of the loan. (A browser search for **afr** will quickly give you a website with the rates!)

Often the minister's employer would rather not charge him interest for a loan. But Sec. 483 says interest is required. This requirement has a **positive tax benefit** for the minister employee.

When the loan is secured by the home, the interest will qualify for deductible "home interest" on Schedule A and also as a part of tax-free parsonage allowance. Therefore, we recommend the following procedure: (1) pay an additional salary factor to equal the correct interest (annually or monthly); (2) increase the designated parsonage allowance as needed; (3) accept the interest payment from the minister (annually or monthly). The amount of interest deductible on Sch A reduces the minister's taxable income, while the extra salary is tax-free housing, subject only to social security.

Loan principal forgiveness: In the event the employing church who loans their minister money for a down payment or major improvement desires or decides to forgive the principal of a loan we recommend the following procedure: (1) secure the loan with the home and record it at the courthouse; (2) forgive a portion of the loan principle each year so that the "top limit" is not exceeded; (3) increase the designated parsonage allowance as needed; (4) treat the amount of principal forgiven as income.

In Sec. 7872, loans with "below-market interest rates," not involved with real or personal property, require that the Applicable Federal Rate be charged for loans over $10,000.

Good tax planning for a minister is to **"overdesignate"** his parsonage allowance and allow for unexpected expenses and increases in utility costs to be covered. The "unused parsonage allowance" will be shown as income on Form 1040, line 7.

● *Part-Time Ministers*

For a minister who is serving part-time and is not fully supported by the employer, it is possible to designate all or 100% of his salary as parsonage allowance. Since parsonage allowance is not required to be shown on Form W-2, a Form W-2 generally does not need to be prepared.

When a minister is employed outside the church and a new or small congregation cannot fully support him, it is good tax-planning for the minister to make substantial Schedule A contributions to the church. The church will then have the funds to pay an adequate salary, designate it as parsonage allowance, and allow him to take full advantage of Sec. 107 parsonage allowance. The minister who is not exempt from social security will have to pay social security taxes on the parsonage allowance.

● *What If Your Home Is Debt Free?*

Obtaining a new mortgage or equity line of credit that is used for major home improvements is always allowable principle and interest for parsonage allowance. However to refinance and use the proceeds for investments or any non-home purchases, payment of the principal and interest will not be available for parsonage allowance.

In Swaggart v. Commissioner, TC Memo 1984-409, the taxpayer argued that rental allowance was fully excludable from gross income regardless of how the funds were spent.... In rejecting such argument, the court concluded that Congress intended to exclude from the minister's gross income only that portion of his compensation paid by the church which was **actually used** by the minister for providing a home for himself. In a previous case, Reed et al, 82 TC 208, the court had also restricted tax-free parsonage to out-of-pocket expenses. For the minister whose home is paid for or nearly so, the amount of actual expenses for taxes, insurance, upkeep, utilities, etc., does not allow as much tax-free parsonage allowance.

In Private Letter Ruling 9115051, the IRS tells us their position in regards to "refinancing the debt-free parsonage." It is important to understand that Sec. 6110(j)(3) of the Code provides that a letter ruling may not be used or cited as precedent.

The IRS was asked to respond to these questions: "Are payments made on a home equity line of credit (secured by the debt-free home) expenses for which a parsonage allowance may be granted by the church? Would taking out a loan secured by a mortgage on the home result in expenses for which a parsonage allowance may be granted by the church?"

The response of IRS was: "Neither payments made on the home equity line of credit nor on the mortgage secured by the house are being used to rent or provide a home as required by Sec. 107 and the regulations. Therefore, amounts designated by the church to pay for these expenditures are not excludable from the minister's gross income as a parsonage allowance under Sec. 107."

What is Meant By "Official Designation"?

"Official designation" means that the employer designates, by official action, **IN ADVANCE**, the amount the dual-status minister expects to spend for all the expenses of his home. The designation can be done by the official board or the congregation, and should be recorded in their minutes. **The amount designated as parsonage allowance must be a specific dollar amount or a specific percentage of salary.** Reg. 1.107-1(b) says:

> *"The term 'rental allowance' means an amount paid to a minister to rent or otherwise provide a home if such amount is designated as rental allowance pursuant to official action..... taken **in advance** of such payment by the employing church or other qualified organization.*
>
> *The designation of an amount as rental allowance may be evidenced in an employment contract, in minutes of or in a resolution by a church or other qualified organization or in its budget, or in any other appropriate instrument evidencing such official action. The designation referred to in this paragraph is a sufficient designation if it permits a payment or a part thereof to be identified as a payment of rental allowance as distinguished from salary or other remuneration."*

Because the IRS will accept **a perpetually worded designation**, we recommend using a perpetual clause as a **safety net.** Example: "As long as .....the above amount....shall apply to all future years until modified." We recommend that a minister "tax plan" annually and consider if the amount designated needs to be modified for the coming year.

If you were not aware of how to designate your parsonage allowance or you have had an inadequate amount designated, there is no way to fix the problem for the past. **Now** is the time to designate an adequate parsonage allowance for the future or the rest of the year. In advance of paying for a major expense or a changing from a parsonage provided to buying your own home, do not hesitate to **amend and increase** your designation.

• *Qualified Organization*

This regulation requires that an independent party make the designation and prevents "self-designation." A qualified organization does not have to be a religiously affiliated entity to be able to designate parsonage allowance. Nor is it necessary that the designation come from the payor of a minister's compensation. In C.T. Boyd, Jr. v. Commissioner, T.C. Memo 1981-528, the advance designation requirement was considered to be met by designation of the Church Federation of Greater Indianapolis, Inc., a nonprofit corporation, even though Boyd was employed by the Indianapolis Police Department as Senior Chaplain. As a police chaplain he was under the direct supervision of the Chief of Police. The Federation retained supervision over Boyd's ecclesiastical performance and maintained day to day contact with him.

IRS Letter Ruling 9052001 involved a chaplain employed by a state prison. The chaplain's employment, supervision, evaluation and termination were strictly the responsibility of the warden. The chaplain's church had designated a housing allowance. However, since written reports or contacts between the chaplain and his church were voluntary, he was not entitled to exclude a housing allowance as a civil servant of the State.

• *Ministers Who Own*

Ministers who own their homes will want to designate an amount to cover the total cost of owning, cost of their furnishings, cost of decorating, utilities, and etc.

When the title to the home and the real estate mortgage is in the minister's name, the employer should not make the payments for him. Pay the minister enough salary to pay all the home expenses, and designate an adequate amount as parsonage allowance. The minister who owns his own home should pay his payment and all of the home expenses himself. **Keep it simple**. Hybrid arrangements where the employer pays some of the expenses and the minister pays others, cause confusion and may result in an inadequate designation of parsonage allowance.

Do not do this: When the home is being purchased by the minister it will be subject to real estate tax. If the home is being purchased by the employing church it will not be subject to real estate tax. Any attempt to creatively place the minister's home in the name of the church to avoid paying real estate tax is absolutely wrong. A future transfer of the title to the minister who has paid for the home would result in the FMV of the home to be taxed as salary.

● *Ministers Who Rent*

Ministers who rent their homes will want to designate an amount to cover the actual rent paid, cost of their furnishings, cost of decorating, insurance, utilities, and etc.

● *Church Owns The Parsonage*

If the employer provides the home and/or pays the utilities, its value is automatically free from income tax. The minister then needs to estimate how much he expects to spend in all of the other categories of home expenses and have that amount of his cash salary designated. It is important to understand that the minister living in a church-owned parsonage has **"two pieces"** to his parsonage allowance:

1. a value provided and
2. a designated portion of his cash salary for the additional home expenses.

● *Evangelists*

According to Revenue Ruling 64-326, a traveling evangelist may exclude amounts he receives from various churches or meetings as tax-free parsonage allowance. There are two ways to handle the designation in advance: (1) A supporting or home church could designate an annual amount even though they do not pay or handle the honorariums, or (2) individual host churches can designate a portion of his honorarium as parsonage allowance. This involves communicating with the various churches in advance and sending them a statement requesting that they take action to "designate" a portion of your honorarium as parsonage allowance. We recommend that you get duplicate, non-carbon copies of the "Statement of Parsonage for An Evangelist" printed. Each church on your itinerary can keep a copy and easily provide you a copy.

A traveling evangelist or conference speaker with a permanent home will incur deductible travel expenses for lodging and meals while on the road and use parsonage allowance exclusion for his permanent home. If he lives in a motor home or travel trailer and does not have a permanent home, his lodging and meal expenses will not be deductible as business expenses. His tax home for tax purposes is wherever he "hangs his hat." He may treat the motor home as his parsonage but his meals will not be deductible. The cost of transportation between engagements would qualify as business expense.

An evangelist who forms his own nonprofit corporation, will be an employee of the corporation. An evangelist, as long as the services he performs is that of conducting worship and the ministration of sacerdotal functions, is a dual-status minister for tax purposes. The organization's board can easily designate his parsonage allowance.

● *Missionaries*

Sec. 911 foreign earned income exclusion allows most missionaries serving outside of the United States to be able to earn as much as $80,000 in 2005 and pay no income tax. If they do not qualify to use the $80,000 exclusion, the mission should definitely designate the parsonage allowance for the dual-status missionary. Missionaries who are dual-status ministers should always designate a parsonage allowance so that their home expenses will be excluded while on furlough or sick leave. Chapter Five contains a detailed discussion of the special tax situation for missionaries serving outside of the United States.

● *Retired Ministers & Parsonage Designation*

A **retired minister** receiving an otherwise taxable distribution from a qualified Sec. 401(a), Sec. 401(k), Sec. 403(b), Sec. 408(k), Sec. 408(p) or Sec. 414(e) plan may have a **"parsonage allowance"** designated by the former employer or denominational pension board according to Rev. Ruling 63-156. We recommend that a perpetually worded designation state that 100% of the retirement income be designated as parsonage allowance and be tax free to the extent spent for housing. **(See sample wording in this Chapter)** Language found in the Department of Labor Regulations under ERISA indicate that both types of contributions to a Sec. 403(b) plan (forfeitable and non-forfeitable) are considered as contributions to an employer's plan and both types are eligible for parsonage allowance designation.

According to Rev. Ruling 72-249, the parsonage allowance exclusion is not available to the surviving spouse who continues to receive retirement income as a beneficiary.

Distributions from an IRA or a Keogh retirement plan may not be eligible to be designated as non-taxable housing because their contributions are not identifiable as being based on earnings from the ministry.

Third party payors of retirement plan distributions **will include** the gross distribution on Form 1099-R, Box 1. Not being able to determine the taxable amount Box 2a could be left blank and Box 2b could be checked. As a retired minister receiving distributions from a retirement plan that has been designated as "parsonage allowance" you are to enter the gross amount on Form 1040, line 16a. It is the responsibility of the retired minister to show as taxable on Form 1040, line 16b, any designated distributions not spent for parsonage expenses. If all of the distribution has been spent for parsonage expenses enter -0- on line 16b.

Steps in Designating & Deducting Parsonage Allowance

1. The dual-status minister is to estimate the amount he expects to spend for the coming year and present this to his employer. It is good to overestimate and allow for unexpected expenses and utility cost increases. In advance of a major unexpected expense, or a change from a parsonage provided to buying your own home, do not hesitate to "amend" and increase your designation for the balance of the year.
2. The employer then makes an official written designation based on the dual-status minister's estimate. You may use the suggested wordings we provide.
3. At the close of the tax year, the dual-status minister then compares his actual expenses with the amount designated. If he has incurred any major expenses he will compute the FRV limit. The smallest amount is allowed as his parsonage allowance exclusion.

Parsonage expense details, receipts, and records are **not to be submitted to the employer.** They are handled differently than the professional business expenses we will discuss in Chapter Three. The personal home expenses can **remain confidential**. If the designated amount is greater than the amount substantiated, it is the responsibility of the individual minister to show the "excess parsonage allowance" as income on Form 1040, line 7. Use the "Worksheet for Form 2106" provided in this publication to compute taxable unused parsonage allowance, if any.

A minister who moves and/or changes amounts of parsonage allowance during the year should allocate the annual designations by the week. For example: You were at ABC Church for 17 weeks and your annual parsonage allowance was $5,200. You were at XYZ Church for 35 weeks and your annual parsonage allowance was $13,000. Compute as follows:

$$\$ 5,200 \div 52 = \$100 \times 17 \text{ weeks} = \$1,700$$
$$\$13,000 \div 52 = \$250 \times 35 \text{ weeks} = \$8,750$$

Total parsonage allowance for the two positions would be:

$$\$1,700 + \$8,750 = \$10,450.$$

Once the parsonage allowance has been timely designated, there is no need to attach a copy of the official designation to the tax return itself. Merely show the amount properly designated on the "Worksheet for Form 2106." In the event you are chosen for an audit, the IRS will ask for a verification of the timely official designation from the church records.

Suggested Wording of the Official Designation

When The Church Owns The Parsonage

The chairman informed the meeting that under the tax law, a minister of the Gospel is not subject to federal income tax on "the parsonage allowance paid to him as a part of his compensation to the extent used by him to rent or provide a home."

The parsonage is owned by the church and the actual utility expenses will be paid by the church.

After considering the estimate of Rev. _____ of his additional home expenses, a motion was made by _____, seconded by _____ and passed to adopt the following resolution:

Resolved that of the total cash salary for the year _____, $_____ is hereby designated as parsonage allowance.

Resolved that as long as Rev. _____ is our employee the above amount of designated parsonage allowance shall apply to all future years until modified.

When A Minister Owns Or Rents His/Her Own Home

The chairman informed the meeting that under the tax law, a minister of the Gospel is not subject to federal income tax on "the parsonage allowance paid to him as part of his compensation to the extent used by him to rent or provide a home."

After considering the estimate of Rev._____ of his home expenses, a motion was made by _____, seconded by _____ and passed to adopt the following resolution:

Resolved that of the total cash salary for the year _____, $_____ is hereby designated as parsonage allowance.

Resolved that as long as Rev. _____ is our employee the above amount of designated parsonage allowance shall apply to all future years until modified.

When A Minister Is Employed By A School, College, Or Mission

Most teachers and administrators working for a church or integral agency of a church have an annual contract of employment with that organization. It is convenient to include the necessary written designation within the contract itself. An "Agreement for the Designation of the Parsonage Allowance" could be worded as follows:

According to the provisions in income tax law, a minister of the Gospel is not subject to federal income tax on the "parsonage allowance paid to him as part of his compensation to the extent used by him to rent or provide a home."

Based on Rev._____'s estimate of his home expenses, it is agreed to officially designate $_____ of his total cash salary as parsonage allowance.

Resolved that as long as Rev. _____ is our employee the above amount of designated parsonage allowance shall apply to all future years until modified.

Statement Of Parsonage For An Evangelist

Evangelists can have a supporting or home church designate an annual amount of the honorariums they will receive as parsonage allowance or they can send a statement to churches on their itinerary and have a portion or all of the honorarium designated as parsonage allowance, in advance of the engagement. **Get duplicate, non-carbon sets printed of the following statement:**

According to the provisions in income tax law, a minister of the Gospel is not subject to federal income tax on the "parsonage allowance paid to him as a part of his compensation to the extent used by him to rent or provide a home."

After considering the request of Rev._____, our evangelist, to designate $_____ or _____% of his honorarium as parsonage, a motion was made by _____, seconded by _____ and passed to adopt the following resolution:

Resolved that of the total cash honorarium paid to our evangelist, we hereby designate $_____ or _____% as parsonage allowance.

Name of Church _____   Date _____

Signature _____   Title _____

When A Retired Minister Receives Pension and/or Honorariums

According to the provisions in income tax law, a retired minister of the Gospel is not subject to federal income tax on ministerial retirement distributions or honorariums designated as parsonage allowance to the extent used by him to rent or provide a home.

Resolved that 100% of any retirement distributions, honorariums, or interim salaries are hereby designated as parsonage allowance for Rev. _____.

Resolved that the above amount of 100% of designated parsonage allowance shall apply to all future years.

Name of Church _____   Date _____

Signature _____   Title _____

Computation of Parsonage Allowance -"Worksheet For Form 2106"

● *Value of Parsonage Provided by Church*

Enter the value of a home and utilities provided by the employer in the box provided. It is subject to social security tax. Though it seems to be contradictory, we do not have to use the same formula we used earlier in the chapter for computing the "top limit" for the minister who owns his own home. The fair rental value of the parsonage provided should be reasonable, but has historically been allowed to be a conservative amount in audits. **Do not be guilty of understating your rental value** below a reasonable amount and thereby understating your social security liability.

You may wish to consult a local realtor for an appraisal, or make inquiries of local landlords. **The condition, location, local market demand, and local economic conditions will help you to determine a reasonable value.** The fact that you must live in a particular home as a part of your employment, gives reason for a more conservative estimate of the value of a parsonage provided.

We would like to refer you to the guidelines in Sec. 119 for qualified campus lodging. (See discussion in Chapter One, Lay Employees - Sec. 119.) The guidelines for Sec. 119 are not necessarily applicable to Sec. 107, but they do represent guidelines for housing in another setting. A "bare minimum" rental value should be at least 5% x the appraised value of the home provided. Example: 5% x $150,000 = $7,500 annual FRV of home including utilities. The guidelines for Sec. 119 further require that the appraised value be determined at the end of each year by an independent appraiser, not the employer. However, it is intended that the appraisal be reviewed annually without undue cost to the employer.

A conservative, but realistic rental value estimate of Rev. Snodgrass's $150,000 home including utilities, considering all the facts and circumstances stated above, might be **$13,000 to $15,000** a year.

● *If You Own Your Home - Use Column B and Column A if Computing FMV*

Enter amounts for all parsonage allowance expenses the minister pays or provides for himself on a cash basis in this column. The actual expenses of the home, furniture, utilities, decorating, and miscellaneous expenses are to be shown in Column B. Enter their total on line 14 of the worksheet.

In a year of incurring major expenses, show the computation of fair rental value of furnished home, utilities, etc., in Column A, on line 14. Examine the sample computation we have shown on Rev. Snodgrass's return in Chapter Seven. Enter the lesser of line 14, Column A or Column B on line 15.

Show the amount that has been officially designated as parsonage allowance by the employer on line 16. If line 16 is greater than line 15, enter the "excess parsonage allowance" on line 17 and as income on Form 1040, line 7.

Parsonage allowance, as an exclusion, **is not to be included on Form W-2, Box 1 according to Publication 15-A, page 9.** When the parsonage allowance is included in error on Form W-2, Box 1, we recommend that a corrected Form W-2c be prepared. When it becomes necessary to deduct a large negative parsonage allowance amount on Form 1040, line 7 or line 21, IRS audit exposure is greatly increased. Though not required, we recommend using Form W-2, Box 14, to show a memo of the amount designated as parsonage allowance.

Computation of Social Security Base -"Worksheet For Form 2106"

Parsonage allowance is free from income tax, but subject to social security and medicare tax. Enter the value of parsonage provided and/or the amount of parsonage allowance designated from line 16 on the lines provided. A minister who has elected to be exempt from social security and has an approved Form 4361 does not have to compute this value for Schedule SE.

Earned income credit may be available for some ministers who did not qualify in the past. We refer you to the final page of Chapter Three, "Definition of Earned Income for Ministers," for the changed definitions.

Professional Expenses

In any profession, the ordinary and necessary expenses incurred in order to be able to earn income are deductible according to Sec. 162. In this chapter we will explain how to have an accountable reimbursement plan. The IRS provides very detailed regulations on how to handle reimbursed employee business expenses. It is good stewardship to take the time to learn the rules and legally reduce income tax by adopting a written accountable plan for professional expenses.

● *Contributions ARE NOT Allowable as Professional Expenses*

Contributions, tithes, or offerings paid to a nonprofit organization are **always Schedule A itemized deductions**. Therefore, regardless of a person's occupation, contributions and tithes are **always** deductible on Schedule A as an itemized deduction.

CAUTION: Over the years we have heard and read creative illegal proposals concerning how a minister's contributions could be a salary reduction or reimbursed as a business expense. The concept was especially attractive to ministers who live in parsonages provided by employing churches and are unable to itemize their Schedule A deductions. Computing social security and medicare tax on the reduced income was also attractive. Even if a contract or other arrangement states that excessive dues must be paid by the employee to retain their position, examination of the facts and circumstances will generally determine that taxable compensation has been wrongly reduced.

The following citations are very clear; contributions are Schedule A deductions:

According to Sec. 61, the assignment of income rule, "Income received for personal services is taxable to the person who earns it, even though he assigns it to another."

The **MSSP for Ministers,** an IRS training manual for their auditors, contains this comment, *"Ministers often pay a small annual renewal fee to maintain their credentials, which constitutes a deductible expense. However, ministers' contributions to the church are not deductible as business expenses."*

The **business expense code Sec. 162(b)** specifically states that contributions are Schedule A deductions: *"No deductions shall be allowed under subsection 162(a) for any contribution or gift which would be allowable as a deduction under section 170 (Schedule A) were it not for the percentage limitations, the dollar limitations or the requirements as to the time of payment, set forth in such section."*

● *Babysitting Expenses Are Not Allowable as Professional Expenses*

The cost of babysitting for your children is never a business expense. Child care incurred while both parents are working results in a potential credit to be computed on Form 2441. When an employer pays for an employee's child care, it is generally a taxable fringe benefit and should be included as income on the employee's Form W-2, Box 1. (Exception: a qualified Sec. 129 Dependent Care Assistance Program or a qualified Sec. 125 Cafeteria plan that provides the choice of dependent care assistance.)

● *Different Tax Treatment for Parsonage Expense and Professional Expense*

It is important to separate in our thinking the parsonage expense from professional expense since their tax treatment is very different. **Parsonage expense** details, receipts, and records **are not to be submitted to the employer.** The personal home expenses can remain confidential. If the designated amount is greater than the amount substantiated, it is the responsibility of the individual minister to show the "excess parsonage allowance" as income on Form 1040, line 7. For the best tax advantage, professional expenses must be adequately accounted to the employer and be reimbursed. An IRS regulation requires there to be a written reimbursement plan between an employer and an employee. **Professional expense** details, receipts and records **must be submitted** to the employer for reimbursement.

- *Professional Expense Rules are not Unique to Ministers*

The professional expenses discussed in this chapter are available to all religious workers, both the dual-status minister and lay employee. All of the information in this chapter about auto, travel, and professional expenses is also applicable to for-profit employers and their employees. Independent contractors or evangelists may also adequately account their expenses to a payor.

- *Volunteer Workers*

When a religious worker receives no income as a volunteer for a qualified organization, but incurs out-of-pocket expenses, they are deductible as contributions on Schedule A. Any miles driven for charitable work are deductible at the rate of 14¢ per mile or actual cost of gas and oil. Do not deduct the miles driven for personal worship to regular church services. Do not deduct any value for your time, it is not allowable. Travel away from home expenses are limited to actual cost of lodging and meals.

A welcome change allows volunteer workers who are reimbursed for travel and ministry expenses to be reimbursed using the business standard mileage rate of $40\frac{1}{2}$¢ per mile, January 1, 2005 until September 1, 2005. On September 1, 2005 the rate changed to $48\frac{1}{2}$¢ until December 31, 2005. The Katrina Act, effective September 23, reduced the amount to be reimbursed to volunteers to $48\frac{1}{2}$¢ X 70% = 33.95¢. (2006 the rate of $44\frac{1}{2}$¢ X 70% = 31.15¢)

A volunteer must adequately account to the organization making the reimbursement to be a "bona fide volunteer" according to IRS INFO 2000-0235, released August 24, 2000. If a volunteer does not submit diaries and receipts to the organization, the organization will be required to treat the payments as compensation, prepare Form W-2, and withhold taxes.

Recordkeeping a Must!!

We recommend a careful reading of **IRS Publication 463**, "Travel, Entertainment, Gift and Car Expenses." Recordkeeping rules have always existed. Adequate records or sufficient evidence must be available to support deductions for auto and professional expenses. A record of the elements of an expense made at or near the time of the expense, supported by sufficient documentary evidence, has more value than a statement prepared later, when generally there is a lack of accurate recall. A log maintained on a **weekly basis** is considered a record made at or near the time of the expense. It can not be stressed enough — **adequate records and receipts must be kept to substantiate all expenses.** Good stewardship means keeping good records!

IRS regulations require that careful and adequate records be kept to submitt to the employer for reimbursement. "Adequate accounting" means you will give your employer the same type of records and supporting information that you would be required to show to the IRS if they questioned a deduction on your return. There is **no relief** from keeping adequate records! Receipts are always required for lodging. Receipts are also required for other expenses that exceed **$74.99.** You may maintain an **account book or diary** for any **expense under $75.00** according to IRS Publication 463, page 25.

According to Rev. Ruling 2003-106, if you charge business expense items on your employer's credit card or charge account, you must submit a record of the details as required in Sec. 274. Employee's can be provided a monthly printout of their transactions, add the required details, and submit back to the employer with receipts for lodging and items costing $75.00 or over.

We have available a **"Professional Tax Record Book"** for ministers, religious workers, and professional individuals. It is designed to provide a convenient and efficient way to keep the auto, travel, and professional expense record details required by the IRS. Monthly summary pages are provided. You can easily photocopy the pages and receipts and submit them to your employer for reimbursement. For those who only need to keep records for auto business miles and auto expenses, we have available an **"Auto Log."** Information for ordering these books is given in the back of this publication.

Unreimbursed Professional Expenses

There is no dispute that in order to adopt a written accountable reimbursement plan both the employer and the employee must understand the rules. Therefore, the following results of not establishing such a plan will hopefully provide the motivation to do so and save tax dollars legally. **It is good stewardship** to reduce income tax by **adopting a written accountable plan** for professional expenses!

Unreimbursed professional expenses, other than auto and travel, carry the extra burden of being "required by your employer" and as "a condition of your employment". Establishing an accountable plan and becoming reimbursed for them by your employer is a good way to show they meet these requirements.

If an employer chooses to provide an expense allowance arrangement that **does not meet** the accountable plan requirements, the employer **must report all amounts paid** under the non-accountable plan **as wages** on the employee's Form W-2, Box 1, even though an employee might voluntarily substantiate expenses to the employer and return any excess amounts to the employer. Such allowances paid to lay employees are subject to withholding of income tax and social security withholding and matching. The dual-status minister will incur additional income tax, but can still reduce his social security base by the amount of business expenses.

Tax Savings Illustrated: Our sample return for Rev. Snodgrass in Chapter Seven is computed "without reimbursement" and "with accountable reimbursement." The difference in tax liability illustrates the value of establishing an accountable reimbursement plan.

If You Do Not Adequately Account To Your Employer

Reg. 1.162-17(c) says, **"Expenses for which the employee is not required to account to his employer. If the employee is not required to account to his employer for his ordinary and necessary business expenses, e.g., travel, transportation, entertainment, and similar items, or, though required, fails to account for such expenses, he must submit, as a part of his tax return, a statement showing the following information:"**

All amounts received as advances or reimbursements from his employer, that were not adequately accounted for, must be included as income on Form W-2, Box 1. In order to deduct non-accounted professional expenses on his tax return, he must complete Form 2106 based on his records and supporting evidence.

The following consequences happen when there is no accountable plan:

1. The expenses become "below the line" deductions on Form 2106 and Schedule A. Meals and entertainment are first reduced by 50%, then combined with other miscellaneous expenses, and further reduced by 2% of the employee's Adjusted Gross Income. With higher standard deductions, many taxpayers do not have enough deductions to itemize. **UNLESS** they adopt a written reimbursement plan and adequately account to their employer and become reimbursed for all their professional expenses they may lose the income tax deduction entirely. The standard deduction for 2005 is $10,000 for a joint return and $5,000 for a single return. Reimbursed auto, travel, and professional expenses are not reduced by 2% of AGI. Employees can be 100% reimbursed for meals. Employers deduct only 50% of reimbursed meals & entertainment as a business expense. Nonprofit employers are not affected since they have no tax liability.

2. A large amount of unreimbursed professional expenses deducted on Schedule A causes many employees to be audited. It is a high "dif" score area of a tax return. Establishing an accountable reimbursement plan with your employer could prevent the time consuming trauma of proving your expenses to an IRS auditor.

3. Many states do not allow itemized deductions. Therefore, unreimbursed professional expenses cause additional state income tax.

4. Items such as earned income credit, refundable child tax credit, deductible IRAs, percentage of medical deduction limitation, percentage of child care credit allowable, educational credits, taxable social security benefits, etc., are all affected by the amount of the Adjusted Gross Income figure. Establishing a written accountable reimbursement plan with your employer may qualify you for other deductions and credits. **Parents of college students may qualify for more financial aid.**

5. For lay employees the social security base for both the employer and the employee is greater when there are unreimbursed professional expenses. Establishing an accountable reimbursement plan with your employer will allow the employer to compute social security withholding and matching on just the salary. Dual-status ministers have always been able to reduce their social security base by unreimbursed business expenses.

6. When a dual-status minister's income is a combination of taxable salary and Sec. 107 non-taxable parsonage allowance only the percentage of **unreimbursed** professional expenses that were spent in earning the taxable salary are allowable. The percentage of expenses spent in earning the non-taxable housing are not allowed. Read the following explanation.

Sec. 265 - Proration of Unreimbursed Expenses

If you establish a written accountable expense reimbursement plan and are adequately accounting to your employer for your auto, travel, and professional expenses, **the following facts WILL NOT affect you**.

A 1988 court case, Melvin H. Dalan & Lillian J. Dalan, Docket No. 8278-87, T.C. Memo 1988-106, filed March 9, 1988, resurrected an old IRS application of Sec. 265. Unreimbursed ministerial trade or business expenses are not deductible to the extent they are spent to earn non-taxable housing.

Example: A minister receives $40,000, including $16,000 housing allowance. His unreimbursed professional expenses amount to $4,000. ($16,000 divided by $40,000 = 40% X $4,000 = $1,600) $1,600 is the amount of the unreimbursed expenses spent to earn the non-taxable housing that he would not be able to deduct. The proration of unreimbursed expenses is to be computed on Schedule A for the employed minister and on Schedule C for the self-employed evangelist.

History of the issue goes back to the David E. Deason case, Docket No. 3993-62, January 10, 1964. During the 60's and early 70's we prorated and did not deduct a minister's expenses spent to earn his non-taxable housing allowance. In 1977, the Internal Revenue Manual Audit, 45(11)3 said that the interpretation of the Service was that Sec. 265 should not be applied to a minister's unreimbursed employee business expenses. The promise of a revenue ruling in the 1977 Memo never happened. Instead, the memo seems to have vanished. Therefore several decisions, such as the Dalan case, were made that were contrary to the IRS's 1977 position. A 1992 court case, Robert H. McFarland and Georgia W. McFarland, Docket No. 28246-90, T.C. Memo 1992-440, filed August 4, 1992, upholds Deason and Dalan cases. The IRS drafted a Revenue Ruling on this allocation issue in December 1990. It stated the IRS position to be parallel to the three court cases, however it was never finalized. The IRS chose to state their position in IRS Publication 517.

● *The Official Position of the IRS*

The official position of the IRS since 1988 has been to follow the Deason and Dalan Court Cases. **IRS Publication 517**, page 9, contains the published position of the IRS: unreimbursed ministerial trade or business expenses are not deductible to the extent they are spent to earn non-taxable housing. If you receive a tax-free rental or parsonage allowance and have ministerial expenses, you must attach a statement to your tax return showing how you computed the percentage of unreimbursed expenses that are not allowed. In Publication 517, pages 11 through 20, a comprehensive example of a completed minister's tax return illustrates the allocation computation.

Our sample return for Rev. Snodgrass, "Without Reimbursement," in Chapter Seven shows the computation for prorating unreimbursed expenses, using the "Worksheet to be Used With Form 2106, Part B."

Reimbursed Professional Expenses

An employee may deduct from gross income, to arrive at adjusted gross income, only those expenses paid or incurred by him in connection with his employment that are reimbursed under a reimbursement or other expense arrangement with his employer.

To be an accountable reimbursement plan, the plan must meet the following three requirements: **(1)** business connection, **(2)** adequate accounting, and **(3)** return of any excess reimbursement. Each requirement is fully discussed in this chapter.

A written reimbursement plan allows both the employer and employee to have a clear understanding of their responsibilities. (**Sample policy wording** is provided later in this chapter.) Reg. 1.62-2(d)(1) requires that the payment for an "adequately accounted reimbursement" be identified either by **making a separate payment** or by specifically indicating the separate amount if both wages and the reimbursement are combined in a single payment. If an employer includes salary, housing, and professional expense reimbursement in one check, they must identify the different amounts on the check and in their accounting.

We recommend that an employee submit his substantiation of employee business expenses for reimbursement no less often than **monthly**. If an employee has a cash flow problem and needs to be reimbursed more often, allow him to submit his records on a **weekly** basis.

CAUTION: When an employer and employee have established an accountable reimbursement plan, it is important to be careful to submit all allowable expenses. An employee cannot deduct expenses on his tax return that he failed to submit to the employer for reimbursement (Drury v. Commissioner, T.C. Memo 1977-199).

CAUTION: When an employer reimburses an employee for non-business meals, overseas travel that does not qualify as business, or personal family members travel expenses it must be reported as **income** on the employee's Form W-2, Box 1.

Tax Law & Regulations

Sec. 62(a)(2)(A) says, "**General Rule. ....the term `adjusted gross income' means, in the case of an individual, gross income minus the following deductions:....**

(A) Reimbursed expenses of employees. The deductions allowed by part VI (section 161 and following) which consist of expenses paid or incurred by the taxpayer, in connection with the performance by him of services as an employee, under a reimbursement or other expense allowance arrangement with his employer...."

Sec. 62(c) says, "**Certain Arrangements Not Treated as Reimbursement Arrangements: For purposes of subsection (a)(2)(A), an arrangement shall in no event be treated as a reimbursement or other expense allowance arrangement if:**

(1) such arrangement does not require the employee to substantiate the expenses covered by the arrangement to the person providing the reimbursement, or

(2) such arrangement provides the employee the right to retain any amount in excess of the substantiated expenses covered under the arrangement.

The substantiation requirements of the preceding sentence shall not apply to any expense to the extent that substantiation is not required under section 274(d) for such expense by reason of the regulations prescribed under the 2nd sentence thereof."

Regulation 1.62-2(d)(3) says: "**Reimbursement requirement   (i) In general. If a payor arranges to pay an amount to an employee regardless of whether the employee incurs (or is reasonably expected to incur) business expenses of a type described in paragraph (d)(1) or (d)(2) of this section, the arrangement does not satisfy this paragraph (d) and all amounts paid under the arrangement are treated as paid under a nonaccountable plan.**"

Business Connection

This business connection requirement means that no part of an employee's salary may be **recharacterized** as being paid under a reimbursement arrangement or other expense allowance arrangement.

The Past: Employees of nonprofit organizations have often had to absorb the "cost of doing ministry business." Especially small to medium size congregations have said, "Pastor, we understand you will incur auto and professional expenses and we will include enough in your salary to cover them. Just do not bother us with the details." **Before 1991**, temporary regulations permitted the employer to subtract an employee's adequately accounted business expenses from the gross salary and only report the remaining portion as taxable salary. It was not necessary to change the "cash flow." **This was recharacterization**.

The Present (Since January 1, 1991): Regulation 1.62-2(d)(3)'s narrow definition of "business connection" was not included in the temporary regulations in effect before 1-1-91. To establish an accountable plan that satisfies this "business connection" requirement can cause a change in the "cash flow." The tax benefits and reduced audit exposure gained by having an accountable reimbursement plan should convince employers and their employees to carefully meet the requirements of an accountable plan. There are two choices for the employer: (**Sample policy wording** is provided later in this chapter.)

1. If the employer is willing to bear the burden of the "cost of doing ministry business" they can adopt a policy to fully reimburse the employee for all adequately accounted business expenses incurred.

2. If the employer feels that they can not assume the unknown amount of the "cost of doing ministry business" they can adopt a policy to reimburse the employee for adequately accounted business expenses up to a fixed limit. If the employee does not incur enough employee business expenses to **"use"** all of the fixed limit amount, he can not be paid the difference nor can it be carried over from one calendar year to the next.

● *How to Start a New Reimbursement Policy or Fix a Partial Reimbursement Policy Already in Place*

It is important to understand that it can be accomplished without **any additional cost to the employer**. It is also possible that the employer will want to **increase** the employee's compensation package by **providing "new money"** for the reimbursement policy for business expenses.

Make a conservative estimate of the amount of business expenses expected to be incurred for the year. When available, examine the employee's past business expense records and deductions on his tax returns. After a determination of the average business expenses incurred in the past, consider if there will be any changes or major expenses for the coming year. From the current amount of compensation, including any partial reimbursements being paid, subtract this **conservative** amount. The reduced salary and the amount available for business expense reimbursement become two completely separate budget amounts.

Employers who initially adjust the employee's salary and adopt an "unlimited" policy will simply reimburse the employee each year for the actual expenses adequately accounted.

Employers who initially adjust the employee's salary and adopt a "fixed limit" policy, according to Private Letter Ruling 9822044 can, prior to the start of a calendar year, determine the amount the "fixed limit" will be in the succeeding year. Computing the "fixed limit" amount annually is a welcome relief. It is acceptable policy to readjust the "fixed limit" amount and the salary amount for the following calendar year. To be an accountable reimbursement plan, the policy must state that the employee will not receive any unused portion and that any unused portion will not be carried over to another year. This **"use it or lose it"** nature of an accountable reimbursement plan is similar to the tax treatment that applies to self-insured medical reimbursement and cafeteria fringe benefit plans.

When a "fixed limit" policy is adopted this is what happens:

1. If the employee's expenses are greater than the fixed limit amount, he can deduct what was not able to be reimbursed as "below the line" Schedule A itemized deductions, subject to limitations.

2. If the employee's expenses are less than the fixed limit amount, the difference between the expenses and the fixed limit amount can not be received by the employee and can not be carried over from one calendar year to the next.

Because of the **"use it or lose it"** nature of an accountable reimbursement plan, we recommend that an accountable reimbursement plan be carefully planned and not overstated.

● *Examples*

Example (1). Community Church pays its minister $500 per week or $26,000 annually. $10,400 has been designated as parsonage allowance. At the end of the month he adequately accounts his employee business expenses of $265 for the month. Community Church designates $265 of the $500 as paid to reimburse the minister's employee business expenses. Because Community Church would pay the minister $500 a week regardless of whether the minister incurred employee business expenses, the arrangement **does not satisfy** the reimbursement requirement of Reg. 1.62-2(d)(3)(i). Community Church must report ($26,000 - $10,400) $15,600 as wages on Form W-2. (This plan would have been an accountable plan for years ending before 1-1-1991.)

Example (2). Community Church pays its minister $500 per week or $26,000 annually. Community Church initially adjusts its minister's salary to $23,000, designates parsonage allowance of $10,400 and adopts a fixed limit reimbursement plan of $3,000. Each month the minister received an expense reimbursement check for the amount of employee business expenses he adequately accounted to his employer. At the end of the year, Community Church had paid their minister expense reimbursements of only $2,400. They decided that they would give him a bonus of $600. The entire $3,000 must be included on Form W-2. Community Church must report ($26,000 - $10,400) $15,600 as wages on Form W-2. The plan **does not satisfy** the reimbursement requirement of Reg. 1.62-2(d)(3)(i)

Example (3). Community Church pays its minister $500 per week or $26,000 annually. Community Church initially adjusts its minister's salary to $23,000, designates parsonage allowance of $10,400 and adopts a fixed limit reimbursement plan of $3,000. Each month the minister received an expense reimbursement check for the amount of employee business expenses he adequately accounted to his employer. At the end of the year, Community Church had paid their minister expense reimbursements of $2,400. Community Church correctly included ($23,000 - $10,400) $12,600 on Form W-2 for their minister. Their reimbursement plan **does satisfy** all the conditions of an "accountable plan."

Example (4). Community Church pays its minister $500 per week or $26,000 annually. Community Church initially adjusts its minister's salary to $23,000, designates parsonage allowance of $10,400 and adopts an unlimited reimbursement plan for employee business expenses. Each month the minister received an expense reimbursement check for the amount of employee business expenses he adequately accounted to his employer. At the end of the year, Community Church had paid their minister expense reimbursements of $3,600. Community Church correctly included ($23,000 - $10,400) $12,600 on Form W-2 for their minister. Their reimbursement plan **does satisfy** all the conditions of an "accountable plan."

Adequate Accounting

- **Definition Of Adequate Accounting**

    Reg. 1.274-5A(e)(4) says, **"Definition of an `adequate accounting' to the employer.... means the submission to the employer of an account book, diary, statement of expense, or similar record maintained by the employee in which the information as to each element of an expenditure is recorded at or near the time of the expenditure, together with supporting documentary evidence, in a manner which conforms to all the 'adequate records' requirements of paragraph (c)(2) of this section."**

    Regulations further instruct us that a responsible person other than the employee must verify and approve the records and amounts of expense. Such a person should be careful not to allow personal expenses to be submitted. Employers are to maintain or keep records of reimbursed business expenses for at least three years after the due date of the employee's tax return. Even though it is not required, we would recommend that the records and receipts be photocopied and that both the employee and the employer keep the records. Our **"Professional Tax Record Book"** contains monthly summary pages, is easily photocopied, and has been designed to make it easy to adequately account to your employer. **The instructions for each section of the record book outline the requirements of Sec. 274 and the necessary details to record for each category of expense.**

    The details of time, place, destination, business purpose, business discussion, etc., are very important details to record at or near the time of the business expense or trip. Each type of business expense and Sec. 274 requirements that apply to it are discussed in more detail later in this chapter. A record of the elements of an expense made at or near the time of the expense, supported by sufficient documentary evidence, has more value than a statement prepared later when generally there is a lack of accurate recall. A log maintained on a **weekly basis** is considered a record made at or near the time of the expense. If you charge business expense items on your employer's credit card you must submit a record of the required details and receipts for lodging and expenses over $75.00 to your employer.

    You must have **actual receipts** for **lodging** and any other **professional expense of $75.00** or more. Request and get receipts. Keep credit card receipts and/or statements that are itemized. Keep canceled checks or use the duplicate style if your bank or credit union does not return canceled checks. You may maintain an **account book or diary** that includes all of the required details for any **expense under $74.99** according to IRS Publication 463, page 25.

    It is **not sufficient** if an employee merely groups expenses into broad categories such as "travel" or reports individual expenses through the use of vague, nondescriptive terms such as "miscellaneous business expenses," according to Reg. 1.62-2(e)(3).

- **If You Do Adequately Account To Your Employer**

    Reg. 1.274-5A(e)(2) says, **"Reporting of expenses for which the employee is required to make an adequate accounting to his employer (i) Reimbursements equal to expenses. For purposes of computing tax liability, an employee need not report on his tax return business expenses for travel, transportation, entertainment, gifts, and similar purposes, paid or incurred by him solely for the benefit of his employer for which he is required to, and does make an adequate accounting to his employer and which are charged directly or indirectly to the employer (for example, through credit cards) or for which the employee is paid through advances, reimbursements, or otherwise, provided that the total amount of such advances, reimbursements and charges is equal to such expenses."**

If you do adequately account to your employer the following will occur:

1. You do not report on your tax return the reimbursement for professional business expenses when you establish an accountable reimbursement plan with your employer.
2. You do not have to keep records for possible IRS audit. You do not have to substantiate your expense account for the IRS auditor as you have already done so with your employer. The employer must retain the records and receipts submitted by you. If your return is audited, show the IRS auditor a copy of the written accountable reimbursement plan you established with your employer.
3. The employer does not include the reimbursements on the W-2, Box 1.

Other references to support the above discussion of reimbursement policies are Reg. 1.62-2 and Reg. 1.162-17.

If you are reimbursed more than your allowable expenses, you must return the excess reimbursement to your employer. If your employer has an "accountable plan" and you fail to either adequately account or return excess reimbursement, it will be deemed to be a "non-accountable" plan for you and your employer is required to report all of your reimbursements as salary on Form W-2. You will be required to treat such non-accountable expenses as "below the line" deductions on Form 2106 and Schedule A, subject to the limitations.

● *Adequate Accounting Requirement Is Satisfied by Mileage Allowance & Per Diem*

Adequate accounting requirement is satisfied when:

1. The amount of reimbursement is based on the auto mileage allowance of **40½¢** per mile and the employee's log of business miles, date, place, and purpose. Announcement 2005-71 increased the mileage allowance to **48½¢** per mile, effective September 1, 2005 until December 31, 2005.
2. The amount of reimbursement for travel away from home is based on the per diem allowance of **$204 or $129** per day and the employee's record of number of days, place, and purpose of travel. (see IRS list of eligible high cost cities later in the chapter)
3. The amount of reimbursement for meals away from home (incurred without cost of lodging) is based on the city by city M&IE rate from the IRS tables per day and the employee's record of number of days, place, and purpose. (Rev. Proc. 2005-10)

Per diem rates are adjusted for inflation and cover a convenient calendar year time period now. Employee mileage allowances and per diem travel subsistence allowances that are not in excess of IRS-set maximums may relieve difficulty of substantiation and generate a deduction that is greater than actual travel expenses. You must use the same method of accounting for the whole year. We will give more detailed discussion under "travel" later in this chapter. Compare the options shown in our discussion of "travel," and use the method that allows the greater deduction.

Rev. Proc. 2004-64 announced the **40½¢ mileage allowance rate** for **2005**. With or without a reimbursement plan, taxpayers are allowed **40½¢** per mile for all of their business miles. Announcement 2005-71 increased the mileage allowance to **48½¢** per mile, effective September 1, 2005 until December 31, 2005.

IRS has announced in Rev. Proc. 2005-78 that the **mileage allowance rate for 2006 is 44½¢.**

● *When Actual Auto Expenses Exceed The Cents Per Mile Computation*

If you are incurring more than **40½¢** per mile (**48½¢** after September 1, 2005) to operate your auto, it may be beneficial to submit your business percentage of actual expenses to your employer. Otherwise, any unreimbursed excess expense becomes a Schedule A deduction subject to the 2% of AGI limitation and the Sec. 265 limitation. **Annually** choose to become reimbursed for actual expenses **or** mileage allowance. Rev. Proc. 2004-64, Sec. 8, describes a fixed and variable rate (FAVR) allowance that is acceptable to the IRS. However, we recommend the following procedure of computing actual:

1. Compute auto depreciation for year and divide by 12.
2. Total actual monthly expenses for gas, oil, repairs, etc., (omit auto payment).
3. Estimate what your annual percentage of business use will be or use the business percentage that you recorded for previous year.
4. Multiply business percentage by the total of depreciation and expenses for the month and submit to your employer for reimbursement.
5. At the end of the year: Divide business miles by total miles for the year to know what your ACTUAL business percentage is.

6. Multiply actual business percentage by the total of depreciation and expenses for the full year.
7. Submit the difference between the annual auto expense computed and what has been reimbursed during the other 11 months of the year to your employer for December's reimbursement.

Return of Amounts Exceeding Expenses

If you are advanced more than your allowable expenses, you must return the excess reimbursement to your employer within a reasonable time. Reg 1.62-2(f)(2) states: in cases when an employee is reimbursed by the employer on **the basis of a per diem or auto mileage allowance up to the IRS-specified rates,** there is deemed to be **no excess retained** by the employee. An "above the line" deduction is allowed up to the IRS-specified rate. Any reimbursement to an employee in excess of the IRS-specified rates can be treated by the employer as "above the line" deductions when the employee submits proof of actual expenses that equal the amount of reimbursement.

An accountable plan must generally require the employee to return any amount paid under the arrangement over and above substantiated expenses within a reasonable period of time. Advances for expenses must be reasonably calculated to not exceed anticipated expenses and any excess must be returned to the employer within a reasonable period of time after receipt. Under the "fixed date method," the following are treated as having occurred within a reasonable period of time:

1. an advance made within 30 days of when an expense is paid or incurred,
2. an expense substantiated to the payor within 60 days after it is paid or incurred, or
3. an amount returned to the employer within 120 days after an expense is paid or incurred.

We recommend that nonprofit employers **avoid adopting a plan that allows for payment of "advances."** If an "advance" is not paid to an employee this more complex bookkeeping procedure is automatically satisfied. Employers who have volunteer treasurers should choose the **simplicity** of periodically reimbursing their employees for actual expenses and/or IRS-specified rates as they are submitted.

Although the "reasonable time" periods do not specifically apply to plans without "advances," we do recommend that an employee account for his expenses within the guidelines. We also recommend that an employee submit his substantiation of employee business expenses for reimbursement no less often than **monthly**. If the employee has a cash flow problem and needs to be reimbursed more often, allow him to submit his records on a **weekly** basis.

Adopt One of the Following Reimbursement Plans

One of the following plans should be adopted for each employee. An employer does not have to have the same plan for all employees. An accountable reimbursement plan is very important to your employees' economic health! **A written reimbursement plan** allows both the employer and employee to have a clear understanding of their responsibilities.

If you and your employer do not have a written reimbursement plan, you must report your expenses as "unreimbursed" on Form 2106 and Schedule A. A plan is not able to be retroactive; it becomes effective for the future at the time it is adopted. Adopting a reimbursement plan on a calendar year basis causes less confusion than a fiscal year plan.

You may customize one of the following policies to clearly state the agreement between the employer and the employee. For example, if you wish to state that the amount of reimbursement will be at the IRS-specified mileage allowance and/or per-diem allowances for travel, add a sentence that clearly states this in your agreement.

Salary Plus Unlimited Reimbursement

The chairman informed the meeting that according to Sec. 62(a)(2)(A), an employee that adequately accounts to the employer the details of their professional expenses, is allowed a deduction from gross income. Sec. 62(c) further requires an employee to return any excess reimbursement or advance to the employer within a reasonable time. Reg. 1.62-2(d)(3) further requires that no part of our employee's salary be recharacterized as being paid under this reimbursement arrangement.

A motion was made by_____, seconded by_____and passed to adopt the following resolution:

Resolved that in addition to the salary provided our employee, we will reimburse him/her for auto, travel and professional expenses considered ordinary and necessary for him/her to carry out his/her duties. (Add special modifications here.)

It is further understood that a person other than the employee will examine the adequately accounted records and that the records will be kept for at least four years by the employer.

Salary Plus Fixed Limit Reimbursement

The chairman informed the meeting that according to Sec. 62(a)(2)(A), an employee that adequately accounts to the employer the details of their professional expenses, is allowed a deduction from gross income. Sec. 62(c) further requires an employee to return any excess reimbursement or advance to the employer within a reasonable time. Reg. 1.62-2(d)(3) further requires that no part of our employee's salary be recharacterized as being paid under this reimbursement arrangement.

A motion was made by_____, seconded by_____and passed to adopt the following resolution:

Resolved that in addition to the salary provided our employee, we will reimburse him/her for auto, travel and professional expenses considered ordinary and necessary for him/her to carry out his/her duties up to a fixed limit of $_____. (Add special modifications here.) If his/her actual expenses are less than this fixed limit, he/she cannot be given the difference as bonus or salary, nor can it be carried over to the next year. If his/her actual expenses are greater than this fixed limit, he/she will be required to deduct the extra expenses on Form 2106 and Schedule A.

It is further understood that a person other than the employee will examine the adequately accounted records and that the records will be kept for at least four years by the employer.

Typical Professional Expenses for a Minister

Auto Expense

The cost of business travel is the largest employee business expense that a minister typically incurs. Therefore, it is very important to understand how to arrive at the "largest" deduction or reimbursement that is allowable. We encourage you to read **IRS Publication 463,** "Travel, Entertainment, Gift and Car Expenses."

● *Effect of Employer Reimbursement Plans*

When you **lease an auto and you adequately account to your employer** for your business mileage, you do have the **choice** of being reimbursed at the mileage allowance rate or the business percentage of your actual expenses. If the business percentage of the cost of your lease (reduced by inclusion factor discussed later), combined with other operating expenses, is greater than the mileage allowance rate, you will want to adequately account to your employer the business percentage of your actual expenses.

When you **own an auto and you adequately account to your employer** for your business mileage, you have the **choice** of being reimbursed at the mileage allowance rate or the business percentage of your actual expenses.

Log Your Business Miles

Dedicate one auto for business use when possible. Because of depreciation limits placed on less than 50% business use autos, it is advisable to concentrate business use to one auto at a time to keep the percentage of business use above 50%. Because the sale or trade of your auto used for business is a reportable transaction, a separate mileage log for each auto used in business must be kept to prove the business percentage of each auto's basis. It is not easy to **keep a log of miles traveled** for business, **but you must.** When you experience the amount of tax savings generated by being able to fully deduct your business mileage expense, you will agree that keeping a business mileage log is very worthwhile.

Revenue Ruling 99-7 clarifies the circumstances under which daily trips between a residence and a work location will be deductible as business mileage. In general, daily trips incurred in going between your residence and a work location is **nondeductible commuting expense**. However, the following circumstances permit deductible business miles:

1. Daily trips between your residence and a temporary work location outside the metropolitan area where you live and normally work qualify as business miles. Daily trips between your residence and a temporary work location within that metropolitan area are not deductible as business miles unless (2) or (3) below applies.

2. If you have one or more regular work locations away from your residence, you may log as business miles the distance between your residence and a temporary work location in the same trade or business, regardless of the distance.

3. If your residence is your principal place of business according to Sec. 280A(c)(1)(A), you may log as business miles the distance between your residence and another work location in the same trade or business, regardless of whether the other location is regular or temporary and regardless of the distance.

Multiple trips between your residence and work location during the day are all non-deductible commuting miles. The distance between your residence and the **first business stop** of the day and/or between the **last business stop** of the day and your residence are non-deductible as commuting miles. Careful planning of your itinerary and daily entries in your mileage log may legally lessen your non-deductible commuting for some days according to Shea v. Commissioner, T.C. Memo 1979-303.

Revenue Ruling 99-7 defines a "temporary work location" as one that is expected to last (and does in fact last) one year or less.

How to Log Business Miles: One entry in your mileage log is sufficient to record a daily business trip consisting of several stops without interruption or a business trip consisting of several days away from home. De minimis personal use, such as a lunch stop between two business stops, is not an interruption in business use. Our **"Professional Tax Record Book"** and our **"Auto Log"** have been designed to make it easy to record all the details necessary for your mileage log and actual auto expenses. Your mileage log should contain the following information:

1. Date
2. Odometer reading at beginning of trip
3. Odometer reading at end of trip
4. Business miles driven for the day
5. Place and purpose of the trip

Sale Or Trade Of Business Auto

It is very important that you keep a record of your auto's basis because, upon sale or trade, you must properly compute the gain or loss. The only way to accurately compute each auto's basis is to keep **separate** mileage records for each auto used.

Regardless of whether you have used optional mileage allowance or actual expense method, the sale or trade of an auto with business use results in a reportable transaction on Form 4797 or Form 8824. **A sale** will result in **a gain that is taxable** or **a loss that is deductible** on Form 4797. **A trade** will affect the basis of the new auto, according to Sec. 1031. Form 8824, Like Kind Exchanges, is required to be attached to your tax return to report a trade transaction. We have included an example of an auto trade and Form 8824 in Chapter Seven for Rev. Snodgrass.

Knowing the basis of your auto makes it possible to tax plan. If the potential value of your auto would cause a **gain upon sale**, generally it would be **best to trade autos.** If the potential value of your auto would cause a **loss upon sale**, generally it would be **best to sell the auto outright,** deduct the loss and buy the replacement auto outright. (IRS Publication 463, page 24)

● *Depreciation Adjustment to Basis*

If the actual cost method and MACRS method of depreciation are chosen in the first year, you must use the Modified Accelerated Cost Recovery System (MACRS) depreciation for the life of the auto. Even if your employer reimburses you under an accountable plan at the optional rate, you still must use your choice of MACRS to determine your basis.

If the optional mileage allowance method to deduct the business use of your auto is chosen for the first year your auto is placed in service, an optional depreciation factor reduces the basis of your auto in determining the adjusted basis when you dispose of it. All business miles should be multiplied by the factor to determine the optional depreciation factor.

The rate for years **2005** and 2006 is **17¢**) (Rev. Proc. 2005-78) The rate for years 2003 and 2004 was **16¢**. The rate for years 2001 and 2002 was **15¢**. The rate for year 2000 was **14¢**. The rate for years 1994 through 1999, was **12¢**.

Exception: If the actual cost method is used to deduct the business use of your auto for **any year other than the first year**, you must use 5 year straight line as the depreciation method. You will combine the optional factor for years of mileage allowance method with the actual depreciation for years of actual expense method to determine your basis.

We have designed a **"Worksheet to Compute Auto Basis."** The backside of the worksheet contains the technical rules that we are detailing in this chapter. We advise you to enter your auto information on our worksheet each year, unstaple it each year and bring it forward to the current return. In a year of sale or trade you will have the necessary information to make the required basis calculations. Information for ordering this form is given in the back of this publication. We feel the best way to illustrate the basis computation on the worksheet is to include an auto trade situation in our sample problem for Rev. Snodgrass in Chapter Seven.

If you are sending your information to us for preparation of your return, please give us the type of information you see on the form and **copies of prior year tax returns** showing how your auto basis has been handled. Our **"Checklist"** in the back of the book allows for your auto information to be separated for each auto.

Auto Interest & Personal Property Tax

Auto interest and personal property tax are not available as an employee business expense. Do not become reimbursed for the business percentage of auto interest and personal property tax. Interest on an auto for an employee is considered "personal interest" and is not deductible on Schedule A. Personal property or excise tax is deductible on Schedule A by employees. Sales tax for the purchase of an auto used in business is to be added to the cost basis as a capital expense or may be deducted on Schedule A.

Self-employed business use or farm use have the advantage of being able to deduct the business percentage of interest and personal property tax on Schedule C or F. Based on Revenue Ruling 80-110, Sec. 1402(a) and Sec. 62(1), it is correct to **use the business percentage of auto interest and personal property tax as a subtraction from a minister's social security base**.

The portion of tax preparation fee that is attributable to the reporting of ministry transactions can also be a subtraction from a minister's social security base according to Revenue Ruling 92-29.

Lease or Own

Although leasing an auto is subject to luxury limitations, it could be advantageous to lease rather than to own. Lease payments may generate more deduction since auto interest is considered to be nondeductible personal interest for the employee. **The question of whether to lease or own is a difficult question to answer.** Our advice is to shop and negotiate for the best deal that provides you with dependable and comfortable travel. Be sure to read the "fine print" conditions of the lease. There is usually a limit as to how many miles you can drive the leased auto before an extra charge per mile is assessed.

Spending additional dollars for transportation because it is tax deductible is not sensible. To spend an additional $500 and be in the 15% tax bracket would only reduce your tax by $75. The difference of $425 is a real cost out of your pocket.

Choose the Best Method of Deducting Auto Expenses

There are two methods of computing the deduction for the cost of operating your auto for business. It is important to keep records of your actual expenses so that you can compare optional with actual and use the method that results in the largest deduction. In the past, due to the luxury auto limitations on depreciation and better gas economy, fewer taxpayers benefited from the actual expense computation. **New tax law has changed the scene**. If any of the following circumstances have happened, the actual method of computing your auto expenses may be greater than optional.

A taxpayer purchasing a clean-fuel or electric auto after August 5, 1997 can use increased luxury auto limits.

The luxury auto limitations are now split into three categories: passenger auto, trucks and vans (mini-vans and SUVs), and electric autos. Different tables are provided for each category. Generally new vehicles **weighing over 6,000 pounds** are not limited by Sec. 280F luxury auto limits or less than 50% business use. Effective October 22, 2004, Sport Utility Vehicles (SUVs), not weighing more than 14,000 pounds, are limited to $25,000 Sec. 179 expensing according to Sec. 179(b)(6)(B).

Mileage Allowance Method

IRS allows you to be reimbursed or deduct **40½¢** a mile for all business miles driven in **2005**. Announcement 2005-71 increased the mileage allowance to **48½¢** per mile, effective September 1, 2005 until December 31, 2005. In addition, you may be reimbursed or deduct your actual business tolls and parking fees. A daily log book of miles driven must be kept in order to use this method. The IRS mileage allowance may be used if you own or lease an auto.

IRS has announced in Rev. Proc. 2005-78 that the mileage allowance rate for **2006** is **44½¢**.

You cannot use the standard mileage rate for **unreimbursed** business use if you:
1. Use the auto for hire (such as a taxi),
2. Operate five or more autos at the same time (as in fleet operations). Rev. Proc. 2003-76 changed this from two or more autos, effective January 1, 2004.
3. Claimed a depreciation deduction using ACRS or MACRS in an earlier year,
4. Claimed a Sec. 179 deduction on the auto.
5. Claimed actual auto expenses after 1997 for a car you leased, or
6. Are a rural mail carrier who received a qualified reimbursement.

Actual Method

This is an itemized list of your actual auto expenses such as: gas, oil, lubrication, repairs, parts, tires, batteries, tune-ups, auto washes, insurance, auto club dues, licenses, parking fees, tolls, and auto depreciation or auto lease.

If the actual cost method and MACRS method of depreciation is chosen in the first year, you must use the MACRS depreciation for the life of the auto. Even if your employer reimburses you under an accountable plan at the optional rate, you still must use your choice of MACRS to determine your auto's basis.

If the actual cost method and Alternative Depreciation System (ADS) of 5 year straight line method of depreciation is chosen in the first year, you will have left open the option to use actual or optional method on an annual basis. You will combine the optional factor for years of mileage allowance method with the actual depreciation for years of actual expense method to determine your basis.

If the actual cost method is used to deduct the business use of your auto for **any year other than the first year**, you must use 5 year straight line ADS as the depreciation method. You will combine the optional factor for years of mileage allowance method with the actual depreciation for years of actual expense method to determine your basis.

Auto Depreciation Rules

Methods and limits of depreciation apply to autos according to the date placed in service. Follow the same column of the table **applicable in the year placed in service** until you change autos.

● *Listed Property - Deductions Limited For Less Than 50% Business Use*

Tax Reform Act of 1984 began to limit depreciation deductions for autos, computers, cellular phones, etc. placed in service after June 18, 1984 that are not **predominantly used in business**. When less than 50% use of the property is business, Sec. 179 expensing is not available. The auto's basis must be recovered over five years using the straight-line method.

● *Depreciation Recapture*

Depreciation recapture is to be computed when an accelerated depreciation method is used in the year placed in service and business use drops below 50% in any future year during the 5 year life. Recapture means "pay back." If you used your auto more than 50% in your business in the year you placed it in service, but 50% or less for business in a later year, you must include in gross income the difference between depreciation and all Sec. 179 expensing claimed and the amount of depreciation recomputed at the 5 year straight line method. You must continue using 5 year straight line ADS even if business use rises back above 50%.

The recapture amount is shown as a memo on Form 4797. Employees enter the recapure amount on Form 1040, line 21 and dual-status ministers also include the recapure amount on Schedule SE.

● *Deductions Limited For Luxury Automobiles*

When an automobile is used more than 50% for business purposes, the law placed further limits on the amounts of annual depreciation deductions that could be taken on automobiles. The amount of annual limits are based on 100% business use. If the business use is less than 100%, the maximum annual limits must be reduced to reflect the actual business use percentage. The depreciation limit amounts apply to regular depreciation and Sec. 179 expensing. The limits are indexed for inflation.

Luxury Limits for Vehicles Since 1991

Date Passenger Auto, Truck, or Van Placed in Service Before 2003

	1-1-91 thru 12-31-91	1-1-92 thru 12-31-92	1-1-93 thru 12-31-93	1-1-94 thru 12-31-94	1-1-95 thru 12-31-96	1-1-97 thru 12-31-97	1-1-98 thru 12-31-98	1-1-99 thru 12-31-99	1-1-00 thru 9-10-01	9-11-01 thru 12-31-02
1st year							30% Special Bonus Depreciation Allowance			$7.660
1st year	$2,660	$2,760	$2,860	$2,960	$3,060	$3,160	$3,160	$3,060	$3,060	$3,060
2nd year	$4,300	$4,400	$4,600	$4,700	$4,900	$5,000	$5,000	$5,000	$4,900	$4,900
3rd year	$2,550	$2,650	$2,750	$2,850	$2,950	$3,050	$2,950	$2,950	$2,950	$2,950
4th- 6th	$1,575	$1,575	$1,675	$1,675	$1,775	$1,775	$1,775	$1,775	$1,775	$1,775

Date Passenger Auto, Truck, & Van, Electric Auto Placed in Service During 2003 and After

		Passenger Autos				Trucks & Vans				Electric Autos		
		Before 5-6-03	5-5-03 thru 12-31-03	1-1-04 thru 12-31-04	1-1-05 thru 12-31-05	Before 5-6-03	1-1-03 thru 12-31-03	5-5-04 thru 12-31-04	1-1-05 thru 12-31-05	Before 5-6-03	5-5-03 thru 12-31-03	1-1-04 thru 12-31-04	1-1-05 thru 12-31-05
1st year	30% Special Bonus Depr'n	$7,660	$7,660			$7,960	$7,960			$22,880	$22,880		
	50% Special Bonus Depr'n		$10,710	$10,610			$11,010	$10,910			$32,030	$31,830	
	No Bonus Allowance	$3,060	$3,060	$2,960	$2,960	$3,360	$3,360	$3,260	$3,260	$9,080	$9,080	$8,880	$8,880
2nd year		$4,900	$4,900	$4,800	$4,700	$5,400	$5,400	$5,300	$5,200	$14,600	$14,600	$14,300	$14,200
3rd year		$2,950	$2,950	$2,850	$2,850	$3,250	$3,250	$3,150	$3,150	$8,750	$8,750	$8,550	$8,450
4th- 6th		$1,775	$1,775	$1,675	$1,675	$1,975	$1,975	$1,875	$1,875	$5,225	$5,225	$5,125	$5,125

● *MACRS Depreciation for Autos Purchased After 12-31-86*

Under Modified Accelerated Cost Recovery System (MACRS) autos are 5-year Class property. The percentage method is based on 200% declining balance method. The alternative recovery method is 5 year straight-line. **Sec. 179 expensing** of up to $24,000 (2001 & 2002), **$100,000 (2003 - 2005),** and $25,000 (2006), can very rarely be used within the luxury auto limits. If business use is 50% or less in year of purchase, then the auto's basis must be recovered over five years using the straight-line method and the half-year convention. The most depreciation allowed per year, regardless of your auto's basis, is the business percentage of the luxury auto limits shown above. MACRS allows depreciation deduction in the year of sale. The IRS tables below have computed the mid-year and mid-quarter factors for the year of purchase automatically.

Mid-year convention allows one half of the annual percentage available in the year placed in service and in the year of sale.

Mid-quarter convention allows the mid-quarter computation percentage depending on which quarter the purchase or sale occurs. If more than **40% of the year's** depreciable assets are placed in service in the **final quarter**, then all non-realty assets for that year **must** be depreciated using "mid-quarter" convention instead of the normal mid-year convention.

The percentages for both mid-year and mid-quarter for autos and other 5-year class equipment are listed below.

Depreciation Table - MACRS 5-year Class Property

Year	Mid-year	Mid-quarter (1st)	(2nd)	(3rd)	(4th)
1	20.00%	35.00%	25.00%	15.00%	5.00%
2	32.00%	26.00%	30.00%	34.00%	38.00%
3	19.20%	15.60%	18.00%	20.40%	22.80%
4	11.52%	11.01%	11.37%	12.24%	13.68%
5	11.52%	11.01%	11.37%	11.30%	10.94%
6	5.76%	1.38%	4.26%	7.06%	9.58%

Leased Automobiles

Autos leased after December 31, 1997 can use the IRS mileage allowance. When you lease an auto for business use, you can choose the greater of the **40½¢ (48½¢ Sept 1 to Dec 31 2005.)** IRS mileage allowance or the business percentage of the actual cost of the lease, gas, oil, etc. You cannot deduct any part of a lease payment that is for commuting or other personal use of the auto. When you lease an auto for business use, the **luxury auto limitations** are applied by the computation of an **income inclusion factor**. **IRS Publication 463** contains special tables to compute the income inclusion factor. Enter the rental cost on line 24(a), Part II, of Form 2106. The inclusion amount is prorated for the number of days of the lease term included in the tax year. The amount computed would be shown on line 24b. The net amount of vehicle rental expenses will be shown on line 24c. There is **no** additional inclusion amount if you have 50% or less business use for this period. Easy to use tables are in **IRS Publication 463** for regular autos and electric autos.

Employer Provided Autos

The value of an employee's personal use of an employer provided vehicle must be included in his income minus any reimbursement he made to his employer. **IRS Publication 15-B,** pages 17 to 23, "Employer's Tax Guide to Fringe Benefits," contains instructions for the employer providing this "working condition" fringe benefit. **Reg. 1.61-21(c),(d),(e), and (f)** is a thorough presentation of the "working condition" fringe benefit.

It is best for the employer providing the auto to pay for all costs or all costs except gasoline. Hybrid arrangements cause confusion and cause the employee to pay tax on a value he did not receive. Regulations only allow for a gasoline factor of **5½¢** a mile to be added if the employer pays for the gasoline or omitted if the employee pays for the gasoline.

In order for an employer to exclude from the employee's gross income the value of an employer-provided vehicle, the **employee must keep** a log of business miles and submit the log to the employer. If the employer does not receive such a log of business miles, the whole value of the vehicle is income to be reported on Form W-2. Please do not let this happen.

● *General Valuation Rule*

Whenever an employer does not choose one of the special valuation rules by a timely notification to the employee, **the value of the fringe benefit must be determined** under the general valuation rule. Under the general valuation rule, FMV is the amount your employee would have to pay a third party to lease the vehicle in the geographic area where he uses the vehicle.

If you want to adopt one of the three Special Valuation Rules to calculate the value of personal use to report as income for your employee, **you must adopt in writing** what rule you have chosen by the first day you make the vehicle available to the employee.

Three special valuation rules are available:

● *(1) The Automobile Lease Rule*

The value of availability of an auto to the employee must first be determined. This value of availability is then reduced by the percentage of business use to determine the value of the employee's personal use of the auto to be treated as compensation.

1. Employer must request from the employee a statement as to the business mileage and the total mileage driven by the employee. Where the employee supplies such statement or record within a reasonable period of time, the employer must compute the personal use percentage and the amount of payroll taxes to withhold on the basis of such information.

2. Determine the FMV of the automobile on the first date the automobile is available to any employee for personal use. Use the Annual Lease Value Table (shown on next page) to determine an annual value. When an automobile is provided for only part of a year, the value is determined by multiplying the annual lease value by a fraction (days automobile is available to the employee divided by 365).

3. The figures in the annual lease value table are applicable for a four-year period starting on the date on which the special rule is applied and ending on December 31st of the fourth full year following that date. After that period, the annual lease value for each calendar year is based on the fair market value of the auto on January 1st of the applicable year.

4. If an employer provides fuel; its fair market value or **5½¢** per mile must be an additional computation.

● *(2) The Vehicle Cents-per-Mile Rule*

Under this cents-per-mile rule, an employer values the benefit using the standard mileage rate multiplied by the total miles the employee drives the automobile for personal purposes. For **2005,** this rate is **40½¢ (48½¢ Sept 1 to Dec 31 2005.)** (2006 - 44½¢.) All of the following conditions must be met:

1. Employer must request from the employee a statement of the business mileage and the total mileage driven by the employee.

2. This rule cannot be used if the FMV of the auto, as of the first date the auto is made available to any employee for personal use, exceeds **$14,800 or $16,300** for a truck or van (IRS Pub 15-B, pages 17 to 23).

ANNUAL LEASE VALUE TABLE / Automobile Lease Rule
IRS Publication 15-B

Automobile Fair Market Value	Annual Lease Value	Automobile Fair Market Value	Annual Lease Value
$ 0 - 999	$ 600	$ 22,000 - 22,999	$ 6,100
1,000 - 1,999	850	23,000 - 23,999	6,350
2,000 - 2,999	1,100	24,000 - 24,999	6,600
3,000 - 3,999	1,350	25,000 - 25,999	6,850
4,000 - 4,999	1,600	26,000 - 27,999	7,250
5,000 - 5,999	1,850	28,000 - 29,999	7,750
6,000 - 6,999	2,100	30,000 - 31,999	8,250
7,000 - 7,999	2,350	32,000 - 33,999	8,750
8,000 - 8,999	2,600	34,000 - 35,999	9,250
9,000 - 9,999	2,850	36,000 - 37,999	9,750
10,000 - 10,999	3,100	38,000 - 39,999	10,250
11,000 - 11,999	3,350	40,000 - 41,999	10,750
12,000 - 12,999	3,600	42,000 - 43,999	11,250
13,000 - 13,999	3,850	44,000 - 45,999	11,750
14,000 - 14,999	4,100	46,000 - 47,999	12,250
15,000 - 15,999	4,350	48,000 - 49,999	12,750
16,000 - 16,999	4,600	50,000 - 51,999	13,250
17,000 - 17,999	4,850	52,000 - 53,999	13,750
18,000 - 18,999	5,100	54,000 - 55,999	14,250
19,000 - 19,999	5,350	56,000 - 57,999	14,750
20,000 - 20,999	5,600	58,000 - 59,999	15,250
21,000 - 21,999	5,850	over $59,999	Auto's FMV X 0.25 + $500

EXAMPLE: *An employer makes an auto available for all of 2005. Its fair market value is $16,000; its annual lease value from the table is $4,600. Employee uses the auto 20% for personal use. Thus, the employer must include in the employee's income 20% of $4,600 or **$920**. If fuel is provided by the employer and personal use of 20% was 4,000 miles, (4,000 X 5½¢) an additional **$220** must be included in income.*

3. It must be reasonably expected that the auto will be regularly used in employer's business, or actually driven primarily by employees at least 10,000 (personal and business) miles during a calendar year.

4. The cents-per-mile rule includes all costs of operating the auto. Neither the employer or the employee may adjust the rate for services not provided, such as repairs. The only adjustment allowed is that if fuel is not provided by the employer, the cents-per-mile value may be reduced by no more than **5½¢**.

● (3) Commuting Rule

Under this rule, the value of the commuting use of an automobile an employer provides is $1.50 per one-way commute ($3.00 for each round trip) for each employee who commutes in the vehicle. An employer can use this special rule if all of the following requirements are met:

1. Employer owns or leases the automobile and provides it to one or more employees for use in his trade or business.

2. For bona fide noncompensatory business reasons, an employer requires the employee to commute in the automobile.

3. Employer establishes a written policy under which they do not allow employees to use the vehicle for personal purposes, other than for commuting or *de minimis* personal use (such as a stop for a personal errand on the way between a business delivery and the employee's home.)

4. The employee does not use the automobile for personal purposes, other than commuting and de minimus personal use.

5. If this vehicle is an automobile, the employee required to use it for commuting is not a control employee.

A **control employee** of a nongovernmental employer is any employee who (1) is a board-appointed, shareholder-appointed, confirmed, or elected officer of the employer whose compensation equals or exceeds $80,000, (2) is the director of the employer, (3) owns a one percent or greater equity, capital or profit interest in the employer, or (4) receives $170,000 or more in compensation. (IRS Publication 15-B)

● 100% Business Use Rule (Very Unlikely)

If an employer **prohibited all personal use** and commuting by the employee, no value would be taxable to the employee. Without personal use, no log of business miles would be required.

All of the following conditions must be met:

1. The vehicle is owned or leased by the employer and is provided to an employee for use in the employer's trade or business.
2. The vehicle is kept on the employer's premises.
3. Only de minimis stop on the way between a business delivery and the employer's place of business.
4. The vehicle is not being used for personal purposes.
5. No employee using the vehicle lives at the employer's place of business.
6. There must be evidence that the vehicle meets all these conditions.

Withholding of Tax: When an auto is either owned or leased by the employer for an employee's use, the personal value of the automobile's use is a taxable fringe benefit subject to withholding of income tax and social security for the lay employee. The dual-status minister will incur the additional income tax and social security tax for estimated tax purposes.

When an employee pays the employer for personal use, the amount to be included in income is reduced by what the employee pays. If the proper amount is computed (general valuation rule or one of the three special valuation rules timely chosen) and paid to the employer, nothing would need to be shown on the W-2, nor any taxes withheld for the lay employee.

Library & Equipment Purchases

Capital purchases are major purchases of equipment that have an expected useful life of more than a year. IRS depreciation rules are easy to use to compute the right amount of allowable depreciation.

Usually when a minister begins his career he already owns a sizable library. The purchase of books and equipment during college and seminary that did not qualify for deductible educational expense or credits can begin to be depreciated when a minister begins receiving an income from their use. They become business property and are considered "placed in service." The **lesser of the cost or fair market value** of items that are converted from personal to business use should be inventoried and placed on the depreciation schedule. Sec. 179 expensing is not available for converted property.

New purchases of library, office furniture, typewriters, computers, printers, overhead or film projectors, VCRs, cameras, copiers, or cellular phones are examples of items that are capital and need to be depreciated or expensed under Sec. 179. **Tax plan according to your tax liability;** choose to "spread out" or depreciate capital assets in years of no tax liability and choose Sec. 179 expensing during years with a tax liability.

If you are fully reimbursed for the purchase of a capital item in the year of purchase, it will be the same as choosing Sec. 179 expensing. We recommend that a depreciation worksheet be completed to show each purchase and any election to expense capital assets.

To be reimbursed by your employer for library and equipment depreciation, compute what this year's depreciation will be for previous assets on your depreciation schedule, divide by 12 and use it as a monthly amount. Then in December, include an extra amount that is the depreciation for the current year's capital purchases.

● *Guidance and Discussion of Ownership of Equipment*

When the **employer makes the decision** to purchase equipment needed for ministry use, the items will be owned by the employer. When an **employee makes the decision** to purchase equipment needed for ministry use from his accountable reimbursement plan, the items will be owned by the employee.

This concept is best understood when we think of the use of an automobile for business. If the employer makes the decision to purchase an auto for an employee's use, it is titled in the employer's name. The rules provided for "employer provided autos" are followed for proper tax treatment. If an employee makes the decision to purchase an auto, it is titled in the employee's name. The rules for business use deductions or reimbursements are followed.

Reimbursement to an employee from an accountable plan for business purchases of library or any equipment is owned by the employee. Ownership of them does not change to employer.

• *Computers*

Computers of today are so capable and useful that almost everyone has entered into the age of technology. Bible research CD's, web-site promotions, E-mail with missionaries, word processing for sermon preparation and congregation data bases are examples of current ministry business use of computers.

Congress has made dual-use (part business and part personal) of computers complex by placing them in a category called "listed property." Complex depreciation treatment can be avoided by dedicating a computer to 100% business use. Now that the cost of owning a computer is more reasonable, it is advisable to purchase one for business use and a second one for the family and personal use. The computer for personal use can be deducted as a parsonage allowance purchase.

Employers should be willing to own and provide the business use computer for their employees. When the employer owns the computer and it is used exclusively for business use, no log of personal time needs be kept. The time spent learning how to manipulate the peripheral devices is to be counted as business use. (Keyboard exercises and Solitaire)

When employees purchase and own a computer and it is used for both business and personal, a log of time must be kept to know the business use percentage. If less than 50% of computer use is business, you cannot choose Sec. 179 expensing. The cost basis must be recovered over five years using the straight-line method and the half-year convention.

Unreimbursed employee business use of computers has to qualify as being a **mandatory requirement** of the employer and a **condition of employment** to be allowable as an itemized deduction. IRS audit history has not been friendly to the employee. In Cadwallader, T.C. Memo 1989-356 the court allowed the deduction for 100% use. In Muline, T.C. Memo 1996-320 a sales manager convinced the court to allow her a deduction with the help of her supervisor as a witness.

• *MACRS Depreciation for Equipment Purchased After 12-31-86*

Under Modified Accelerated Cost Recovery System (MACRS) the depreciation percentages are based on 200% declining balance method. Items in the 5-year class are computers, typewriters, copiers, and duplicating equipment. Items in the 7-year class are library, office furniture, cell phones, and fixtures. **Sec. 179 expensing thresholds are:** of up to $24,000 (2001 & 2002), **$100,000 (2003 - 2005),** and $25,000 (2006),. The IRS tables below have computed the mid-year and mid-quarter factors for the year of purchase automatically.

Mid-year convention allows one half of the annual percentage available in the year of purchase and in the year of sale.

Mid-quarter convention allows the mid-quarter computation percentage depending on which quarter the purchase or sale occurs. If more than **40% of the year's** depreciable assets are placed in service in the **final quarter**, then all non-realty assets for that year **must** be depreciated using "mid-quarter" convention instead of the normal mid-year convention.

In our discussion of auto depreciation earlier in this chapter we included the MACRS percentages for 5-year class property. The MACRS percentages for both mid-year and mid-quarter for 7-year class property are listed below.

Depreciation Table - MACRS 7-year Class Property

Year	Mid-year	Mid-quarter			
		(1st)	(2nd)	(3rd)	(4th)
1	14.29%	25.00%	17.86%	10.71%	3.57%
2	24.49%	21.43%	23.47%	25.51%	27.55%
3	17.49%	15.31%	16.76%	18.22%	19.68%
4	12.49%	10.93%	11.97%	13.02%	14.06%
5	8.93%	8.75%	8.87%	9.30%	10.04%
6	8.92%	8.74%	8.87%	8.85%	8.73%
7	8.93%	8.75%	8.87%	8.86%	8.73%
8	4.46%	1.09%	3.33%	5.53%	7.64%

Travel

Ordinary and necessary travel expenses incurred in order to be able to earn income include: train, airplane, boat, bus fares, auto rental, taxi, hotel, motel, rooming house, meals, gratuities, telephone, fax, travel insurance, baggage charges, cleaning, and laundry costs. Unreimbursed meals while away from home overnight are subject to a 50% limitation.

To substantiate your travel expenses, you must record the following at or near the time of the travel: the amount spent, the date of the business trip, the place traveled to, and the business reason or purpose of the trip. Receipts are always required for lodging. Receipts are also required for other expenses that exceed **$74.99**. You may maintain an **account book or diary** for any **expense under $75.00** according to IRS Notice 95-50.

"Tax home" is defined as a taxpayer's place of business or employment where he earns most of his income regardless of where the family residence is maintained. Travel **away from home overnight** is necessary for the above expenses to be deductible. "Overnight" does not necessarily mean a 24-hour period but there must be enough time allowed for you to be released from activities for 6 hours of sleep, even if it is from noon to 6 p.m. **Do not** deduct or adequately account to your employer for **meal expenses when you are not away from home overnight.**

A **traveling evangelist** or conference speaker with a permanent tax home will incur deductible travel expenses for lodging and meals while on the road and use parsonage allowance exclusion for his permanent home. If he lives in a motor home or travel trailer and does not have a permanent home, he is considered a transient or itinerant. His tax home for tax purposes is wherever he "hangs his hat." His lodging and meal expenses **will not** be deductible as business expenses. He may treat the motor home as his parsonage but his meals **will not** be deductible. The cost of transportation between engagements does qualify as business travel expense.

Temporary work location: If employment at a work location is realistically expected to last (and does in fact last) one year or less, the employment is temporary in the absence of facts and circumstances indicating otherwise. You can deduct transportation expenses to a temporary work location outside your metropolitan area.

Second Job: If you regularly work at two or more places in one day, you can deduct your transportation expenses of getting from one workplace to another.

A minister may incur away-from-home expenses for the following: attendance at a church convention, speaking engagements, lectures, travel to perform a wedding or a funeral, travel for pulpit supply, evangelistic meetings, deputation for missionaries, travel to youth camps, etc.

Most overseas travel will not qualify as deductible. The primary purpose of a trip has to be business and your employer has to send or require you to make the trip. Be sure the rules are satisfied before deducting or becoming reimbursed for overseas travel. No deduction is allowed for costs of travel claimed as a **form of education**. **For example, a trip to the Holy Land is not deductible.** Enrollment in a formal course of study in the Holy Land **may** qualify as an education expense.

If a trip is primarily for business and you extend your stay for a vacation or have other nonbusiness activities, you may deduct the travel expense to and from the business destination. You would not be able to deduct side-trip mileage or the extra cost of the meals and lodging for the personal time.

If a trip is primarily for business and you have weekend or off duty days, all of the meals and lodging will be deductible. Personal side-trip miles would not be deductible. Saturday lodging and meals is considered an allowable business day when required to obtain a cheaper air fare.

If a trip is primarily for vacation or personal reasons, the entire cost of the trip is a nondeductible personal expense. However, you can deduct any expenses while there that are directly related to your business.

Travel expenses for business reasons are only allowable for the person earning an income. Expenses for a nonsalaried spouse and children to accompany you on a trip are personal and not allowable as business expenses. The single room rate can be used instead of one half of double room rate. Except for bona fide entertainment the spouse's meals are not deductible.

Reconciliation Act of 1993 added Sec. 274(m)(3) and states: "No deduction shall be allowed under this chapter for travel expenses paid or incurred with respect to a spouse, dependent, or other individual accompanying the taxpayer (or an officer or employee of the taxpayer) on business travel, unless--

    (A)   the spouse, dependent, or other individual is an employee of the taxpayer,

    (B)   the travel of the spouse, dependent, or other individual is for a bona fide business purpose, and

    (C)   such expenses would otherwise be deductible by the spouse, dependent, or other individual."

A welcome change allows volunteer workers, **including a non salaried spouse**, attending a convention, who are reimbursed for travel and ministry expenses to be reimbursed using the business standard mileage rate of 40½¢ per mile, January 1, 2005 until September 1, 2005. On September 1, 2005 the rate changed to 48˙¢ until December 31, 2005. The Katrina Act, effective September 23, reduced the amount to be reimbursed to volunteers to 48½¢ X 70% = 33.95¢. (2006 the rate of 44½¢ X 70% = 31.15¢) A nonsalaried spouse must be attending a convention as an official delegate or representative of a church or organization. A volunteer must adequately account to the organization making the reimbursement to be a "bona fide volunteer" according to IRS INFO 2000-0235, released August 24, 2000.

Unreimbursed lodging, meals, fares, and auto mileage at **14¢** per mile as a delegate are allowable as a contribution deduction on Schedule A.

CAUTION: When an employer reimburses an employee for non-business meals, overseas travel that does not qualify as business, or personal family members travel expenses it must be reported as **income** on the employee's Form W-2, Box 1.

Lodging, Meal, And Incidental Expense Per Diem Rates

Periodically, the IRS publishes per diem rates that may be used by employers who reimburse employees for their traveling expenses. The IRS per diem rates are adjusted for inflation. These per diem rates include an individual's lodging, meals and incidental (M&IE) travel expenses. **Incidental expenses** covered by a per diem arrangement include laundry, cleaning, and tips for services, but do not include cab fares, business calls, fax, or other communication costs. An optional method of deducting for incidental expenses only, when no meal expenses are incurred, is **$3** a day.

The applicable per diem amount depends on the locality of travel. For travel within the continental United States (CONUS) and for foreign and non-foreign travel outside the continental 48 states (OCONUS), separate lodging and M&IE rates are published periodically in the Federal Register, U.S. Government Printing Office. **IRS Publication 1542** contains the CONUS tables. For travel in **2005**, the rate is **$31** a day for most areas in the United States. Other locations are designated as high-cost areas, qualifying for higher standard meal allowances. Locations qualifying for rates of **$35, $39, $43, $47, $49, $51, $54, $59, or $64** a day are listed in IRS Publication 1542. You can access the federal per diem rates on the internet at: **http://www.gsa.gov**

How to prorate partial travel days: You can use either of the following methods to prorate the full-day rate for M&IE:

1. use ¾ of the M&IE rate for the day of departure and the day of arrival back home, or
2. use any method that you consistently apply and that is in accordance with reasonable business practice. For example, for travel away from home from 9 a.m. of one day to 5 p.m. of the next day can be treated as 2 full days of M&IE, even though federal employees are limited to 1½ days of M&IE.

Unreimbursed employees and self-employed individuals may only use the per diem rate established for meals and incidental expenses found in the IRS CONUS tables. The entire M&IE rate is subject to the 50% limitation on meal expenses. **Actual lodging** expenses must be used. In addition, the high-low rate available to employers and discussed below may not be used by unreimbursed employees and self-employed individuals.

● *Alternative Method for Employers*

A **high-low per diem method** is available to simplify the administrative burden of sifting through some 36 pages of per diem rates in order to determine the correct rate for an employee's particular areas of travel. Under the high-low per diem method, the IRS publishes a list of localities that are classified as high-cost areas. All other localities within the continental United States are classified as low-cost areas. The IRS then establishes a per diem rate for the two types of localities. The **2005** per diem rates are **$204** for high-cost localities and **$129** for low-cost localities. The M&IE portion of the alternative method is **$46** for high-cost localities and **$36** for low-cost localities. The remaining **$158 or $93** is the lodging portion of the per diem allowance. There is no optional standard lodging amount similar to the standard meal allowance, you can not combine actual meal cost and lodging high-low per diem rates.

The high-low method may not be used to reimburse an employee for M&IE expenses only. The employer can use the M&IE rate from the IRS tables if the employer pays for lodging, provides lodging or the employee does not incur lodging.

The **same method of reimbursement** must be used for the whole year of travel within the continental United States. Annually compare the four options for computing your best travel reimbursement and use the greater of:

1. Individual location rates from the conus or oconus tables
2. High-low per diem alternative method (both lodging & M&IE)
3. Your actual cost of lodging and M&IE from the conus or oconus tables
4. Your actual cost of lodging and actual cost of meals

Become reimbursed throughout the year according to the method you expect to be the greater, then at year end, calculate all three. If another method is greater, become reimbursed for the adjusting differential at the end of the year.

The locations listed on page 70 are eligible for the high cost rates. Some locations are high cost for **only a portion** of the year. Effective date for the list from **Rev. Proc. 2005-67** was October 1, 2004. IRS published Rev. **Proc. 2005-10** early in 2005 for calendar year 2005. Transition rules state that an employer who used Rev. Proc. 2005-10 for an employee during the first 9 months of calendar year 2005 may not use the rates in Rev. Proc 2005-67 until January 1, 2006.

High-low Per Diem Rates

Effective Dates	Lodging & Meals	Lodging Only	Meals & Incidentals
10/1/05 - 12/31/06	$226 high/$141 low	$168 high/$96 low	$58 high/$45 low
10/1/04 - 12/31/05	$204 high/$129 low	$158 high/$93 low	$46 high/$36 low
11/1/03 - 12/31/04	$207 high/$126 low	$161 high/$90 low	$46 high/$36 low
10/1/02 - 12/31/03	$204 high/$125 low	$159 high/$90 low	$45 high/$35 low
10/1/01 - 12/31/02	$204 high/$125 low	$162 high/$91 low	$42 high/$34 low
1/1/00 - 12/31/01	$201 high/$124 low	$159 high/$90 low	$42 high/$34 low
1/1/99 - 12/31/99	$185 high/$115 low	$143 high/$81 low	$42 high/$34 low

Entertainment

Entertainment expenses and meals for entertainment that are not reimbursed will be subject to the 50% limitation, then combined with other unreimbursed professional expenses and further limited by 2% of AGI and Sec. 265 allocation limitation as a deduction on Schedule A. An employee can be reimbursed for 100% of meal and entertainment expense. Employers will deduct only 50% of reimbursed meals and entertainment as a business expense. Nonprofit employers will not be affected since they have no tax liability.

Restrictive tests for meals and entertainment require that the event is directly related to the active conduct of your job and directly preceding or following a substantial and bona fide business discussion on a subject associated with the active conduct of your business or ministry.

The record-keeping rules for entertainment, **Sec. 274**, are very strict. The entertainment diary section in our **"Professional Tax Record Book"** is designed to help you keep all of the necessary facts. **You must have the name of the persons entertained, their title or position, where the entertainment took place, what purpose or discussion took place and the amount of the expense.** Receipts are important if the expense exceeds $75.00. When the entertainment is in the home and the occasion is over the $75 threshold, keep the receipt from the grocery store.

By adopting an accountable reimbursement plan, you will be submitting your expense records to your employer. **Due to the confidential nature of a minister's entertainment activity,** we recommend that the diary showing who was entertained and what business was transacted should be retained by the minister and a dollar amount be submitted to your employer for reimbursement. An IRS regulation allows this confidential treatment, Reg. 1.274-5T(c)(2)(ii)(D).

Most ministers are required to do substantial entertaining in their home. Since the cost of the home itself is nontaxable as parsonage allowance, the main expense of entertaining is the cost of meals provided. Special speakers, missionaries, board members, prospective faculty, etc., are entertained and a record of the number of meals provided in the home, multiplied by an average cost per meal, will result in a sizable deduction. A reasonable amount per meal, depending on your actual circumstances and service practices, might vary between $8.00 to $11.00 per meal. Those afternoon meetings with refreshments, or after evening service snacks for the youth group, etc., might vary between $2.50 to $3.50 per person.

High Cost Localities for High-Low Per Diem Method

State	Key City	County or other defined locations	Effective Dates 2005 (Rev. Proc. 2005-10)	Effective Dates 2006 (Rev. Proc. 2005-67)
AZ	Phoenix/Scottsdale	Maricopa	1/1-5/31	1/1-3/31
CA	Monterey	Monterey	2/1-11/30	N/A
CA	Napa	Napa	5/1-10/31	All Year
CA	Palm Springs	Riverside	1/1-5/31	N/A
CA	San Diego	San Diego	All Year	All Year
CA	San Francisco	San Francisco	All Year	All Year
CA	Santa Barbara	Santa Barbara	All Year	N/A
CA	Santa Monica	City limits of Santa Monica	All Year	All Year
CA	South Lake Tahoe	El Dorado	12/1-8/31	N/A
CO	Aspen	Pitkin	All Year	12/1-3/31
CO	Crested Butte	City limits of Crested Butte (Gunnison County)	12/1-3/31	N/A
CO	Crested Butte/Gunnison	Gunnison	N/A	12/1-4/30
CO	Silverhome/Breckenridge	Summit	12/1-3/31	12/1-3/31
CO	Steamboat Springs	Routt	N/A	12/1-3/31
CO	Telluride	San Miguel	12/1-9/30	10/1-4/30
CO	Vail	Eagle	All Year	12/1-3/31
DC	Washington, D.C.	Also the cities of Alexandria, Falls Church and Fairfax, and the couties of Arlington, Loudoun and Fairfax in Virginia; and the counties of Montgomery and Prince George's in Maryland.	All Year	All Year
DE	Lewes	Sussex	7/1-8/31	N/A
FL	Daytona Beach	Volusia	2/1-3/31	N/A
FL	Fort Lauderdale	Broward	1/1-5/31	N/A
FL	Key West	Monroe	All Year	All Year
FL	Miami	Miami-Dade	10/1-5/31	1/1-4/30
FL	Naples	Collier	1/1-3/31	2/1-3/31
FL	Palm Beach	Palm Beach (also the cities of Boca Raton, Delray Beach, Jupiter, Palm Beach Gardens, Palm Beach, Palm Beach Shores, Singer Island, and West Palm Beach)	10/1-5/31	2/1-3/31
IL	Chicago	Cook and Lake	2/1-4/30 & 9/1-11/30	10/1-6/30 & 9/1-9/30
LA	New Orleans	Orleans and St. Bernard Parishes	All Year	All Year
LA	New Orleans	Orleans, St. Bernard, Jefferson, and Plaquemine Parishes	N/A	10/1-5/31
ME	Bar Harbor	Hancock	N/A	7/1-8/31
	(for counties of Montgomery and Prince George's, see District of Columbia)			
MD	Baltimore	Baltimore County and Baltimore City	All Year	All Year
MD	Cambridge/St. Michaels	Dorchester and Talbot	6/1-8/31	6/1-8/31
MD	Ocean City	Worcester	7/1-8/31	6/1-9/30
MA	Boston	Suffolk	All Year	All Year
MA	Cambridge	City limits of Cambridge	All Year	All Year
MA	Hyannis	Barnstable	7/1-8/31	N/A
MA	Martha's Vineyard	Dukes	5/1-8/31	7/1-8/31
MA	Nantucket	Nantucket	All Year	6/1-8/31

State	Key City	County or other defined locations	Effective Dates 2005 (Rev. Proc. 2005-10)	Effective Dates 2006 (Rev. Proc. 2005-67)
MI	Traverse City	Grand Traverse	7/1-8/31	N/A
NH	Conway	Caroll	N/A	7/1-8/31
NJ	Atlantic City	Atlantic	5/1-10/31	N/A
NJ	Cape May	Cape May (except Ocean City)	6/1-8/31	N/A
NJ	Cape May/Ocean City	Cape May	N/A	7/1-8/31
NJ	Ocean City	City limits of Ocean City	6/1-10/31	N/A
NJ	Princeton/Trenton	Mercer	All Year	N/A
NM	Santa Fe	Santa Fe	7/1-8/31	N/A
NY	Carle Place/Garden City/Glen Cove/Great Neck/Plainview/Rockville Centre/Syosset/Uniondale/Woodbury	Nassau	All Year	N/A
NY	Floral Park/Garden City/Glen Cove/Great Neck/Roslyn	Nassau	N/A	All Year
NY	Lake Placid	Essex	7/1-8/31	7/1-8/31
NY	Manhattan	Boughs of Manhattan, Brooklyn, Queens, the Bronx, and Staten Island	All Year	All Year
NY	Riverhead/Ronkonkoma/Melville	Suffolk	All Year	All Year
NY	Riverhead/Ronkonkoma/Melville/Smithtown/Huntington Station/Amagansett/East Hampton/Montauk/Southampton/Islandia/Commack/Medford/Stony Brook/Hauppauge/Centereach	Suffolk	N/A	All Year
NY	Saratoga Springs/Schenectady	Saratoga and Schenectady	N/A	7/1-8/31
NY	Tarrytown	Westchester (except White Plains)	All Year	
NY	Tarrytown/White Plains/New Rochelle/Yonkers	Westchester	N/A	All Year
NY	White Plains	City Limits of White Plains	All Year	N/A
NC	Kill Devil	Dare	4/1-10/31	N/A
PA	Hershey	City limits of Hershey	All Year	All Year
PA	Philadelphia	Philadelphia	All Year	All Year
RI	Jamestown/Middletown/Newport	Newport	5/1-10/31	10/1-10/31 & 5/1-9/30
RI	Providence	Providence	All Year	All Year
SC	Hilton Head	Beaufort	4/1-10/31	N/A
UT	Park City	Summit	12/1-3/31	12/1-3/31
VA		(for cities of Alexandria, Fairfax, and Falls Church, and the counties of Arlington, Fairfax and Loudoun, see District of Columbia.)		
VA	Virginia Beach	Cities of Virginia Beach, Norfolk, Portsmouth, Chesapeake, and Suffolk	6/1-8/31	N/A
WA	Seattle	King	5/1-10/31	All Year

If the meals are eaten outside the home, then the receipt for the actual cost of the meals is deductible. If you entertain business and non-business individuals at the same event, you must divide your entertainment expenses between business and non-business. For example, if you entertain a group of individuals that **includes yourself**, three business prospects, and seven social guests, 4/11 of the expenses qualifies for the deduction.

If your spouse is present during an occasion of entertainment because the spouse of the person being entertained is present, you may deduct the meal cost for both spouses. Meal expenses for your children are not business deductions.

Educational Expenses

Educational expenses incurred for the purpose of maintaining or improving present job or professional skills or meeting the expressed requirements of an employer to retain the job are deductible. The deduction will not be allowed if the education qualifies you for a new trade or business or satisfies the minimum requirements of your present job.

For education costs to be deductible as a business expense, you are unable to be absent from your profession for more than a year. A minister who has not been gainfully employed as a minister will not be able to deduct his seminary education. Most seminary degrees require three or more years. Seminary students who have the opportunity to serve as a "part-time" minister while obtaining additional education will be more likely to qualify for the education expense deduction. IRS considers you to have changed careers if you work a secular job while obtaining additional education for a period of more than 12 months.

Tuition, fees, books and supplies, any transportation to school away from your hometown, meals and lodging (if necessary to be away from home overnight to attend classes) are typical educational expenses. Unreimbursed meals are only 50% deductible.

No deduction is allowed for costs of travel claimed as a **form of education.** For example, a trip to the Holy Land is not deductible. Enrollment in a formal course of study in the Holy Land **may** qualify as an education expense.

● *Education Incentives for Taxpayer and Family*

Education tax-planning has become very important. Unreimbursed educational expenses deducted on Form 2106 are not eligible for either the HOPE or Lifetime Learning Credits. If you have qualified business education deductions, calculate your tax liability both ways, either the deductions or the educational credits, and claim the larger tax benefit. (IRS Publication 970, "Tax Benefits for Higher Education")

Comparison of the Credits:

Hope Credit - You may be able to claim up to $1,500 credit per eligible student. Credit is available ONLY until the first two years of post-secondary education are completed and only for two years per eligible student. Student must be pursuing an undergraduate degree or other recognized education credential. Student must be enrolled at least half time for at least one academic period. There can be no felony drug conviction on a student's record.

Lifetime Learning Credit - You may be able to claim up to $2,000 credit per return, for the entire family. Credit is available for all years of postsecondary education and for courses to acquire or improve job skills for an unlimited number of years. Student does not need to be pursuing a degree or other recognized education credential and can be enrolled in one or more courses. Felony drug conviction rule does not apply.

Eligible Expenses for Hope and Lifetime Learning Credits. Qualified tuition and related expenses **paid to the institution** as a condition of enrollment or attendance are eligible. Related expenses include course-related books, supplies and equipment, and required student activity fees **paid to the institution**. Noneligible expenses include room and board, insurance, student health fees, and transportation even if paid to the institution. Noneligible expenses also include books, supplies, and equipment that are not purchased from the institution. Qualified tuition and related expenses must be reduced by tax-free funds received from scholarships, Pell grants, employer-provided educational assistance, educational bonds, Coverdell distributions, and veterans' educational assistance.

Who is Eligible for Hope and Lifetime Learning Credits? You, your spouse, or any child claimed as your dependent. If the child is your dependent, the money is *considered* to be paid by you even if it *is* paid by the child.

Phase Out for Hope and Lifetime Learning Credits. The credits phase out as your **2005** AGI ranges from $87,000 to $107,000 ($43,000 to $53,000 for single filers). Thresholds are inflation indexed.

Coverdell Education Savings Accounts. Maximum annual contribution you can make to a Coverdell ESA is **$2,000**. Contributions must be for a child under age 18 or a special needs beneficiary. Contributions are *not deductible*. Saving and investing in a mutual fund could *compound and grow* to a significant amount if begun when the child is young. The money is *completely tax-free* when taken out if it is used to pay for qualifying elementary, secondary and post-secondary education expenses.

Contributions to a Coverdell ESA for any year can be made by the due date of your return for that year (not including extensions).

If you file a joint return, the amount you can contribute to a Coverdell ESA will be **phased out** if your modified adjusted gross income is more than $190,000 but less than $220,000. ($95,000 to $110,000 for single filers.)

You can claim the Hope or lifetime learning credit in the same year you take a tax-free distribution from a Coverdell ESA, provided that the distribution from the Coverdell ESA is not used for the same expenses for which the credit is claimed.

Student Loan Interest of up to **$2,500** can be deducted—even if you do not itemize. The deduction is allowed only for interest paid on qualified education loans. For joint filers the threshold for phase out is **$105,000 to $135,000** and it is **$50,000 to $65,000** for single filers. You can deduct interest paid during the remaining period of your student loan.

College Tuition Deduction. In **2005**, joint filers with modified adjusted gross income that is less than $130,000 to $160,000 can claim a **$4,000** "above the line" deduction. For single filers, the adjusted gross income threshold is $65,000 to $80,000. **After 2005 it sunsets or ends**. If your MAGI exceeds the income ceiling, no deduction at all is allowed. You may be able to take the Hope or Lifetime Learning Credit for your education expenses instead of a tuition and fees deduction. You can **choose the one** that will give you the lower tax. Expenses eligible for the deduction are reduced by any tax-free distribution from a Coverdell ESA.

Office Expense and Supplies

Typical expenses an employee might have in their ministry are stationery, pens, erasers, ink, stapler, paper clips, record books, secretarial or typing expenses, postage, copier supplies, computer supplies, etc. Any office furniture or equipment that have useful lives of more than one year should be depreciated or Sec. 179 expensed. (See depreciation discussion)

If you are required to provide an office outside of your home, any cost to you would be a deductible expense. Rent, furniture, utilities, etc., would be allowable expenses.

Office-In-Home deduction is not available if your employer provides an office on their premises. It is generally not available when you have 100% of your home expenses tax-free under Sec. 107 parsonage allowance.

To deduct a portion of your home as an office-in-home, it must be used regularly and exclusively as the principal place of business. Qualifying office-in-the-home use results in the favorable absence of **personal commuting miles** for business use of the automobile.

A home office that is used regularly and exclusively qualifies if:

1. the office is used by the taxpayer to conduct administrative or management activities of a trade or business, and
2. there is no other fixed location of the trade or business where the taxpayer conducts substantial administrative or management activities of the trade or business.

In a year of no or inadequate parsonage allowance designation, and you have a qualifying office-in-the-home situation, deduct it. To compute the amount allowable, divide the square footage used as an office by the square footage in your entire home. Use this percentage of the allowable home expenses and depreciation. A qualified "office-in-the-home" deduction would reduce your social security base and if "adequately accounted" to your employer would not increase income tax.

Final Regs for Sec. 121, the tax free exclusion of gain for the sale of a personal residence, provide that only post-May 6, 1997 depreciation will be taxable when both residential and non-residential portions of the property are within the same dwelling unit. (IRS Publication 523)

Generally, it is best for you to have 100% of your home expenses be tax-free under Sec. 107 parsonage allowance.

Religious Materials

Many trips to the religious bookstore add up to considerable expense for most employees in the ministry. Tracts and booklets purchased for distribution in the visitation ministry, music and musical supplies for the choir; gifts for presentation at marriages, baptisms, or holidays; teaching aids, including video and cassette programs, are but a few of the usual expenses a dual-status or lay employee incurs.

Clothing for the minister is usually not deductible. Tax law states that if something is required as a condition of employment and is not adaptable for general wear, it is deductible. Pulpit robes or special shirt collars and their cleaning expense would qualify as a deduction. Suits and shirts that are adaptable for general wear are not deductible for a salesman, businessman, or a minister.

Seminars And Dues

Fees charged to attend seminars or conference meetings and dues to professional organizations that are directly related to your profession are deductible.

Subscriptions, Paperbacks, Tapes And CDs

A number of periodicals and journals find their way into your mail box. The cost of the subscriptions that is directly related to your ministry is deductible. Magazines and local newspapers give the current events so necessary for sermon illustrations and provide news of the local community. Except for one subscription to a local newspaper (which IRS claims must be personal), deduct the subscriptions you use directly in your ministry.

Small booklets, paperback books, tapes, and CDs should be separate from regular library books and the whole cost deducted in full in the year of purchase. **DO NOT deduct** magazine subscriptions, tapes, and books that are purchased for **personal reasons and interests.**

Business Telephone

Long distance business calls need to be separated from the personal portion used in the parsonage allowance computation because as a business expense they will reduce income tax as well as social security and medicare tax. The base rate portion of your home telephone cannot be used as a business expense. However, it is a utility that is a parsonage allowance expense.

The business portion of your cellular phone bill is a legitimate professional expense. When a cellular phone is used outside of the home, do not use the personal portion as parsonage allowance.

The business portion of your internet connection is a legitimate professional expense. When used in the parsonage, the personal portion would be a utility for parsonage allowance expense.

Earned Income Credit

Beginning in 2002, the earned income that is included in the taxpayer's gross income is used to calculate earned income credit. The former inclusion of nontaxable earned income no longer applies. As a result, many ministers qualify for earned income credit!!

For **2005**, earned income credit is available for the low-income taxpayer who maintains a household in the U.S. for more than one-half of the taxable year and has taxable earned income of less than **$13,750** (married joint) or **$11,750** (single) without a qualifying child; **$33,030** (married joint) or **$31,030** (single) with one qualifying child; **$37,263** (married joint) or **$35,263** (single) if you have more than one qualifying child. It is a refundable credit and, if there is no tax liability, the government "gives" it to the taxpayer.

The amount of the credit was increased and became available for low income individuals without a qualifying child for the first time in 1994. The maximum basic credit for **2005** is **$399** without a qualifying child; **$2662** with one qualifying child; **$4,400** with two or more qualifying children.

Earned income credit will be denied for taxpayers who have "disqualified income" of over **$2,700** for the taxable year. "Disqualified income" consists of (a) interest (taxable and tax-exempt); (b) taxable dividends; (c) gross income from Schedule E less expenses; (d) capital gain net income; (e) net passive income that is not self-employment income.

A modified definition of AGI is used for phasing out the earned income credit by disregarding certain losses.

• *Definition of Earned Income for Ministers*

For tax years before 2002, earned income was based on modified AGI. Salary deferrals such as Sec. 403(b), 401(k) and salary reductions such as Sec. 125 cafeteria plans were treated as "earned income" for Earned Income Credit purposes. Sec. 107 parsonage allowance and Sec. 119 meals and lodging for the convenience of the employer were also treated as "earned income."

Beginning in 2002, earned income no longer includes certain nontaxable employee compensation. Earned income credit will generally be figured using your AGI, **not** modified AGI. According to the instructions for Earned Income Credit, Sec. 107 parsonage allowance **is still included** as "earned income" for a minister subject to social security and **is not included** for an exempt minister who is an employee of an organization.

Sec. 32(c)(2)(A) says: "The term "earned income" means—

(i)   wages, salaries, tips, and other employee compensation, but only if such amounts are includible in gross income for the taxable year, plus

(ii)   the amount of the taxpayer's net earnings from self-employment for the taxable year (within the meaning of section 1402(a), but such net earnings shall be determined with regard to the deduction allowed to the taxpayer by section 164(f)."

Rev. Ruling 79-78 defines "earned income" for the dual-status minister to include parsonage allowance and to include the income of a minister who elected to be exempt from social security if he is **an employee.**

Use the following outline to guide you in determining if you are entitled to earned income credit.

1.   Ministers who are **subject** to social security and medicare tax:
   a.   An employee of an organization - Earned income includes wages, value of parsonage and/or parsonage allowance, and Schedule C net honorariums, less adjustment for one half of self-employment tax, Form 1040, line 27.
   b.   An independent evangelist - Earned income includes Schedule C net honorariums and parsonage allowance, less adjustment for one half of self-employment tax, Form 1040, line 27.

2.   Ministers who have become **exempt** from social security and medicare tax:
   a.   An employee of an organization - Earned income includes wages entered on Form 1040, line 7, including "excess parsonage allowance", **but not Schedule C net honorariums**.
   b.   An independent evangelist - **Sch C net honorariums do not qualify** for earned income credit.

IRS Publication 596 and Instructions for Form 1040, line 66a and 66b, contains detailed instructions and worksheets to calculate the correct amount of earned income credit.

Social Security and Retirement Planning

Dual-status ministers are treated as self-employed individuals in the performance of ministerial services for social security purposes as a result of written law. Sec. 1402(a)(8) is an exception to the "common law" rules for determining whether a person is an employee or self-employed. **Dual-status means** that the minister is an **employee** for income reporting, fringe benefit, and expense deducting purposes and **self-employed** for social security purposes.

Social Security for Religious Workers

Dual-Status Minister

Detailed information presented in Chapter Two helps you determine your correct treatment for social security purposes. **Summary:** The same regulations for determining if a minister qualifies for self-employed status for social security purposes are used to determine if a minister is entitled to parsonage allowance. Generally, you must be employed by a church or an integral agency of a church, perform the duties of a minister, and be ordained or "the equivalent thereof" to be treated as if you were self-employed for social security purposes. When, according to the regulations, you are to be treated as self-employed for social security purposes, **it is mandatory**. For your employer to withhold and match social security would be in error.

In the absence of a formal ordination, licensing, or commissioning, it is the date a church called or hired you as their minister and gave you the authority to perform substantially all of the religious duties that your self-employed status begins. It is necessary for your church to have formally ordained, licensed, or commissioned you as a minister before they can "assign or designate" you to a position at a "non-integral agency" and qualify you for dual-status treatment. It is also necessary for your church to have formally ordained, licensed, or commissioned you as a minister if you conduct worship and administer ordinances or sacraments, but are not employed by a church or an integral agency of a church.

Before 1968, services performed by ministers were exempt from social security unless they filed a certificate (Form 2031) stating that they wished to be covered by social security.

Since 1968, ministers are automatically covered under social security unless they file an application for exemption on the grounds of conscientious or religious opposition to social security and the government's involvement in public insurance. **If you choose to be covered, YOU DO NOTHING**. You are automatically liable for paying social security on Schedule SE.

An individual who had elected to be covered by social security by filing Form 2031 (before 1968) made an irrevocable decision and could not file Form 4361 and elect to be exempt. Anyone engaged in the ministry at the time of the law change in 1968 had until April 15, 1970, to file Form 4361 and continue not being covered by social security. A minister is often unaware of his **opportunity to choose** between paying social security or becoming exempt from paying Social Security. Once a minister begins to pay social security and the time expires for filing Form 4361 **and he does not have a change of belief accompanied by a change to another faith**, there is no way for him to become exempt. (See discussion "When to File Form 4361-Including 'New Belief' Opportunity")

Computation Of Social Security Base - "Worksheet to be Used with Form 2106"

In Chapter Six we have a chart showing the types of income common to a minister and indicate what is required to be entered as salary on Form 941, line 2, and Form W-2, Box 1. **Parsonage provided and/or parsonage allowance designated is to be omitted from Form W-2, Box 1.** However, both the parsonage provided and/or the parsonage allowance must be added to the taxable amount of salary for social security and medicare tax purposes. On the "Computation of Social Security Base" section of the "Worksheet to be Used with Form 2106," enter the value of the parsonage provided on line 2, and enter the parsonage allowance designated from Part D, line 16, on line 3.

Because a dual-status minister is treated as "self-employed" for social security purposes, you can subtract **all unreimbursed professional expenses** from your income to arrive at the amount of income upon which to compute social security. Revenue Ruling 80-110 clearly states that unreimbursed auto, travel, and professional expenses can be used to reduce the social security base for the dual-status minister. Based on Revenue Ruling 80-110, Sec. 1402(a) and Sec. 62(1), **it is correct to use the business percentage of auto interest and personal property tax as a subtraction** from a minister's social security base. The portion of tax preparation fee that is attributable to the reporting of ministry transactions can be a subtraction from a minister's social security base according to Revenue Ruling 92-29.

Qualifyied fringe benefits are not subject to social security and are correct to be omitted from employee's Form W-2, Box 1. Nonqualifyied and taxable fringe benefits receive the same treatment as taxable salary. They are to be included in the employee's Form W-2, Box 1 and they are subject to social security.

Contributions to a Sec. 403(b) tax sheltered account by a dual-status minister are not subject to social security according to **Revenue Ruling 68-395**.

If you have filed Form 4361 and are exempt from social security, write "Exempt - Form 4361" on the self-employment line, Form 1040, page 2. If you are exempt from social security on your earnings from the ministry, but have secular self-employment income, use Schedule SE, page 2. Check the box on Line A to report that you have filed Form 4361 and compute social security on your secular earnings.

• *Social Security Deductions For Self-Employed*

On Schedule SE the gross social security base is adjusted to allow one half of social security as a deduction. On Form 1040, page 1, an adjustment for one half of the social security paid by the self-employed taxpayer is allowed.

Social Security Exemption

Form 4361 includes a statement that, because of your religious principles, you are conscientiously opposed to accepting, for services performed as a member of the clergy, any public insurance (governmental insurance that makes payments in the event of death, disability, old age, or retirement). This includes public insurance established by the Social Security Act. Your conscientious opposition must be based on the institutional principles and discipline of your particular religious denomination **OR** it must be based on **your individual religious principles**. Opposition based on the general conscience or for economic reasons will not satisfy this requirement.

A dual-status minister must prayerfully make his/her own decision as to whether he/she wants to be covered by social security. After a personal study of the **scriptures for biblical principals** that would show opposition to public or government insurance, a minister choosing to be exempt from social security should informally make sufficient notes of his study and conclusions.

As tax professionals, our job is to inform and teach you that, as a dual-status minister, you have an important decision to make regarding social security. No tax professional can make the choice for you nor should they advise you either way. **You must prayerfully make your own decision**. If you choose to remain subject to social security, you will compute it on Schedule SE and timely prepay your estimate of income tax and social security and medicare tax liability. If you choose to become exempt from social security you must timely file Form 4361. If you choose to become exempt **it must be for the religious and conscientious grounds** stated above.

Ministers who have filed Form 4361 are opposed to **only public** insurance and must provide their own alternative to social security. They most certainly **can** and **should** have a private investment plan for retirement needs and disability insurance coverage.

• *Form 4361 Filed For Invalid Reason*

You may not become exempt for solely economic reasons. If you file an application for exemption only for economic reasons, you have not made a valid election. In **Rev. Ruling 70-197** a minister established *"that his application was made as a result of erroneous advice and was predicated solely on a judgement determination that a private insurance program was preferable from an economic standpoint for his insurance needs over that of the social security program rather than because he was conscientiously opposed to, or because of religious principles opposed to, the acceptance of any public insurance as specified in the form."* Accordingly it was held that the minister did not qualify for the exemption and his net earnings from ministry was subject to social security.

Rev. Ruling 82-185 concluded that Social Security tax can not be assessed later than three years after the taxpayer files a Form 1040 and fully reports all income but makes no entry with respect to self-employment tax.

● *What Happens To What I Have Already Paid In?*

Form 4361 does not cause you to waive the right to receive social security benefits. Any secular employment or work that is **NOT** in the exercise of your ministry will be subject to either social security or self-employment tax. Any social security you pay on secular earnings will be credited to your account.

If vested, you will be entitled to receive social security benefits from all mandatory contributions on secular earnings. **Ten years or forty quarters** of social security contributions result in your being vested and eligible for benefits based on your lifetime average. You can find out the number of quarters you have been credited for by contacting the Social Security Administration. Since secular work is always subject to social security, it would be possible to earn additional quarters by performing secular work after filing Form 4361. Earnings required for a quarter of credit in **2005 is $920** and in **2006 is $970**. When you retire, you can choose the **greater source** of benefits, either from **your account** or **your spouse's** account.

If vested, or your spouse is vested, Medicare Insurance Part A **will be provided** for you and your spouse.

If not vested, nor is your spouse vested or you are single, Medicare Insurance Part A **can be purchased** by an exempt minister. Medicare Part A would cost **$375** a month if you have less than 30 quarters and **$206** a month if you have between 30 and 39 quarters. You would pay for Medicare B also. This should bring **peace of mind** to exempt ministers who have been given wrong information and have been told they will not qualify for Medicare. **www.medicare.gov**

● *Disability Coverage*

Disability coverage under social security will discontinue after you become exempt. When it will discontinue for you, depends upon your age and the number of quarters of credit you have. Knowing how many credits you need to remain covered by social security disability is very important. You could obtain a secular job to add credits or you could purchase private disability insurance coverage. Foreign missionaries have difficulty obtaining comparable life and disability insurance coverages and may wish to remain covered by social security.

● *Irrevocable Unless Congress Creates a "Window" for Revocation*

The exemption, once obtained, is basically irrevocable. Except when Congress gives a "window" of time for an exempt minister to revoke it, the decision is permanent. Historically, there have been three times that Congress has made provisions for revocation. **Ministers who revoke their election can never become exempt again**. If filed by the due date of the 1978 return, Form 4361-A gave opportunity for ministers who were exempt to revoke their election. If filed by the due date of the 1987 return, Form 2031 gave the second opportunity for ministers who were exempt to revoke their election. If filed by the due date of 2001 return, Form 2031 gave the third opportunity for ministers who were exempt to revoke their election.

● *When To File Form 4361 - Including "New Belief" Opportunity*

When a minister has the belief of opposition to public insurance at the time he begins **his initial ministry** he will have until the due date (April 15th) of his tax return, including extensions, for the **second tax year** in which he has net self-employment **earnings of $400** or more from services as a minister to **timely file** Form 4361, "Application for Exemption." Net earnings is the salary and/or honorariums, minus unreimbursed business expenses, plus parsonage provided and/or parsonage allowance designated.

It is very important for a minister who wishes to become exempt from social security to be aware that the date his ministry begins is when he assumes the duties of the ministry. In the absence of a formal ordination, licensing or commissioning, it is the **date a church called or hired** you as their minister and gave you the authority to perform substantially all of the religious duties.

Here is a very important court definition of a "duly ordained, licensed, or commissioned" minister. In J.M. Ballinger, U.S. Court of Appeals, 10th Circuit, No. 82-1928, 3/7/84, it was stated:

> *"Not all churches or religions have a formally ordained ministry, whether because of the nature of their beliefs, the lack of a denominational structure or a variety of other reasons. Courts are not in a position to determine the merits of various churches... We interpret Congress' language providing an exemption for any individual who is `a duly ordained, commissioned, or licensed minister of a church' to mean that the **triggering event** is the assumption of the duties and functions of a minister."*

Several of the tax court cases we reviewed in Chapter Two were concerning ministers who wanted to become exempt from social security. After waiting until they received their formal or permanent credentials, they were denied exemption because their applications were untimely filed. Services they performed with temporary or limited credentials were still being performed **with the same employer** when they received their permanent credentials. Not realizing that their initial date of hire was the beginning of their ministry caused them to have their applications disapproved because of untimeliness. When an application to become exempt from social security is filed late, it will be disapproved. A minister who files untimely and has his application disapproved has no future opportunity to become exempt. **A timely filed Form 4361 will be approved.**

Example of timing: you had net earnings of $5,000 in 2004 and $38,000 in 2005, the deadline for filing Form 4361 would be April 15th, 2005. The two years need not be consecutive. If a minister had net earnings of $700 in 1998, less than $400 in 1999 through 2004, and $4,000 in 2005, the deadline for filing Form 4361 would be April 17th, 2006.

Change of belief accompanied by a change to another faith: When a minister does not have the belief of opposition to public insurance at the time of his initial date of hire, and does not file an application to be exempt, he may experience **another opportunity to become exempt**. It depends upon the church polity of his employing church. In a **connectional** (not self-governing) church polity, a minister is typically appointed to a congregation and generally is moved by an overseer to a different congregation within the denomination. In an **autonomous** (self-governing) church polity, a minister is typically hired or called directly by a congregation and generally makes his own decision as to when he wants to resign and change church employers.

1. A change of faith **does not happen** when an employee is transferred between connectional church congregations.
2. A change of faith **does happen** when a minister leaves a connectional church denomination and goes to another connectional church denomination or to an autonomous church employer.
3. A change of faith **does happen** when a minister resigns from one autonomous church and goes to another autonomous church or to a connectional church.

When a minister has the belief of opposition to public insurance at the time he begins **his "change of faith"** ministry, he will have until the due date (April 15th) of his tax return, including extensions, for the **second tax year** in which he has net self-employment **earnings of $400** or more from services as a minister to **timely file** Form 4361, "Application for Exemption." Net earnings is the salary and/or honorariums, minus unreimbursed business expenses, plus parsonage provided and/or parsonage allowance designated. No formal reordination or relicensing is necessary. In filling out a "new belief, new faith" Form 4361, enter the new date of hire in Box 3 and enter the year of hire as the first year on line 5.

The Ballinger and Hall tax court decisions require the Internal Revenue Service to approve "**change of belief accompanied by a change to another faith**" applications for social security exemption. We had communication with one service center that said they had no knowledge of this provision and sought help from the national IRS office on the issue. The Form 4361 that they had denied was resubmitted and finally approved.

A **summary** of the **two tax court cases** that have brought about the ability for a minister to have more than one "window" of time to acquire an opposition to social security follows:

J.M. Ballinger, U.S. Court of Appeals, 10th Circuit, No 82-1928, 3/7/84: Taxpayer was ordained as a minister of the First Missionary Baptist Church, on November 22, 1969. He became minister of the Maranatha Church in September, 1973. He received net earnings from the ministry in excess of $400 during 1973, 1974 and 1975. On March 8, 1977 he incorrectly filed Form 4029 instead of Form 4361. It was disapproved by the IRS because he was not a member of a religious order described in Sec. 1402(g). On May 2, 1978 he was reordained by the Maranatha Church. On July 7, 1978 he filed the correct Form 4361 showing May 2, 1978 as the beginning of his ministry. The IRS initially approved the application. Upon discovery that Rev. Ballinger had first been ordained in 1969 and hired by Maranatha Church in September, 1973, the IRS revoked the exemption. Had Rev. Ballinger filed Form 4361 by April 15, 1975, the judges stated that it would have been a different case. The three judge panel said:

> *"The statute makes no distinction between a first ordination and subsequent ordinations. Courts are not in a position to determine the merits of various churches nor an individual's conversion from one church to another. Nor can we hold that an individual who has a change of belief **accompanied** by a change to another faith is not entitled to the exemption."*

Having **untimely filed** his Form 4361, the taxpayer's exemption from social security **was disapproved**.

James B. Hall, U.S. Court of Appeals, 10th Circuit, No 93-9027, 7/19/94: The same court ten years later upheld their decision and the three judge panel said, *"We anticipated a case like this when we decided Ballinger v. Commissioner."* Taxpayer was ordained as a deacon in the United Methodist Church in 1979 and earned more than $400 per year from his ministerial services in both 1980 and 1981. Taxpayer's activities as a deacon made him potentially eligible to apply for a 1402(e)exemption. At that time, however, the taxpayer was not religiously or conscientiously opposed to the acceptance of public insurance, thus he was not eligible and did not apply for an exemption. He left the ministry and spent five years as an engineer. Taxpayer was ordained by the Community Church and began a new ministry and accepted a new belief in opposition to public insurance. Rev. Hall applied for exemption in the first tax year immediately following his second ordination and the commencement of his new ministry. It was initially denied as untimely (after April 15, 1982.) A lower Tax Court affirmed this denial. The U.S. Court of Appeals judges said:

> *"We ultimately concluded that the statute permits all ministers who oppose public insurance on religious grounds to qualify and, as we interpret the statute, permits ministers who change churches to qualify."*

> They also stated: *"We are not concerned that our decision will open the floodgates for conniving Elmer Gantrys to dupe the Internal Revenue Service and opt out of the social security system without a sincere religious objection."*

Having **timely filed** his Form 4361, taxpayer's exemption from social security **was approved**.

Private Letter Ruling 200404048: A minister who because of religious principles was opposed to the acceptance of public insurance, had filed Form 4361 untimely after his first date of hire. It had been denied as untimely. Upon changing faiths he filed a new Form 4361 and it was also denied. Both the Ballinger and Hall cases are discussed in the letter ruling. The minister had a change of faith **without** a change in belief. His belief of opposing the acceptance of public insurance was made evident when he filed the first Form 4361.

● *Exemption is Retroactive to Beginning of Ministry*

An approved Form 4361 is retroactive back to the date your ministry or change of faith began. If you paid social security for the first year of your ministry or change of ministry and have chosen to file Form 4361 during the second year, you can receive a refund of the first year's social security payment. Upon receiving an approved Form 4361, file Form 1040X as a claim for your refund. Attach a photocopy of your approved Form 4361 to Form 1040X. **The IRS does not automatically send** social security refunds.

● *How To File Form 4361 and Attachments*

For efficient processing of your exemption application it is important to include all of the required attachments and information.

Attach proof of the beginning of your initial ministry or change of faith ministry: a copy of your certificate for ordination, license, commissioning or a letter from the church who hired you verifying the date you were hired as their minister.

Extra statement required for applicants without ordination certificate: If your church or denomination both ordains and licenses ministers, Form 4361, line 6, requires that you attach a copy of the by-laws stating that a licensed or employed minister is invested with the authority to perform substantially all of the duties of the church or denomination. If no such by-laws exist, then type the following statement on your church's letterhead, have a person in authority sign it, and attach it to your application:

> _"Our church/denomination does not have specific by-laws regarding the powers of ordained, licensed, commissioned or employed ministers. We do give the same authority to perform all of the ecclesiastical duties to our licensed, commissioned or employed ministers as we do to those who are ordained."_

Notify church: The ordaining, licensing or commissioning body of your church must be informed that you are conscientiously opposed to or because of religious principles you are opposed to the acceptance of public insurance benefits based on ministerial service. In the absence of a formal ordination, licensing or commissioning, it is the church that hired you that you must notify. When you sign Form 4361 you are certifying (line 7) that you have performed this notification. Individual opposition is sufficient for a minister to be exempt; it does not matter that the position of the employer is different.

Prove your church is a church: You must establish that the organization that gave you the authority to do ministerial services **is a church**. The IRS requires the exemption applicant to establish or prove that the church that ordained him or "the equivalent thereof" is a religious organization described in **Sec. 501(c)(3)** and also in **Sec. 170(b)(1)(A)(i).**

IRS Publication 78, published quarterly, lists organizations, denominations or churches that have filed Form 1023 requesting exempt status. If your church is a part of a major denomination, your church will be under its group exempt status. If the church that ordained you or "the equivalent thereof" is independent or autonomous and voluntarily filed Form 1023 and received a determination letter, it is listed in IRS Publication 78. Attach a copy of their determination letter to your Form 4361.

Churches are not required to file and submit the information requested on Form 1023. Form 8718 must accompany the Form 1023 and requires either a $150 or a $500 fee to be paid to the IRS.

If the church on your application has not voluntarily filed Form 1023, you must provide proof that it is a church with your Form 4361. The service center to which you send your Form 4361 will accept the following types of information from you to establish that the church is a church:

1. On church stationery provide the name of organization, address, and Employer Identification Number. Make this statement, "We are a church described in Sec. 501(c)(3) and also in Sec. 170(b)(1)(A)(i)." Include a description of the characteristics that qualify the organization as a church such as regular worship, evangelism and membership. The statement should be signed by someone authorized to represent the church.

2. If your church is incorporated attach copies of the organization's creating instrument and a copy of the constitution and bylaws.

3. Provide copies of church bulletins, newsletters, photos of the church and members, etc., to show the regular times of worship and other activities that are typical of a church.

● _How To Send Your Form 4361_

Make photocopies of the completed Form 4361 for your records and keep in two or three safe places. Send **three** signed copies with the attached documents we have discussed by **Certified Mail** so that you can prove that it was timely filed. Form 4361, page 2 instructions give the address to which it should be sent. All Form 4361s are to be sent to one national office. **File your Form 4361 by itself**. Never file it with your Form 1040.

Watch For Letter: The Secretary of Health and Human Services has the responsibility of communicating with the applicant to further verify that the applicant understands the grounds (basis) for exemption and is seeking the exemption on those grounds. Applicants receive a letter asking for their signature again, verifying that they understand the grounds under which they filed Form 4361. **The letter must be returned to the IRS within 90 days** or the effective date of the exemption will not begin until it is received by the IRS.

Eventually a copy is sent back to you marked **"approved"**. The process can take several months. If you fail to get an approved copy back in 6 to 8 months, call IRS and ask that they put a tracer on it. Applications sometimes get lost and need to be refiled.

● _Put Your Approved Copy In Several Safe Places_

Once you receive your "**APPROVED COPY**" from the IRS — copy it, protect it, and treat it as a valuable document. We recommend making several copies. Give a copy to your tax accountant. If your approved copy has been misplaced or lost, request a copy from the Social Security Administration. Call 1-800-772-1213 or visit their website: http://www.ssa.gov/

- **_What If You Timely Filed, But Have Never Received An Approved Copy From IRS_**

Ministers who failed to receive their "Approved Copy" of Form 4361 should take steps to obtain one. Often during an audit event they are unable to prove their exempt status and are billed for social security in the audit report. Common reasons for not receiving the "Approved Copy" are (1) minister moved before receiving approval; (2) application got lost in the mail or in the processing system; (3) original application lacked complete information and was denied because of lack of information. **The Good news** is that anytime you have proof that Form 4361 was timely filed, you can refile it! By resubmitting a new Form 4361, containing correct original information, with a letter stating the history and proof of timely filing, we have been successful in obtaining for several clients an "Approved Copy" back, effective to the original date ministry began. Any social security tax assessed can then be canceled or refunded.

Social Security & the Religious Sects Opposed to Insurance

A completely different set of rules apply to members of religious orders. **Sec. 1402(g)** allows any self-employed member of a religious order that opposes both private and public insurance to file **Form 4029** and be exempt from social security regardless of his work activity (farming, construction, etc.). Since November 10, 1988, **Form 4029** can be filed at any time. This exemption is a statement that the individual is opposed to both **public and private insurance** and **is an actual waiver** of ever receiving any benefits from social security. It is necessary that the religious order has a history and a plan to provide for the members when they become dependent through disability or old age. **It is also necessary that the order was organized before 1950.** New religious orders described in Sec. 1402(g) cannot be formed. If a member ceases to be a member of the order their exemption is revoked. Members who have filed Form 4029 for exemption from social security and have made contributions to a private retirement annuity revoke their exemption and will have to pay back-years' social security tax according to Revenue Ruling 77-88. According to Private Letter Ruling 8741002, funding of an IRA through a CD in a bank did not constitute insurance, and thus, did not disqualify the taxpayer from exemption. However, earnings exempt from Social Security under Sec. 1402(g) are not eligible earnings from which to make an IRA contribution. Beginning in 2002, Simple and Keogh plans will be allowed for self-employed exempt under 1402(g) according to Sec. 401(c)(2)(A))

Because Revenue Ruling 77-88 has often been taken out of context and thought to apply to **Sec. 1402(e)** for ministers who have filed Form 4361, it is important for you to know that it does not apply to ministers. Ministers who have filed Form 4361 are opposed to **only public** insurance and must provide their own alternative to social security. They **can** and **should have a private investment plan for retirement needs**.

Social Security and the Lay Employee

A religious worker who does not qualify for dual-status tax treatment must be treated as a lay employee of the employer for social security and medicare tax purposes. He does not have an individual choice of being exempt or subject to social security.

Prior to 1984, a nonprofit religious organization as described in Sec. 501(c)(3) had been automatically exempt from withholding social security from their employees and matching it with their share. So an organization that wished to remain exempt from withholding social security for all its employees did not have to file any form. Prior to 1984, if an organization and its employees desired to be covered by social security, they had to file Form SS-15.

Since January 1, 1984, the Social Security Amendments Act of 1983 extended social security coverage **on a mandatory** basis to all lay employees of nonprofit organizations.

Electing Churches Form 8274

The Tax Reform Act of 1984 provided for an election by a church or qualified church-controlled organization that is **opposed for religious reasons** to the payment of social security taxes not to be subject to such taxes. (Sec. 3121(w)) The election merely **transfers** the social security liability **from the electing church to the lay employee**.

The electing church is required to withhold income tax and to report the compensation paid to each lay employee who earns **more than $100.00** on Form W-2. The electing church should withhold additional amounts of income tax so their employees will have an adequate amount of tax prepaid to cover the cost of the social security to be computed on their Schedule SE. Form 941, with the box on Line 4 marked, is the correct quarterly report for an electing church. The electing church **must communicate** to their employees their responsibility to compute and pay their own social security on their Form 1040, Schedule SE. In Chapter Six we show a filled out example of Form 941 and W-2's for an electing church. The memo "Electing church employee to pay social security on Schedule SE" is what we recommend to include on Form W-2, Box 14.

- ### *When To Make The Election - Form 8274*

Church employers with lay employees, as of October 1, 1984, had until October 31, 1984 to file Form 8274. To become an "electing church," a church must file Form 8274 (two copies) before the first date on which a quarterly employment tax return would otherwise be due. Existing churches that have never had lay employees, only dual-status minister employees or volunteers, may file Form 8274 by the due date of the quarter in which they first hire a lay employee. Churches not aware when to timely file for the election have no recourse. In Private Letter Ruling 199911025, a church asked for an extension of the time period for filing the Form 8274 and it was denied.

Example of timely filing: A church was organized many years ago and has had a dual-status minister as their only employee. On October 15, 2005, they hired a secretary to work in the office and based on opposition for religious reasons, they should timely file Form 8274 before January 31, 2006.

If an electing church fails to provide the required Form W-2's for two years and fails to furnish the information upon request by the IRS, the IRS will revoke their election.

Employees of "electing churches" do not qualify to claim exemption from paying social security by filing Form 4361. The wages subject to social security on Schedule SE are the wages in Box 1 of their Form W-2 plus any Sec. 403(b), 408(p), or 401(k) voluntary contributions. Such wages from an electing church can not be reduced by losses from other self-employment activity or unreimbursed employee business expenses. (Sec. 3121(b)(8); 3121(w)) (IRS Publication 557, page 10)

- ### *How To Revoke The Election - Form 8274*

The Tax Reform Act of 1986 **made it easy for electing churches to revoke their election**. By simply filing a Form 941 on or before its due date for the first quarter for which the revocation is to be effective, accompanied by payment in full of the social security taxes that would be due for the quarter, the election is revoked.

How To Do Correction For Wrong Treatment

Are you a dual-status minister but your employer **wrongly treated you as an employee for social security purposes**? When, according to the regulations, you are to be treated as self-employed for social security purposes, **dual-status tax treatment is mandatory**. For your employer to withhold and match social security is in error. This can be corrected for all three "open" years that are allowed to amend returns. The rates for 2002, 2003, 2004 and 2005 have been the same: 15.3% withheld and matched for employees and 15.3% for the self-employed.

Even though it is advisable to correct the wrong treatment of the minister's status, there has not been an underpayment or overpayment of tax liability. Some employers may choose to correct the wrong treatment for the current and future years.

We want to give adequate information for making corrections if you choose to correct the open years. The amount of social security matched by the employer is not required to be credited or paid to the employee. The social security withheld from the employee's salary must be paid back to the employee. If the employer chooses to allow their matched portion to be credited to their employee, it must be counted as extra salary on the W-2c in the year of the correction.

Because a dual-status minister can deduct unreimbursed employee business expenses from his social security base, the social security and medicare tax computed on Schedule SE may be less than the amount withheld and matched in error.

- ### *Two Ways To Handle The Corrections*
    1. When the employer is willing to count their matching portion as extra salary for the minister:
        a. Prepare 941c and an amended 941 to reflect the changes made. You will not be requesting a refund on the 941c.
        b. Prepare W-2c and W-3c showing matching portion added to "Wages, tips, other compensation" as additional salary.

    c. Include total amount of social security withheld and matched as income tax withheld in "federal income tax withheld."

    d. Prepare an amended return for the minister. The minister will have credit on his 1040X for the total social security amount withheld and matched. Depending on the level of his total income, he may have a small refund or owe a small amount of additional tax, plus interest on the balance.

2.   When the employer wishes to keep their matching portion:

    a. Prepare 941c and an amended 941 to reflect the changes made and claim a credit on the next quarter's 941 or file Form 843 to claim a refund for the employer's matching portion.

    b. Prepare W-2c and W-3c showing original salary in "Wages, tips, other compensation."

    c. Include amount of social security withheld as income tax withholding in "federal income tax withheld."

    d. Prepare an amended return for the minister. The minister will have partial credit on his 1040X for social security computed on Schedule SE and will incur interest on the balance owed.

It is important when making changes to your federal Form 1040 to remember to amend your state income tax return when it is affected. **Do not hesitate to seek** professional accounting help in preparing corrections to payroll reports. The staff at **Worth Tax & Financial Service** is available to prepare payroll reports, W-2's, and corrections for organizations.

Should the Minister's Spouse be on the Payroll?

No one will dispute the fact that a minister's spouse works many hours for the church and usually receives no paycheck. To establish a salary, it is necessary that there is a true employer/ employee relationship. The amount of the salary should be reasonable and paid on the basis of time spent in working for the employer. Employed ministers **should not personally pay** their spouse a salary. It is not allowed under the "assignment of income" portion of tax law according to Sec. 61 and Revenue Ruling 74-32.

● *Benefits - When Both Spouses Have Earned Income*

When both spouses have income from salaries it qualifies them for claiming Child Care Credit on Form 2441 for babysitting expenses incurred while both are at work. Babysitting expense **is never to be treated as an employee business expense.**

Travel and professional expenses can be justified for both employed spouses. For a husband and wife to both be receiving a salary and conducting bona fide business activities, travel away from home expenses, auto travel, entertainment, etc., are able to be claimed.

At retirement the ability to receive two semi-retired salaries and be within the social security earnings limitation can be very advantageous. Those who retire early, between age 62 and 65 will still benefit from this situation. **The earnings limitation has been lifted for those who reach full retirement age!** A history of both spouses having earnings before retirement is wise. To establish a salary for your spouse at retirement time would cause the Social Security Administration to notice the absence of your spouse's earnings before your retirement.

Estimated Tax, Form 1040ES

It is necessary for all taxpayers to "prepay" their income tax and their social security tax. An employee has tax withheld from each paycheck and "prepaid" by the employer each quarter. **Withholding by the employer of a dual-status minister is optional.** The dual-status minister is generally required to "prepay" tax by making quarterly payments based on an estimate of the amount of tax he expects to owe for the year. The current year's estimate is to be calculated at the time you prepare the previous year's tax return and the first installment of ¼ of the total is due on **April 15th**. Other due dates are **June 15th, September 15th, and January 15th**. Instead of paying the final January 15th installment, you may elect to file your return early, by January 31st, and pay any tax due with the return.

If you or your spouse are an employee and earn other wages from which tax is withheld, you may be able to arrange to have enough withheld to cover your combined tax liability. To claim less exemptions or allowances at the other job is usually more convenient than to make quarterly payments.

It makes no difference **how you prepay your tax liability;** either **estimated payments** or **adequate withholding** will meet the requirements. An estimate is exactly what the word means. No one can predict the correct amount of tax a year in advance. If you anticipate no tax or **less than $1,000** for the year, no estimate is necessary. If circumstances change during the year you may always amend or change your estimate and increase or decrease the quarterly payments.

Underpayment Penalties

You may be charged a penalty for not paying enough estimated tax or for not making the payments on time. The amount of underpayment penalty is the same as the rate of interest the IRS charges on late payments and it is announced each quarter. For individuals (other than high-income individuals) the penalty does not apply if **each required payment is timely** and the total tax paid is based on:

1. 90% of the total tax liability due on the return for the current year (income tax, social security tax, early withdrawal penalties, alternative minimum tax, etc.) or;

2. 100% of your total tax liability shown on the previous year's return, commonly referred to as a **safe harbor estimate.** When you expect your tax liability will increase, pre-pay 100% of the liability shown on the previous year's return in timely installments, and pay any remaining balance with the return by April 15th and you will not incur a penalty.

Higher income taxpayers: If your adjusted gross income (AGI) was more than $150,000 ($75,000 for married separate), substitute 110% for 100% in (2) above.

File your estimated tax on **Form 1040ES** and keep in mind that the estimate includes income tax and social security and medicare tax.

Waiver of Penalty

A waiver of penalty is available if you did not make a payment because of a casualty, disaster, or other unusual circumstance. Also, a waiver may be claimed if you retired (after reaching age 62) or became disabled during the tax year a payment was due or during the preceding tax year and your underpayment was not due to willful neglect. To claim the waiver, follow the instructions given for Form 2210 or in IRS Publication 505, page 46.

Optional Withholding Agreement

A withholding agreement can be made between an employer and a dual-status minister. It is to be a written agreement. A Form W-4 can be prepared with the amount to be withheld each pay period entered on line 6 rather than claiming any allowances on line 5. The employer should withhold enough **income tax** to prepay the minister's total income tax and social security and medicare tax liability. Form W-2 will show the amount that has been withheld in Box 2.

Retirement Planning For Religious Workers

All religious workers should establish retirement plans to **supplement** social security income during retirement. Dual-status ministers who have become exempt from social security must have a disciplined savings plan for retirement to take the place of social security. **It would be foolish to become exempt from social security and do nothing to provide for one's needs in retirement.**

We want to present some ideas and information that will make it possible to have the option to retire or semi-retire. Financial planning for retirement has been neglected by many religious workers. We can blame low compensation, busy work schedules, and even a hopeful expectation that the Lord will return before retirement, but the fact is many ministers and religious workers can not afford to retire.

Investments that are diversified are the best way to plan for meeting your needs during retirement. Through mutual funds it is possible to invest regular amounts in a diversified portfolio. The principle of investing regularly and over a long time horizon results in amazing compound growth. Investments in common stocks or stock funds have historically outperformed savings in fixed income investments. **You should never feel it is too late** to begin an investment plan. Most Americans do not begin to save regularly until the children are raised and the mortgage is nearly paid. The increase in life expectancy creates a greater need for investment planning and at the same time allows a longer time for the magic of compounding to function.

Let us give you an example of **the magic of compounding.** If you began investing at age 25 and invested $150 a month for 40 years and had a 10% rate of return, you would be a millionaire at age 65. If you began investing at age 45 and invested $1,316.88 a month for 20 years and had a 10% rate of return, you would also be a millionaire at age 65.

Mutual Funds

Over meaningful time spans of 10 years or more, well-managed stock funds have performed better than other investments. The growth of an investment in a mutual fund comes from two sources: income dividends and capital appreciation. While there have been times when the value of an investment in mutual funds have declined, over the years such an investment has produced much better results than savings deposits. There is no doubt that a savings account or certificate of deposit is a good place to put money you want to keep in reserve for short-term needs. However, well-managed stock funds are the best place for your long-term **investment** or retirement dollars.

Investing in the stock market can be confusing if you do not have much time to devote to it. Some publications would encourage you to try to "time" the market and to trade often. Most of us do not have the time to be watching the daily changes in the market place. Even investment professionals cannot always "buy low and sell high." Those who "buy high and sell low" become discouraged and often discontinue investing. A better strategy for investing is to invest regular amounts into a family of mutual funds and let your investment compound over a long period of time. This strategy is often called "dollar cost averaging."

A well managed mutual fund must charge the investors for management costs. Some mutual funds have "loads" or commissions up front or at the time of your investment. Other mutual funds advertised in the Wall Street Journal and financial magazines are "no load" or without a commission at the time of the investment. Generally, the "no load" funds have a higher annual management fee than the "loaded" funds. Some funds have a back end "load" if you do not own the fund long enough. **Before you make any investment in a mutual fund, you will be given a prospectus that fully explains the fees that particular fund will charge.** Choosing a "no load" mutual fund could actually end up costing more over the life of an investment because the annual management fees are charged on the compounded value of the investment. "Loaded" mutual funds typically have much lower annual management fees. "Loaded" mutual funds are marketed through registered representatives and having received a commission at the time of your investment, they are willing to answer your questions and help you monitor your investments.

Life Insurance

Life insurance is an important part of your portfolio because it provides risk protection for your family. One purpose of life insurance is to replace your earnings should you die prematurely. The amount of your debt, the ability of your spouse to earn a living, the age and number of dependent children are a few of the factors to consider in determining how much life insurance coverage you should have. There is no easy formula to use to decide whether it is best to have a term life policy or a universal life policy or a whole life policy. The facts and circumstances of your individual needs can be evaluated by an insurance professional. It is possible to combine life insurance protection and mutual fund investing within a variable life policy. Upon your death, life insurance benefits are not taxable to your beneficiaries on their Form 1040. However, the amount of benefits are to be included in your taxable estate and could cause estate tax.

Annuities

An annuity is a product of life insurance companies that is a contract which promises to pay you for the rest of your life in exchange for a stated cost of premium. A fixed annuity is invested in interest bearing investments and usually has a better rate of return than a bank certificate of deposit. A variable annuity is invested in the capital market through a group of mutual funds. An annuity's earnings are reinvested and are tax deferred, or not currently taxed. If you are receiving social security benefits, and you have a high adjusted gross income that causes a portion of your social security to be taxed, an unqualified annuity, funded with "after tax" dollars, is a good tax planning tool.

At age 65 you can annuitize the investment through several options. If you annuitize an annuity, and die early, the insurance company wins; if you live beyond life expectancy, you win. The option of choosing joint life is usually a good choice. The option of choosing a refund feature means that your named beneficiary will receive any remainder of principal in your contract upon your death. If you choose to annuitize an annuity, an income factor of **about 3%** is used to calculate your monthly distribution.

An annuity does not have to be annuitized. Distributions can be withdrawn from the annuity as you need cash flow without annuitization. The contract can continue to earn at **a higher rate** and any principle remaining at your death can be passed on to your beneficiaries. The value will not be subject to probate expense. However, as the contract passes to your appointed beneficiary, the profit or gain in the contract will be taxable on your beneficiary's Form 1040.

Because annuities have an "end load" or cost if you take more than the allowed minimum withdrawal during the first six or seven years of the investment, they should never be used as a short term investment. The taxable portion of withdrawals before age 59½ or disability do incur the 10% penalty assessed by the IRS. The taxable portion of withdrawals are also subject to regular tax.

Unqualified and Qualified Plans

Investments and annuities are available in unqualified plans and qualified plans. An unqualified plan means that the cost or premium is not subtracted from your taxable income. Qualified investment plans have the added advantage of "sheltering" the cost or contribution to the plan from current tax. To establish a qualified investment or annuity, it is usually a simple procedure of signing an extra document that establishes a custodian for the plan. **See Chapter One** for additional details for Tax Sheltered Accounts (TSAs) and Individual Retirement Accounts (IRAs).

Tax Sheltered Account or 403(b) Plan

Tax Sheltered Accounts are available to public school employees and employees of nonprofit organizations. Ministers employed by a nonprofit organization are eligible for making contributions to a Sec. 403(b) retirement account. Since January 1, 1997, a minister or chaplain, who in connection with the exercise of his ministry is a self-employed individual or is working for an employer that is not a qualified nonprofit organization, can also contribute to a TSA. TSAs are the most popular retirement plans to be established by nonprofit employers.

This code section provides **two methods of funding.** An employer can provide a 403(b) plan that includes **both** forfeitable contributions by the employer and non-forfeitable contributions made by the employee through a salary reduction plan. Or an employer can provide a 403(b) plan that includes either method of funding without the other. An employer can provide a Sec. 403(b)(7), voluntary salary reduction plan **without** the complexities and cost of a 403(b)(9) plan.

Employer Contributions - Forfeitable (employee loses if not vested) can be made by the **employer** to a Sec. 403(b)(9) account on the behalf of its employees. The maximum limit for a defined contribution plan applies (lesser of $42,000 or 100% of pay). The cost to establish and administer this type of Sec. 403(b)(9) employer plan that must meet discrimination testing, causes it to not be cost effective for an employer with a small staff.

Salary Reduction Contributions - Non-Forfeitable (employee is always 100% vested) can be made for the **employee** to a Sec. 403(b) account established by the employer for voluntary salary reduction contributions. For 2005, an employee can contribute up to 100% of compensation limited to **$14,000** annually, with an additional **$4,000** available if age 50 or over by end of year. (2006 - $15,000, with an additional $5,000 available if age 50 or over by end of year.)

Contributions to a TSA account by a dual-status minister **are not** subject to social security and medicare tax according to **Revenue Ruling 68-395**. However, contributions to a TSA account by a lay employee **are** subject to social security and medicare tax withholding according to **Revenue Ruling 65-208**.

A Sec. 403(b) retirement annuity or a Sec. 403(b)(7) mutual fund account can be established to accept only **non-forfeitable** voluntary salary reduction contributions from one or several employees. The employer is required to notify all of the employees that they have the opportunity to make voluntary salary reduction contributions to the 403(b) plan. It is not necessary that they choose to participate. Many employers provide Sec. 403(b)(7) plans that only allow salary reduction non-forfeitable voluntary contributions because **they are quick to establish and involve very little cost of administration.** Plans established with a mutual fund family as custodian typically cost a nominal $5 to $25, regardless of how many employees participate. Employees of nonprofit organizations who change employers from time to time like the "portability" of a Sec. 403(b) non-forfeitable type of plan. A change of employers requires a new custodial agreement to be established.

● _Retired Ministers & Parsonage Designation_

A **retired minister** receiving an otherwise taxable distribution from a qualified Sec. 401(a), Sec. 401(k), Sec. 403(b), Sec. 408(k), 408(p) or Sec. 414(e) plan may have a **"parsonage allowance"** designated by the former employer or denominational pension board. It is possible for 100% of the retirement income to be nontaxable to the extent it is used for parsonage expenses according to Revenue Ruling 63-156. Language found in the Department of Labor Regulations under ERISA indicate that both types of contributions to a Sec. 403(b) plan (forfeitable and non-forfeitable) are considered as contributions to an employer's plan and both types are eligible for parsonage allowance designation.

Distributions from an IRA or a Keogh retirement plan may not be eligible to be designated as non-taxable housing because their contributions are not identifiable as being based on earnings from the ministry.

According to Rev. Ruling 72-249, the parsonage allowance exclusion is not available to the surviving spouse who continues to receive retirement income as a beneficiary.

Individual Retirement Account

A qualified tax shelter that we are all familiar with is the Individual Retirement Account or the IRA. You can set up and make contributions to an IRA if you received taxable compensation during the year and have not reached age $70\frac{1}{2}$ by the end of the year.

You can establish an IRA that is invested in mutual funds. You can establish an IRA with an insurance company that is an annuity contract. You can establish an IRA with a bank that is invested in a Certificate of Deposit. **IRAs** are now **flexible** and have the capability of being **qualified or unqualified.** Since 1998, active participation in an employer-sponsored plan by one spouse does not prevent the non-participating spouse from making a deductible contribution to an IRA unless their AGI reaches the phaseout level between $75,000 to $85,000 for a joint taxpayer and $50,000 to $60,000 for a single taxpayer. You can choose to designate contributions to an IRA as "nondeductible" on Form 8606 in a year that you have no tax liability.

Contributions to a Roth IRA are nondeductible in the year of the contribution. Their earnings will accumulate tax free and qualified distributions will be tax free. Total individual contributions to all IRAs for tax year **2005** cannot exceed **$4,000**, with an additional **$500** available if age 50 or over by end of year. (2006 - $4,000 plus $1,000 catch up.) The AGI Phaseout for Roth IRA is $150,000 to $160,000 for joint filers and $95,000 to 110,000 for single filers.

A Roth IRA is a wonderful choice for the non-tax paying minister's retirement planning. A Roth IRA invested in a mutual fund will capture the long term growth of the capital market. Qualified distributions are those made after a 5 year period, and in addition, made after age $59\frac{1}{2}$, after death to a beneficiary, after becoming disabled or distributed to pay for "qualified first time home buyer expenses."

According to Reg. 1.219-1(c)(1), for IRA purposes, compensation does not include Sec. 911, foreign earned income and/or housing that is excluded from income and consequently contributions to an IRA are not allowed.

When Should You Have A Qualified Plan?

When you have an income tax liability, it is good tax planning to consider making contributions to a sheltered or qualified retirement plan. Even when you have no income tax liability you may wish to contribute to a Sec. 403(b) retirement plan and reduce your social security base if you are a dual-status minister. In any year you have **no income tax** liability and if you are exempt from paying social security (Form 4361), it would be best to invest in a Roth IRA or an unqualified investment.

Tax Planning for the Retired or Semi-retired Minister

Between the ages of 62 and 65, most ministers consider the possibility of semi-retirement. **Between age 62 and full retirement age**, an employer can pay salary and parsonage value and/or allowance up to the limitation shown on the next page and the minister will receive all of his social security benefits. If his earned income is more than the limitation, his social security benefits will be reduced by $1 for each $2 of extra earned income. Sign up and receive all benefits available to you. Social Security will obtain the information from your tax return. Always have your tax advisor examine any Social Security proposed adjustments. Often they add your wages from Form 1040, line 7 and your Schedule SE earnings in error. The amount of the limitation is adjusted for inflation every year and is announced in October.

The Retirement Earnings Test **has been eliminated for individuals when they reach full retirement age**. A modified test applies for the year an individual reaches full retirement age.

In the year an individual reaches full retirement age, the limitation shown on the next page will only apply to the earnings for the months prior to attaining full retirement age. If his earned income is more than the limitation his social security benefits will be reduced by $1 for each $3 of extra earned income. **There is no limit on earnings beginning the month an individual attains** full retirement age.

After the year in which you reach full retirement age, and the earnings limitation ends, you can earn $1,000,000 and still draw your full social security benefits!

The amount of earnings a person can receive, before it affects the amount of social security benefits available, are as follows:

	2004	2005	2006
Before Full Retirement Age	$ 11,640	$ 12,000	$ 12,480
Year Reaches Full Retirement Age	$ 31,080	$ 31,800	$ 33,240

Year of Birth	Full Retirement Age
1937 or earlier	65
1938	65 & 2 months
1939	65 & 4 months
1940	65 & 6 months
1941	65 & 8 months
1942	65 & 10 months
1943-1954	66
1955	66 & 2 months
1956	66 & 4 months
1957	66 & 6 months
1958	66 & 8 months
1959	66 & 10 months
1960 & later	67

Definition of Earned Income

Salary and the value of a home provided and/or the parsonage allowance ARE considered "earned income" by social security.

Fringe benefits, an accountable employee business expense reimbursement plan, and nonforfeitable contributions to a salary reduction TSA ARE NOT "earned income" and can be provided in addition to $12,000/$31,800 salary and housing limitation.

Income from pensions, interest, dividends, rents and sale of property ARE NOT earned income. You can receive **unlimited** amounts of such **nonearned income** and still receive all of your social security benefits.

Social Security Benefits are Sometimes Taxed

Social security benefits you receive may be taxable in some instances. You will receive Form SSA-1099 showing the total benefits paid to you during the year and the amount of any social security benefits you repaid during the year. For the first threshold of $32,000 ($25,000 for single) the maximum amount of your social security benefits that can be taxable is 50%. For the second threshold of $44,000 ($34,000 for single) the maximum amount of your social security benefits that can be taxable is 85%. The worksheet provided with Form 1040 helps you compute the "modified adjusted gross income", which for the first threshold is 50% of your social security benefits, plus other taxable income, plus tax-exempt interest, less adjustments. If this amount is less than the threshold of $32,000 ($25,000 for single) none of your benefits will be taxed. It is important for married taxpayers to file a joint return. The threshold for married separate returns is -0-. Married separate returns would cause unnecessary tax.

Is Your Social Security Earnings Record Correct?

Because a law requires that all Americans receive an annual statement of potential Social Security benefits, since October 1, 1999, the Social Security Administration sends a four page annual Social Security Statement to 125 million workers, throughout the year. Workers will automatically receive their statements about three months before their birth month.

It is very important to examine your statement and correct any errors in your account. Anyone can get a copy of their statement by either calling and requesting one or logging onto the internet. Social Security's web site's address is: **www.ssa.gov**

Dual-status ministers often experience mistakes in their social security earnings record. The amount of earnings on Form 1040, line 7, is often combined with the social security base on Schedule SE. This mistake can lead to an overstatement of your earnings. If the amount of earnings on Form 1040, line 7, is recorded as your earnings and the parsonage allowance is omitted, your earnings will be understated. Ministers who begin to receive social security benefits while continuing to work often experience problems receiving correct amounts.

Medicare Prescription Drug Program

The Medicare Prescription Drug Program is known as Medicare D. Web-site **ssa.gov** and toll-free number 1-800-772-1213 are available to obtain information to sign up and participate.

## CHAPTER FIVE

Overseas Missionaries and Religious Orders

Missionaries Serving Overseas

Missionaries who are U.S. citizens serving overseas in a foreign country are subject to the same U.S. income tax laws as those living in the U.S. All income, worldwide, must be reported on their Form 1040. However, they may qualify for the **$80,000** foreign earned income exclusion provided in Sec. 911. Generally, your **initial choice** of the exclusion on Form 2555 **must be filed with a timely filed 1040 return**.

Missionaries are considered to be performing ministerial duties when evangelizing, conducting worship, teaching, etc. They are to be treated as dual-status ministers. You may want to reread Chapter Two for our detailed discussion defining dual-status and the special tax treatment for those who qualify.

When a dual-status minister, serving as a missionary overseas, has an "approved" Form 4361 and is exempt from social security, he is to write "Exempt Form 4361" on the self-employment line, Form 1040, page 2. Disability coverage under social security will discontinue after you become exempt. When it will discontinue for you depends upon your age and the number of quarters of credit you have. Overseas missionaries have difficulty obtaining comparable life and disability insurance coverages. If you are considering an overseas ministry, you may wish to choose being covered by social security.

Missionaries who do secular jobs (carpenters, physicians, nurses, pilots, cooks, mechanics, etc.), are regular lay employees. When employed by an American employer they are subject to withholding and matching of social security and medicare tax. When employed by a foreign employer they are subject to that country's equivalent of social security, if they have one.

● *Statement For Claiming Benefits of Section 911*

Lay employees that are eligible for the foreign earned income exclusion should sign and submit Form 673 to their employer. It permits the employer to not withhold federal income tax on foreign wages.

● *Effect of Sec. 911 Foreign Earned Income Exclusion on TSA and IRA Contributions*

According to Reg. 1.403(b)-1(e)(2), foreign earned income counts as includible compensation if an employee wishes to make contributions to a TSA.

According to Reg. 1.219-1(c)(1), for IRA purposes, compensation does not include foreign earned income and/or housing that is excluded from income and contributions to an IRA are not allowed.

● *Social Security and Binational Agreements*

U.S. Citizens living and working outside of the United States as dual-status ministers are subject to social security regardless of whether their employer is American or foreign. When they are employed by a foreign church or nonprofit organization or they are independent contractors, they may also be subject to that country's equivalent of social security. The United States has entered into **agreements** with several foreign countries to coordinate social security coverage and taxation. If the country you work in has entered into such an agreement, dual coverage and dual contributions (taxes) for the same work is eliminated. U. S. citizens who live and work in a foreign country **five years** or more may be subject to social security in the foreign country. A certificate of coverage issued by one country serves as proof of exemption from social security taxes on the same earnings in the other country.

Independent contractors doing secular jobs, living and working outside of the United States, are subject to social security. The agreements usually eliminate double coverage and double tax for them also.

IRS Publication 54, page 9, gives a list of countries and additional information. We also have copies of the agreements and you may call and ask to consult with our agreement specialist.

● *Form TD F 90-22.1*

"Report of Foreign Bank and Financial Accounts" should be filed for all missionaries who have savings or checking accounts overseas which exceed $10,000 in aggregate value at any time during the calendar year. The Form TD F 90-22.1 is to be filed **separately** from the Form 1040. It is due by June 30th and is to be sent to: U.S. Department of the Treasury, P.O. Box 32621, Detroit, MI 48232-0621.

Bona Fide Residency and Physical Presence Rules

To qualify for Sec. 911 foreign earned income exclusion and/or foreign housing exclusion,the missionary must be able to satisfy the requirements of either bona fide residency or be physically present in a foreign country or countries for a total of at least 330 days during any period of 12 consecutive months.

To be considered a bona fide resident of a foreign country, you must have intentions to remain overseas for an indefinite stay and give evidence by words and acts as to the length and nature of your stay. You will not be treated as a bona fide resident of a foreign country if you have made a statement to the authorities of that country that you are not a resident and have been held not subject to its income tax. To establish your bona fide residency in a foreign country you must reside there for an uninterrupted period **which includes an entire tax year**. If you use the calendar year as your tax year, your entire tax year is the period beginning January 1 and ending December 31. The term "uninterrupted period" refers to your bona fide residence and not to your physical presence. Temporary absence for vacations or business trips is allowable.

The physical presence test does not apply to the type of residence you establish, to your intentions about returning, or to the nature and purpose of your stay overseas. It is concerned only with how long you stay in a foreign country or countries. If, during a period of 12 consecutive months, you are physically present in a foreign country 330 full days (approximately 11 months), you meet the physical presence test. ANY period of 12 consecutive months may be used. If 12 months during the middle of the stay overseas contains 330 days of physical presence, you will satisfy the requirement and be able to be exempt for the whole stay overseas.

Discussion of Form 2555 and Form 2555-EZ

The **IRS Publication 54, Form 2555, and Form 2555-EZ for 2005** are available on **www.irs.gov** as we go to press. IRS Publication 54, "Tax Guide for U.S. Citizens and Resident Aliens Abroad" contains indepth information for missionaries. Form 2555-EZ can be filed if you are a U.S. citizen or resident alien; your income from earned wages/salaries in a foreign country is less than $80,000; you are filing a calendar year return that covers a 12-month period; there are no adjustments to your income such as one half of self-employment tax deduction; and you are not filing a Schedule C with expenses.

● *Foreign Earned Income Exclusion*

Exclusion has been available since 1982. The Tax Relief Act of 1997 provided a gradual increase in the threshold. (See table below.) Individuals meeting either the bona fide residency test or the physical presence test could elect to exclude foreign earned income at the following annual rates:

1987 through 1997	$70,000
1998	$72,000
1999	$74,000
2000	$76,000
2001	$78,000
2002 and later years	**$80,000**

If both you and your spouse work abroad and meet either test you can each choose the foreign earned income exclusion. Together, you and your spouse can exclude as much as $160,000 a year.

The foreign earned income exclusion **is voluntary**. Generally, your initial choice of the exclusion on Form 2555 must be filed with a timely filed return (including extensions), a return amending a timely filed return, or a late filed return (determined without regard to any extensions) filed within one year from the original due date of the return. The amending of Reg. 1.911-7 now provides a fourth time to make a valid election. If no federal tax is owed after taking into account the foreign earned income exclusion or housing cost amount, an election may be made at any time later than the times provided above whether or not the IRS has discovered the failure to make the election. The change applies to taxable years beginning after December 31, 1981. This provision had made it very important for missionaries to timely file their initial tax returns. The $75,000/$80,000 exclusion in 1982 and 1983 was denied a taxpayer, an American citizen, who worked abroad and failed to file timely returns. (William J. Faltesek, Docket No. 48522-86, 6-6-89)

Once you choose to exclude your foreign earned income, that choice remains in effect for that year and all later years unless you revoke it. If you revoke your choice for any tax year, you cannot claim the exclusion again for your next 5 tax years without the approval of the IRS. The government charges a fee for this request. In Private Letter Ruling 9625060, 3/28/96, a taxpayer, having revoked his foreign earned income exclusion election for 1993 and 1994 because taxes were higher in the United Kingdom, **was granted** permission to re-elect the foreign earned income exclusion for1995. He had moved to Hong Kong and their tax rate was less than the United Kingdom. Several other private letter rulings have been submitted to the IRS requesting to re-elect Sec. 911 exclusion. They have all received a positive response.

• *Foreign Housing Exclusion*

In addition to the foreign earned income exclusion, you can separately claim an exclusion or a deduction from gross income for your housing amount if your tax home is in a foreign country and you qualify under either the bona fide residence test or the physical presence test.

For missionaries who earn considerably less than the $80,000 foreign earned income exclusion, it is not advisable for them to choose the foreign housing exclusion. In addition to a complex computation, **if chosen,** the foreign housing exclusion **must be used first** and fully before using the foreign earned income exclusion. In any year that a missionary earns over $80,000, he can initially choose and apply the foreign housing exclusion on a timely filed return by completing the appropriate section on Form 2555. The two exclusions available can be separately chosen and separately revoked. By attaching a statement to the return or an amended return for the first year that you do not wish to claim the exclusion(s), you can revoke either choice for any tax year.

Sec. 911 foreign housing exclusion is unique, and very different from Sec. 107 housing for ministers and Sec. 119 housing. Any year your income exceeds $80,000, take the time to study IRS Publication 54, pages 20-21. Being able to use the foreign earned income exclusion first makes your Form 2555 less complicated.

• *Vacation Computation*

According to Revenue Ruling 76-191, while home in the U. S., (unless on vacation ONLY), income earned is usually taxable on your federal return. Vacation time earned during the last year preceding your leave can be considered eligible Sec. 911 exclusion. If your mission gives you 6 months vacation (without work) for a four year term, one-fourth, or 45 days is eligible for the exclusion. If you are working and traveling on deputation all of your furlough, all of your leave would be taxable.

To determine the amount of U. S. income you should count the number of days in the U.S., subtract the vacation days, divide the result by 365 days, then multiply that percentage times the annual salary. For a missionary, who usually works a 7 day week, you would count 7 days for each week.

Example:	Days in U.S.	75 days
	Less vacation	(21 days)
		54 days
	54 ÷ 365 =	14.79%

Taxable income for U.S. $35,500 X 14.79% =   **$5,250.45**

Moving Expense — Overseas

• *Foreign Moves - Form 3903F*

If you move to a new principal place of work outside the United States and its possessions, it is a "foreign move." If all or part of the income you earn at the new foreign location is excluded under the foreign earned income exclusion, the part of the moving expense that is allocable to the excluded income is not deductible.

Since 1993, both "what" and "where" to deduct moving expenses changed. Qualified moving expenses are an above-the-line deduction subtracted from gross income in arriving at adjusted gross income under Sec. 62(a). More detailed discussion is included in Chapter One.

Qualified moving expenses **are now limited** to the reasonable cost of:

1. Moving household goods and personal effects from the former residence to the new residence; and

2. Traveling, including lodging during the period of travel, from the former residence to the new place of residence. **Meal expenses while moving are non-deductible.**

A special moving rule applies to Form 3903-F: The cost of moving household goods is expanded to include the reasonable expenses of moving household goods and personal effects to and from storage and of storing them for all or part of the time the new workplace continues to be your principal workplace. If you moved in an earlier year and are claiming only storage fees during your absence from the United States, you can simply enter the allowable amount on the moving deduction line, Form 1040, page 1. Next to the amount write "Storage Fees."

● *Non-Foreign Move Form 3903*

A move from a foreign country to the U.S. is not a foreign move. The regular moving deduction rules apply. If you permanently retire and your principal place of work and former home were outside the U.S. and its possessions, you do not have to satisfy the 39 work week requirement. You may deduct the move back to the U.S., subject to all of the other requirements and limitations of Form 3903.

When and Where To File As An Overseas Missionary

There is an automatic extension of two months to June 15th for any U.S. citizen with **both their tax home and their abode** outside the U.S. on April 15th. This is an extension of time to file only, tax liability has to be paid by April 15th. If you take advantage of the automatic extension, you are required to attach a statement to your return showing you were residing outside the U.S. on the due date of your return. If additional time is required, the regular automatic 4 month extension, Form 4868, can be filed by June 15th for an extra two months of extension.

File Form 2555 or Form 2555-EZ with Form 1040 and send to:

INTERNAL REVENUE SERVICE CENTER
Philadelphia, PA 19255-0215

● *Special Extensions Of Time For Filing*

A new missionary arriving in an overseas country anytime during the year cannot file Form 2555 or Form 2555-EZ the first year and claim the foreign earned income exclusion. However, after he has established his bona fide residence or met the physical presence test, all of his income is eligible for the special tax treatment from the **date of his arrival.** There are two ways to handle the problem of filing:

1. **File Form 2350** by the due date of your return, requesting an extension of filing your return until after establishing foreign residence. It is necessary to pay any anticipated tax on U.S. income with Form 2350. Then, within 30 days after meeting the residency requirements, file your return along with a copy of the approved Form 2350.

    a. An earlier first year return can often be filed by satisfying the physical presence rules.

    b. After satisfying the bona fide residency rules, it is best to switch to bona fide resident because it does not have to be re-established after a furlough or vacation back in the U.S.

2. *(Not the best choice!)* File the current year's return and pay tax on all income, including income earned abroad. After meeting the residency requirements, file Form 1040X and Form 2555 or Form 2555-EZ within one year of the due date of the original return to claim a refund of taxes on earnings while overseas.

Independent Missionaries

If a missionary has a sponsoring mission or church, it is correct for that organization to treat the missionary as an employee under the "common law rules." Missionaries who perform ministerial duties and are employed by a foreign mission board or an integral agency of a church are entitled to dual-status treatment. Missionaries who do secular jobs (carpenters, physicians, mechanics, etc.), are regular employees subject to withholding and matching of social security and medicare tax.

When a missionary does not have a sponsoring mission or church, the total gross income may include substantial funds for ministry projects. Entering large expenditures and building projects as Schedule C deductions creates a very high IRS audit exposure. Should an independent missionary be chosen for an audit, foreign IRS personnel are apt to be inexperienced concerning typical ministry endeavors. The experience can become costly, difficult, frustrating and time consuming.

We have included further instructions and recommendations for handling independent religious workers in Chapter Six.

Religious Orders — Two Types

Vow of Poverty: Members of qualifying Religious Orders described in Sec. 1402(c)(4) and Sec. 1402(g) who perform services for a religious order in the exercise of duties required by such order are exempt from income tax or social security tax liability according to Sec. 3121(b)(8)(A). Members serving under a vow of poverty are typically held to a strict level of moral and spiritual discipline which requires daily prayer and communion with other members and prohibits the ownership of material possessions. Prorata goods, services, and cash allowances received by members for their needs, whether disabled or able to perform services assigned to them, was deemed to be nontaxable. (Private Letter Rulings 199938013, 199937013, and 9752002)

Protestant Religious Orders Described in Sec. 1402(c)(4)

The idea of non-integral agency protestant ministries adopting the status of "religious order" was popular in the late 70's and early 80's. Some were advised to change their by-laws and declare their organization to be a "religious order." The Social Security Amendments Act of 1983, and the mandatory application of social security coverage to employees of nonprofit organizations made the idea flourish. In order to avoid the cost of withholding and matching social security, several non-integral agency protestant ministries began claiming the status of "religious order." So many requests for determination were received by IRS that they put a freeze on responding to them. During 1985 the IRS responded with letters stating that the question of what constitutes a religious order was under intensive study by the Service and that they would not be able to respond to the requests until their study was completed.

During 1991, IRS issued **Revenue Procedure 91-20, IRB 1991-10**. It sets forth guidelines that will be used by IRS in determining whether an organization is a religious order for federal employment tax purposes. IRS has identified from previous court cases the following characteristics:

1. The organization is described in Sec. 501(c)(3) of the Code.
2. The members of the organization vow to live under a strict set of rules requiring moral and spiritual self-sacrifice and dedication to the goals of the organization at the expense of their material well-being.
3. The members of the organization, after successful completion of the organization's training program and probationary period, make a long-term commitment to the organization (normally more than two years).
4. The organization is, directly or indirectly, under the control and supervision of a church or convention or association of churches, or is significantly funded by a church or convention or association of churches.
5. The members of the organization normally live together as part of a community and are held to a significantly stricter level of moral and religious discipline than that required of lay church members.
6. The members of the organization work or serve full-time on behalf of the religious, educational, or charitable goals of the organization.
7. The members of the organization participate regularly in activities such as public or private prayer, religious study, teaching, care of the aging, missionary work, or church reform or renewal.

Being a 501(c)(3) organization is required. Considering all the facts and circumstances about an organization, it is not necessary that all of the above characteristics be true. If most of the above characteristics are true, the organization will be treated as a religious order. In the absence of one or more of the above characteristics, Rev. Proc. 91-20 says that the IRS will contact the organization and carefully consider the organization's views concerning their status.

We are aware of and have read the IRS's favorable private letter rulings granting Sec. 1402(c)(4) status of religious order to two different organizations during 1992. Several organizations have received favorable private letter rulings affirming their status of a "religious order." (Private Letter Rulings 9322009, 9418012, 9434015, 9448017, 9630011, 199937013, 200106015 and 200143017)

If a nonintegral agency ministry wrongly claims the status of a "religious order," the underpayment of payroll taxes could be so overwhelming that the ministry could find it hard to survive.

• *Information Returns and Proper Tax Treatment for Sec. 1402(c)(4) Religious Orders*

The proper form to report the income paid to a member of a "religious order" is Form W-2. The practice of **issuing Form 1099** to employee-members **is incorrect**. To qualify as an "independent contractor" or a "nonemployee" of a religious order would be impossible, due to the amount of control a religious order has over its members.

1. Member, ordained or "the equivalent thereof," doing duties of the ministry. Tax treatment is the same as a dual-status minister, eligible for parsonage allowance, self-employed for social security purposes and **must timely file Form 4361 to be exempt from social security.** Withholding of income tax is optional, Form W-2 is the proper form to show taxable salary.

2. Member, lay employee of order, performing services required by the order are not eligible for parsonage allowance. Earnings are treated as self-employment for social security purposes and **must timely file Form 4361 to be exempt from social security.** Withholding of income tax is optional, Form W-2 is the proper form to show taxable salary.

3. Nonmember lay employees are automatically covered by social security, cannot become exempt, and are to receive a regular Form W-2 with income tax withholding.

4. Member, employee working for the order, doing duties required by the order, receives no salary, and has no income tax or social security tax liability, does not have to file any forms.

Religious Orders Described in Sec. 1402(g)

Sec. 1402(g) describes Religious Orders that are opposed to both private and public insurance. Examples of such orders are the Amish, Quakers and Catholic Monastic Orders. The term "religious order" is not well defined in IRS Code or regulations. In a 1969 tax court case, Eighth Street Baptist Church, Inc. v. U.S., 295 F.Supp. 1400 (D.Kan. 1969), the judge cited Webster's dictionary as his best source of a definition to determine that Eighth Street Baptist Church was not a religious order. Sec. 1402(g)(1)(E) gives the fact that a religious order or sect has to have been in existence at all times since December 31, 1950. In a court case for the year of 1976, a taxpayer argued that this provision was unconstitutional under the first amendment since it discriminates against religious sects not established prior to December 31, 1950. The judge stated that Congress has great latitude in limiting the exemptions by any general standards, (TC Memo 1980-284, Glen A. Ross, Docket No. 3593-79). Sec. 1402(g)(1)(D) states that a religious order described in Sec. 1402(g) must have for a substantial period of time been making reasonable provisions for its dependent members.

• *Information Returns and Proper Tax Treatment for Sec. 1402(g) Religious Orders*

1. Member, working outside of the order, earnings are given to the order, and duties are the kind that are ordinarily performed by members of the order and they are required to be exercised on the behalf of the religious order as its agent. Examples in Publication 517 indicate that being instructed to be a secretary qualified and being instructed to be a lawyer did not. According to Revenue Ruling 84-13, a psychologist did not qualify either.

    a. If duties qualify, the earnings are not taxable to member and there are no tax liabilities.

    b. If duties do not qualify, even though the order receives the salary, the earnings are taxable to member and subject to federal income tax withholding and social security tax withholding and matching.

2. Member, working outside of the order, self employed doing secular work, profits are subject to regular income tax and self-employment tax. An exemption is available from self-employment tax by filing **Form 4029 at any time.** To be able to file for this exemption, the member must be conscientiously opposed to accepting benefits of **any private or public insurance and waive all rights to ever receive any social security benefits.**

3. Since 1988, members or member partnerships who have filed Form 4029 and are exempt from social security, can employ other members who have also filed Form 4029 and be exempt from withholding and matching social security tax on their wages. An exempt employer will be required to withhold income tax and prepare Form W-2 for exempt employees.

4. Nonmember lay employees are automatically covered by social security, cannot become exempt, and are to receive a regular Form W-2 with income tax and social security tax withholding and matching.

## CHAPTER SIX

Completed Payroll Reports

Now we are ready for the practical application of all the information presented in the preceding chapters! Though the tax laws are complex and every employer/employee relationship is unique, the examples shown in this Chapter are for the purpose of teaching the simplest approach to designing the best compensation package. **Regardless of what creative label** the employer might call money or property "paid" to an employee, **it is taxable** if a section of the Internal Revenue Code **does not exclude it.** Generally, the employee will be taxed on all remuneration that is not a qualified *fringe benefit* (Chapter One), *parsonage allowance* (Chapter Two), or *reimbursement for professional expenses* **under an accountable plan** (Chapter Three). Tax law excludes these categories of a compensation package from federal income tax. Fringe benefits and an accountable reimbursement plan for professional expenses are also excluded from social security and medicare tax.

Our **payroll sheets** are designed with extra columns for parsonage allowance, contributions to Tax Sheltered Accounts and a section to keep record of an accountable reimbursement plan. This is a tell and show chapter. You will benefit greatly by studying the filled out sample payroll sheets and reports at the end of the chapter.

Steps in Establishing a Compensation Package

Whether by a denominational salary formula or simple budget determination, once the total compensation available is determined, we recommend the following four steps to arrive at the best tax treatment. For example, if the salary formula does not allow enough housing, it is important to go ahead and designate an adequate amount. For tax purposes, the compensation package may differ from the formula used to arrive at the total compensation available.

1. **Establish the fringe benefits that will be provided.** The cost of accident and health insurance, contributions to a qualified pension plan, premiums for up to $50,000 group term life insurance, etc., generally are to be paid by the employer directly to the companies providing the plans. The employer provided qualified fringe benefits are not to be included on the payroll record, quarterly reports, or in the W-2 at year end.

2. **Establish an accountable reimbursement plan** for auto and professional employee business expenses. Establish a written reimbursement plan for each employee using the suggested wordings in Chapter Three. Employees must "adequately account" their auto and professional expenses to the employer. The tax benefits to be gained by establishing an accountable reimbursement plan should convince employers to bear the burden of the "cost of doing ministry business." An employer should be willing to reimburse their employees for all auto and professional expenses over and above their salary. Employers who initially adjust the employee's salary and adopt a "fixed limit plan," according to Private Letter Ruling 9822044 can, prior to the start of a calendar year, determine the amount the "fixed limit" will be in the succeeding year. If the employer provides an auto for an employee, they must have a written plan and follow the IRS regulations to determine how much to include in the employee's income for personal use. The employee must maintain and submit a log of business miles to his employer.

3. **Determine the amount of the cash salary**. You may wish to obtain a copy of "compensation guidelines" provided by denominational handbooks or other organizations.

4. **Designate an adequate portion of salary as parsonage allowance in advance for the dual-status minister.** When a church or integral agency of a church owns the house in which the minister lives, they must designate a portion of his cash compensation as parsonage allowance for the additional home expenses he personally incurs. When a church or integral agency of a church does not provide the home and the minister rents or owns his own home, they must designate a portion of his cash compensation as parsonage allowance for the whole cost of providing the home. Use the "Suggested Wordings" in Chapter Two. The amount of **designated housing allowance**, divided by the number of pay periods is shown on the payroll record as a

subtraction from salary and **is not to be shown** as taxable compensation on the **941 quarterly reports or W-2 at year end**. The minister is responsible to show any unused portion as income on his Form 1040, line 7.

Dual-Status Minister - Rev. Snodgrass' Compensation Package

Fringe Benefits Provided:
    Hospital Insurance Premiums .... $ 5,520
    Group Term Life Insurance ($50,000) .... $ 420
Unlimited professional expense reimbursement policy ... $ 11,896
Total Cash Compensation $51,000
    *Parsonage Allowance Designated .... ($24,000)
    Contributions to Salary Reduction 403(b) Retirement .... ($ 6,000)
Taxable Salary on W-2 .... $21,000

* Rev. Snodgrass owns his own home. **The $24,000** parsonage allowance **is not shown in Box 1 of his W-2.** As we illustrate on his tax return in Chapter 7, he is responsible to show the unused portion of $7,517 as income on Form 1040, line 7. (When the parsonage is owned by the church employer, do not include its value in Box 1 of his W-2.) Rev. Snodgrass will include the $24,000 parsonage allowance on his Schedule SE for social security purposes unless he has an approved Form 4361 exemption.

Calculation for Amount of Paycheck: The contributions to the 403(b) retirement will be paid directly to a mutual fund or insurance company by the employer. **$51,000 less $6,000 = $45,000** divided by the number of paydays in the year. Our sample payroll sheet illustrates semimonthly pay periods:

$45,000 ÷ 24 = **$1,875.00** per pay check.

Lay Employee - Joseph Mop's Compensation Package

Value of Home & Utilities Provided (Sec. 119) .... $ 5,700
Fringe Benefits Provided:
    Hospital Insurance Premiums .... $ 3,970
    Group Term Life Insurance ($50,000) .... $ 276
Unlimited professional expense reimbursement policy ... $ 1,568
Total Cash Compensation $28,800
    Contributions to Salary Reduction 403(b) Retirement .... ($ 1,800)
Taxable Salary on W-2 .... $27,000

When an employer provides housing and utilities for a lay employee that satisfies all three conditions of Sec. 119, the value is not to be shown on the payroll report, 941 quarterly reports, or W-2 at year end. It is free from federal income tax, social security, and medicare tax. When one of the tests is not satisfied, the value of housing and utilities provided is subject to income tax, social security, and medicare tax and is to be shown as taxable compensation on the payroll reports. We illustrate Joseph Mop, the janitor, being provided Sec. 119 housing.

Calculation for Amount of Paycheck: The contributions to the 403(b) retirement will be paid directly to a mutual fund or insurance company by the employer. **$28,800 less $1,800 = $27,000** divided by the number of paydays in the year. Our sample payroll sheet illustrates semimonthly pay periods:

$27,000 ÷ 24 = **$ 1,125.00** per pay check.

Organizations Must File Information Returns!

Gone are the days when an employer can get by with handing the minister a piece of paper stating the amount of money paid for his services during the year. The following quotes and facts are provided with the hope that nonprofit employers will take heed, *do what the law requires, and avoid* the frustration of penalties and problems with the IRS.

Who is An Employer?

It is important that a nonprofit organization practice responsible payroll accounting in a **business like manner**. Individuals to whom you make payments for services rendered are not to be given the "choice" of their status treatment. The correct reporting to the IRS of payments for services rendered is very well documented in IRS Publications. Employers have often suffered the consequence of listening to inaccurate opinion or counsel. IRS Publication 15-A "Employer's Supplemental Tax Guide", page 8, states:

"Many nonprofit organizations are exempt from income tax. Although they do not have to pay income tax themselves, they must still withhold income tax from the pay of their employees. However, there are special social security, Medicare, and Federal unemployment (FUTA) tax rules that apply to the wages they pay their employees."

In Chapter One, we discussed fully the "common law rules" that are to be used to determine if an individual who has been paid for services rendered is an employee or an independent contractor. According to **Sec. 3509**, employers who wrongly treat an employee as a non-employee **are liable** for income tax that should have been withheld and the employee's portion of social security tax and medicare tax.

In Chapter One we also discussed the "statutory employee" definition. It is a status limited to four occupational groups and **a status that is not available** for either dual-status ministers or lay employees of a church or organization.

Who Is An Employee?

Payment to janitors, secretaries, paid babysitters, etc., for services rendered, are generally employees when the "common law rules" are applied. **Payment of $100 or more in a year** to a lay employee is subject to withholding and matching of social security and medicare tax. (IRS Publication 15-A, page 9) The threshold of $100 applies to nonprofit employers and for-profit employers. (For-profit employers also have a threshold of $50 per quarter for income tax withholding). Other thresholds: Farm employees—$150 annual; Household employees—$1,400 annual. You must carefully study federal employment tax rules and timely file payroll reports and **Form W-2's**. The sample payroll reports in this chapter will guide you.

Who Is An Independent Contractor?

Payment to guest musicians, evangelists, skilled contractors, and others who provide occasional services usually qualify for "independent contractor" status. At the time of payment for services rendered, have each person provide their social security number on a Form W-9. You are required to prepare **Form 1099** for each "independent contractor" that you paid **$600** or more during the year. Form 1099s are not required for payments made to corporations.

Payments to evangelists and guest speakers can be designated as parsonage allowance in advance and you may reimburse them for adequately accounted travel expense diaries and/or receipts. At the time of payment for the engagement have them fill out a Form W-9. **Designated parsonage allowance and reimbursements are not to be shown on Form 1099.** Report the remaining taxable honorarium on Form 1099 if it is $600 or more for the year. If an evangelist or musical group is employed by a corporation and the check is written to the corporation, a Form 1099 is not required.

Suggestion: There are two types of work most churches pay to have performed, janitorial and yard work, that can be planned to be non-employee engagements. To hire services that advertise in the yellow pages or the classified ads, perform the services for the general public and provide their own equipment, etc., would allow the preparation of Form 1099 and no payroll taxes to be withheld. The **"common law rules"** we discussed in Chapter One must be the basis for your decision to treat payment for services rendered as independent contractor payment or as employee wages.

Informational Return Penalties

IRS's emphasis on informational reporting affects everyone, not just nonprofit organizations. **Computer cross-matching of all informational returns with individuals' tax returns** gives the IRS the ability to detect unreported income. Since 1982 there have been penalties for failure to submit W-2's and 1099's to the IRS. Information return penalties include failure to file an information return, failure to file information returns correctly and on time, failure to file paper forms that are machine readable (must be typed with black ink), and failure to file electronically if filing 250 or more information returns including Form W-2s, 1099s, 1098s, etc. For your reading pleasure the IRS has 123 different tax codes dealing with penalties they can assess various taxpayers! Their current emphasis is on **correct and timely filed information**. The penalty for failure to file information returns is provided for in **Sec. 6652**.

Sec. 6721 imposes a penalty for any failure to file an information return on time, any failure to include all information required to be shown on the return, or for the inclusion of incorrect information. The amount of the penalty is based on how late the return is filed or when the failure is corrected. If corrected by the 30th day after the due date, the penalty is $15 a return, maximum of $75,000 a year. If filed or corrected more than 30 days late but by August 1, the penalty is $30 a return, maximum of $150,000 a year. If filed after August 1st of any year, the penalty is $50 a return, maximum of $250,000 a year.

Willful Or Intentional Disregard

Willful or intentional disregard causes very severe penalties. An example of a longstanding penalty for intentional disregard of doing payroll taxes from **Sec. 6672, is the 100% penalty.**

> *"Any person required to collect, truthfully account for, and pay over any tax imposed by this title who willfully fails to collect such tax, or truthfully account for and pay over such tax, or willfully attempts in any manner to evade or defeat any such tax or the payment thereof, shall, in addition to other penalties provided by law, be liable to a penalty* **equal to the total** *amount of the tax evaded, or not collected, or not accounted for and paid over."*

Late payment penalties and interest are in addition to the above penalties. **Trustees or treasurers** of nonprofit organizations, whether paid or volunteer, **can be held responsible when** the organization fails to pay the taxes.

It is unfortunate that such severe penalties exist. **It is very important** for an employer to **fulfill the informational return filing requirements** rather than having to go before the board or congregation and ask for funds to be raised to pay penalties and interest that could have been avoided by filing timely returns.

United States v. Indianapolis Baptist Temple, KTC 1999-37 and KTC 1999-396: To satisfy a nearly **$6 million** payroll tax debt for the years spanning 1987 through 1992, a U.S. District judge in Indianapolis ordered the church properties to be seized in the fall of 2000. A summary judgement was ordered on June 29, 1999 for $5,319,750.27, plus interest and other penalty additions that had accrued after July 26, 1998. **On February 13, 2001**, dozens of federal marshals swarmed the building and a helicopter hovered overhead during **the peaceful seizure**. Rev. Greg Dixon Sr. and several others were carried out on stretchers.

The timely filing of Form 8274 and timely filed Form 941s and W-2s would have prevented years of court proceedings and unfortunate debt.

Attitude Towards the IRS Should Be One of Cooperation

We recommend that the attitude of any organization towards the IRS or its agents should be one of cooperation. If your organization was not aware of your obligation to withhold income tax and withhold and match social security and medicare tax, it is our recommendation that for all wages paid within the three year statute of limitations, late reports should be filed and taxes paid. It is possible to write a letter and claim "reasonable cause" and lack of knowledge, rather than unwillingness, and have the IRS forgive some or all of the penalties. Interest will be assessed on the late payments.

To be uncooperative may cause the IRS to suspect that your church is a fraudulent one. Avoid being considered as a "tax protest" church. There are those who are not religious or not actually ministers but become "ordained" by mail and establish fictitious nonprofit churches in their homes for the purpose of "tax avoidance" or "tax protest." As in Tweeddale v.Commissioner, 92 T.C. 501, the judge said, "Petitioner was not a lone cowboy riding off on a wild stallion. He paid $1,200 for a set of documents constituting the plan or arrangement, purporting to establish a tax-exempt church with himself as a tax-exempt minister.....a totally meritless claim he abandoned on the eve of trial. Moreover, the organizer of this scheme went to jail for tax crimes as a result of it." The judge cited United States v. Daly, 756 F.2d 1076 (5th Cir. 1985). Daly, who did not himself file Basic Bible Church returns, formed the Basic Bible Church chapters to have the appearance of religious organizations while disseminating information on how to file returns so as to hamper IRS investigation and detection of the tax scheme. The judge further said, "We are bone-tired of seeing the Court's time, respondent's resources, and the national treasury wasted in litigating these phony vow of poverty cases."

If you are aware of anyone involved in this type of "tax protest," go to the IRS website and download **Form 211**, report them, and **be eligible for up to 10%** of tax collected as a **reward** from the IRS!

How To Prepare Information Returns

The employer is responsible for filing informational reports, not the employee. However, **we recommend that the minister take an active part** in helping the treasurer prepare and timely file required reports. Treasurers hold a very responsible position; consider paying them wages for carrying out their duties. When a new person assumes the responsibility, be sure they are properly informed and taught the importance of timely and correctly filed payroll reports.

Do not hesitate to seek professional accounting help in preparing the informational returns. **The staff at Worth Tax & Financial Service is available** to prepare payroll reports and W-2s for employers.

We would encourage the careful reading and study of the following:

IRS Publication 15,   "Employer's Tax Guide"

IRS Publication 15-A, "Employer's Supplemental Tax Guide," contains information for exempt organizations and the "common law guidelines"

IRS Publication 15-B, "Employer's Tax Guide to Fringe Benefits"

2005 Instructions   for preparing Forms W-2 and W-3.

These employer publications are automatically sent to you each year. They are sent to all new organizations that file for an identification number. Preprinted 941s and Federal Tax Deposit coupons are also automatically sent to employers. If you need any type of tax forms, call the IRS toll-free number listed in your phone book and they will provide them free. If you have access to the Internet, connect to **www.irs.gov/formspubs/index.html** IRS publications and forms are available to be downloaded and printed with Adobe Reader! **Efficient :+)**

We will teach you how to prepare the proper payroll forms by example. Rev. Snodgrass and Joseph Mop are employed by Mission Community Church. We have used their sample "compensation packages," shown earlier in this chapter to prepare the reports. Refer to them often as we give you step by step instructions.

Obtain An Employer Identification Number

Does your organization or church have one? The bank where you have your organization's checking account has required you to furnish them with a Employer Identification Number. It looks like this: 00-0000000, nine digits. It is a Federal Identification Number for federal reports, and is not your state incorporation number or sales tax exempt number.

New churches and existing churches without a number should request one with Form SS-4. You can apply for an EIN online, by telephone, by fax or by mail depending on how soon you need to use the EIN. You can receive your EIN by internet and use it immediately to file a return or make a payment. Go the IRS website at **www.irs.gov/businesses/index.html** and click on **Employer ID Numbers** under **Related Topics**.

Lay Employees

It is **important to understand** that dual-status ministers and lay employees are treated differently for withholding purposes.

A lay employee's income **IS** subject to income tax withholding and each lay employee must fill out a Form W-4. The status and number of allowances claimed will determine how much income tax is to be withheld. **IRS Publication 15** contains the tables showing how much income tax is required to be withheld. **IRS Publication 15-A** contains the tables showing a combination of income tax, social security tax, and medicare tax withholding.

Joseph Mop's W-4 shows he is married and wishes to claim "0" allowance. Turn to page 48 of IRS Publication 15 (2005) and find his semimonthly pay of $1,125.00 on the left-hand column. Under the "0" allowance column we see the proper amount to withhold is **$89.00**. For the sample payroll sheet for Joseph Mop, the tables for the Percentage Method of withholding calculated **$89.00** withholding.

A lay employee's income **IS** subject to social security and medicare tax withholding and matching. 2005 combined rate to be withheld for employees was 7.65%. Employers pay an additional 7.65% when they file Form 941. The rate for 2006 remains the same. **The 7.65% combined rate is made up of 6.2% rate for social security tax and 1.45% rate for medicare.**

The only exception to the above paragraph is for **electing churches** that have filed **Form 8274** and are exempt **because of religious reasons**, Sec. 3121(w). The election merely **transfers** the social security liability **from the church to the employee**. Churches which desire to be an electing church must file two copies of Form 8274 after they hire lay employees, but before the first date on which a quarterly employment tax return is due. (See more detailed discussion in Chapter Four.) Lay employees of churches that have filed Form 8274 are subject to paying social security at the 2005 self-employed rate of 15.3% (less adjustments) on their personal return.

Dual-Status Ministers

A dual-status minister's income **IS NOT** subject to withholding income tax according to Sec. 3401(a)(9). The dual-status minister is to "prepay" his taxes by filing Form 1040ES, Estimated Tax for Individuals. When a dual-status minister prepays his taxes on Form 1040ES, we recommend that he does not prepare Form W-4 for the employer.

A dual-status minister's income **IS NOT** subject to withholding and matching for social security and medicare tax purposes. Sec. 1402(a)(8), an **exception** to the normal employer/employee common law rules, states that the dual-status minister is to be treated as self-employed for social security purposes. A dual-status minister who is conscientiously opposed to or because of religious principles opposed to the acceptance of public insurance based on ministerial service can timely file Form 4361 and become exempt from social security. This is discussed fully in Chapter Four. When the employer is a church or integral agency of a church, **it is NEVER correct** to treat a dual-status minister, doing the duties of a minister, **as an employee** for social security and medicare tax purposes.

● *Optional Withholding*

When an employer and a dual-status minister agree to optional withholding as the means for prepaying the minister's tax liability, he should prepare a Form W-4. Entering the amount to be withheld each pay period on line 6 will satisfy the requirement that the agreement be written. (Status and number of allowances on line 5 should be left blank.) We recommend that the dual-status minister "estimate" his total tax liability — income tax, social security, and medicare tax; divide it by the number of pay periods (24 if paid semimonthly) and have the employer "withhold" that amount each payday as **federal income tax withholding**. The amount withheld will be shown as a credit in Box 2 of Form W-2.

This option would take the place of the dual-status minister prepaying his taxes on Form 1040ES. Rev. Snodgrass estimated he needed **$6,000.00** prepaid and had $250.00 withheld each payday.

$$\$6,000.00 \div 24 = \mathbf{\$250.00}$$

His other choice would have been to personally pay 4 estimated tax payments of **$1,500.00** on **Form 1040ES.**

Independent Religious Workers

When an independent religious worker **does not** have a sponsoring mission or church, the total gross income may include substantial funds for ministry projects. Entering large expenditures and building projects as Schedule C deductions creates a very high audit exposure. Should an independent minister/missionary be chosen for an audit, foreign IRS personnel are apt to be inexperienced concerning typical ministry endeavors. The communication between the taxpayer and the IRS agent can be difficult, frustrating, and time consuming.

The **ideal solution** to the Schedule C problem for the independent religious worker is **to establish an employer/employee relationship with a church** in the U.S.

Every independent religious worker or missionary needs to find a supporting organization or church to be willing to function as his employer. A carefully planned compensation plan with fringe benefits, designated parsonage allowance, an accountable reimbursement plan, and salary will provide the best tax advantages and **reduce audit exposure.** A church checking account should be set up with the religious worker having signature privileges. **The religious worker then advises all of his supporters to make their checks payable to the church.** As the religious worker pays for "work projects" and employee business expenses, they become legitimate church ministry expenses of the organization. Copies of all of the financial transactions and detailed receipts should be submitted to the sponsoring church.

The income the religious worker receives for his personal salary is recorded on a payroll record and included on the church's quarterly Form 941 and a **Form W-2 at year end**. The religious worker's uncomplicated Form 1040 will reflect only his true personal earnings. If the religious worker qualifies for dual-status treatment, he will be responsible for his own social security on Schedule SE, the same as any dual-status minister employed by a church or an integral agency of a church. If he does not qualify for dual-status treatment, the support received can be used to provide the necessary social security and medicare tax withholding and matching.

Prepare a Payroll Sheet for each Employee

Employers are responsible for accurate recording of the salary, deductions, and net pay for each individual employee. Computers are wonderful replacements of manual payroll! Most payroll software programs will allow modifications to handle the dual-status minister and the employee of "an electing church."

We have created and have available manual "Payroll Sheets" that contain extra columns needed to show parsonage allowance and TSAs and provide a section to keep a record of the professional business expense reimbursements.

1. Begin entering a paycheck on the "Payroll Sheet" by entering the total cash salary (including parsonage allowance) in the "total" column in the middle. **Also enter** in this column: a bonus or love gift, salary to offset social security cost, any taxable fringe benefits, etc., as they are paid to the employee.

2. The columns to the right of the "total" column allow you to show income tax, social security tax, medicare tax, state income tax, and local income tax deductions. A dual-status minister who "prepays" his federal taxes on Form 1040ES and state taxes on the appropriate state forms will not use these columns.

3. The first column to the left of the "total" column allows you to subtract voluntary contributions to a Tax Sheltered Account. TSA contributions **are subject** to social security and medicare tax withholding and matching for the lay employee according to Revenue Ruling 65-208. They are **not subject** to social security on Schedule SE for the dual-status employee according to Revenue Ruling 68-395. The total contribution is to be entered as a memo on Form W-2, Box 12.

4. The second column to the left of the "total" column allows you to subtract parsonage allowance for the dual-status minister. The parsonage allowance of **$24,000** for Rev. Snodgrass is divided by 24 pay periods to arrive at the semimonthly amount of **$1,000.00**.

5. Use the right hand section to record the checks written to reimburse an employee for adequately accounted employee business expenses. Study Chapter Three and **be sure you have adopted a written reimbursement plan** that satisfies the IRS Regulation 1.62-2.

Chart of Where to Show Transactions

Study our "**Chart of Where to Show Transactions**" shown on page 105. It will guide you as to what portions of the compensation package you are required to include and what portions you are not required to include on the payroll reports. The payroll sheet's "total" column for each employee should include any item from the chart with a "yes" in the "taxable income" column.

● *Use A Blank "Payroll Sheet" As A Summary*

It is important that your "payroll sheets," Form 941s (all four quarters), and the W-2s at year end **reconcile or balance.** Use a blank "Payroll Sheet" as a summary of monthly or quarterly totals if you have several employees.

Make Payroll Tax Deposits as Required

The amount of payroll taxes you owe determines the frequency of deposits. You owe these taxes when you pay the wages. There are penalties for making late deposits. When you make a payroll tax deposit with Form 8109, the bank electronically transmits your payment to the IRS Service Center that day.

There are two deposit schedules for determining when you deposit taxes, monthly or semiweekly. The IRS will notify you each November whether you are a monthly or semiweekly depositor for the coming calendar year. This determination is made based on the aggregate amount of employment taxes reported during a "look back" period. The regulations define a look back period as the twelve-month period ending on the preceding June 30th.

Combine federal income tax withheld with total amount of social security and medicare tax to be paid (15.3%) to determine total liability for each period.

● *Deposits Penalty*

It is important to make timely deposits for payroll taxes. The applicable percentage of penalty for late payment in Sec. 6656 is (1) 2% if not more than 5 days late, (2) 5% if not more than 15 days late, and (3) 10% if more than 15 days late. It is possible to have the penalty waived if it occurs during the 1st quarter that a deposit was required.

● *$2,500 Rule*

If an employer accumulates less than **$2,500** tax liability for the quarter, no deposit is needed and payment can be made with the tax return for the quarter.

● *Monthly Rule*

An employer is a monthly depositor if the aggregate amount of employment taxes reported for the look back period is **$50,000** or less. A monthly depositor must deposit employment taxes for payments made during a calendar month by the 15th day of the following month.

● *Semiweekly Rule*

An employer is a semiweekly depositor if the aggregate amount of employment taxes reported for the look back period is more than **$50,000**. Under the semiweekly deposit rule, those paying wages on Wednesday, Thursday, and/or Friday must deposit employment taxes by the next Wednesday, while those paying wages on Saturday, Sunday, Monday, and/or Tuesday are required to deposit employment taxes on the following Friday.

If the total accumulated tax reaches **$100,000** or more on any given day, it must be deposited by the next banking day.

● *How To Make A Deposit*

Use the Federal Tax Deposit (FTD) Coupons, Form 8109, to make the deposits if you are a monthly or semiweekly depositor with less than $200,000 total payroll tax deposits during the previous year. Write the amount due on the coupon, indicate it is 941 tax liability and which quarter is being paid. Write the check, paid to the order of your bank, and take it to the bank and ask for a receipt.

The Electronic Federal Tax Payment System (**EFTPS**) requires all employers with $200,000 annual payroll tax to make electronic deposits. When you are required to make deposits by EFTPS and fail to do so, you are subject to a 10% penalty. All employers are **encouraged to voluntarily** participate. Call 1-800-555-4477 to enroll in **EFTPS**. The website for information and making electronic deposits is: **www.eftps.gov**

The New Employment Tax e-file System can be used to e-file Form 941. Website is: **www.irs.gov/efile**

● *Example of Computing Monthly Deposits*

Mission Community Church's Form 941 for the 4th quarter shows the monthly liabilities on line 17, Monthly Summary Record of Federal Tax Liability section. **We computed the monthly liabilities as follows:**

Joseph's Social Security tax - $2,400.00 X 12.4%=	$ 297.60
Joseph's Medicare Tax - $2,400.00 X 2.9% =	69.60
Rev. Snodgrass' Federal Tax	500.00
Joseph's Federal Tax	178.00
October Total	**$ 1,045.20**
Joseph's taxable wage - $2,400.00 X 12.4% =	$ 297.60
Joseph's Medicare Tax - $2,400.00 X 2.9% =	69.60
Rev. Snodgrass' Federal Tax	500.00
Joseph's Federal Tax	178.00
November Total	**$ 1,045.20**
Joseph's taxable wage - $2,400.00 X 12.4 =	$ 297.60
Joseph's Medicare Tax - $2,400.00 X 2.9% =	69.60
Rev. Snodgrass' Federal Tax	500.00
Joseph's Federal Tax	178.00
December Total	**$ 1,045.20**

Prepare Quarterly Reports

● *Form 941 - Instructions With Social Security*

LINE 2   will include taxable salaries of both dual-status ministers and lay employees from the extreme left-hand column of the "Payroll Sheets".

LINE 3   Enter the income tax you withheld and all optional withholding for dual-status employees.

LINE 5a   will only include taxable salaries (including TSA contributions) of lay employees. In our 2005 example, the employee's withheld social security tax of 6.2% and the employer's matching portion 6.2% is combined for a total tax of 12.4%. The 2006 rate will be the same.

LINE 5c   will only include taxable salaries (including TSA contributions) of lay employees. In our 2005 example, the employee's withheld medicare tax of 1.45% and the employer's matching portion 1.45% is combined for a total tax of 2.9%. The 2006 rate will be the same.

LINE 10   undeposited taxes due must be less than $2,500 or you will be billed up to a 10% penalty for not paying on time with FTD Coupons at a bank or EFTPS electronic deposits.

● *Form 941 - Instructions Without Social Security - Filed Form 8274*

If an existing church filed Form 8274 by October 31, 1984 (a new church by the first date on which a quarterly tax return would be due), and for religious reasons became exempt from withholding and matching social security, they should use **Form 941 and mark the box** provided on line 4. Their employees will be liable for paying social security and medicare tax at the combined rate of 15.3% (less adjustments) on their personal Schedule SE for 2005.

LINE 2   will include taxable salaries of both dual-status ministers and lay employees from the extreme left-hand column of the "Payroll Sheet".

LINE 3   Enter the income tax you withheld, all optional withholding for dual-status employees and additional withholding for lay employees' social security liability.

LINE 5a   Leave blank - does not apply to electing churches.

LINE 5c   Leave blank - does not apply to electing churches.

LINE 4   Mark the check box

LINE 10   undeposited taxes due must be less than $2,500 or you will be billed up to a 10% penalty for not paying on time with FTD Coupons at a bank or EFTPS electronic deposits.

● *Due Dates for Quarterly Reports*

> January, February, and March ....due on April 30th
> April, May, and June ....due on July 31st
> July, August, and September ....due on October 31st
> October, November, and December ....due on January 31st.

● *When 941 Reports Are Not Necessary*

Employers who withhold income tax on wages, or who must pay social security or medicare tax, must file Form 941 quarterly. **When there is no liability**, the IRS does not require you to file Form 941. When a church employer has only dual-status employees and is not withholding income tax, no quarterly Form 941 is required. IRS computers are programmed to look at lines 3, 5a, and 5c and only cross match tax liabilities with the annual Form W-3. **Always report** the taxable salary for a dual-status employee on Form W-2 annually.

Prepare Year End Reports

Form W-3 and Copy A of all Forms W-2 are to be sent to the Social Security Administration address shown on Form W-3. Since Copy A is imaged and character recognized by machines, **they must be typed with black ink.** Do not use script type, or make any white outs or strike overs. Use decimal points but not dollar signs or commas (00000.00). Specific line by line instructions are given in 2005 Instructions for the preparation of the W-3 and the W-2. If a box **does not apply,** instructions say to **leave it blank.** A dual-status minister's W-2 **must not** have any entry in **Boxes 3, 4, 5, and 6.** If the tax liability figures on the W-3 do not reconcile with the tax liability figures that have been reported quarterly on the 941, you will receive a computer print out from the IRS asking why they are different and a billing of tax liability they think you owe.

> Form 941, Line 2   wages should match   = W-2, Box 1 (but are not cross-matched by IRS)
> Form 941, Line 3   tax should match   = W-2, Box 2
> Form 941, Line 5a   wages should match   = W-2, Box 3
> Form 941, Line 5a   column 2 tax should match   = W-2, Box 4 X 2
> Form 941, Line 5c   wages should match   = W-2, Box 5
> Form 941, Line 5c   column 2 tax should match   = W-2, Box 6 X 2 (odd cents okay)

Year-end reports are to be prepared by January 31st. Employees are to be given their W-2 copies by January 31st. You have until February 28th to actually send Copy A of the W-2 to the Social Security Administration. Some employers have given a W-2 to their employee, then failed to send Copy A to the Social Security Administration. **Be sure to send Copy A to the government** so they can cross match it with your employees' returns. Avoid "failure to file" penalties!

We feel it will be helpful to list a few of the required entries on the W-2 that are typical for religious workers. Enter appropriate codes using capital letters, leave one space blank after the code and enter the dollar amount on the same line. Use decimal points but not dollar signs or commas.

Box 10: Show total amount of dependent care benefits paid or incurred by you for your employee.

Box 12: C 230   ($230 premium for over $50,000 group term life insurance)

          D 1200   ($1,200 elective deferral to 401(k) plan)

          E 1200   ($1,200 elective deferral to 403(b) plan)

          L 4050   ($5,050 reimbursement for 10,000 miles @ $50\frac{1}{2}$¢, enter $1,000 in Box 1 @$40\frac{1}{2}$¢)

          P 825   ($825 reimbursement for qualified moving expenses)

          S 1200   ($1,200 salary reduction contributions to 408(p) SIMPLE plan)

          No Entry   ($4,050 reimbursement for 10,000 miles @$40\frac{1}{2}$¢)

          No Entry   (All reimbursements with accountable plan at IRS rates or actual)

Box 14: You may use this box for any other information you want to give your employee. Please label each item. Examples are parsonage allowance designated, moving expenses paid, or reminder for employee of an electing church to pay social.security on Sch. SE.

Box 14: Show total value of taxable fringe benefits that are also shown in Box 1, such as the value of personal use of employer owned auto **or** provide a statement to employee of calculations.

State and Local Tax Withholding

Call your State and local Departments and ask for materials and instructions for withholding the proper amount of tax for your employees. Some states require that you withhold state tax for the dual-status minister as well as the lay employee.

Unemployment Taxes

Nonprofit employers are not subject to Federal Unemployment Taxes. IRS Publication 15-A, page 8, states this fact. Most states do not require nonprofit employers to pay state unemployment tax. Consult with your state unemployment office to be sure.

Workmen's Compensation Insurance

Most states **require** nonprofit employers to provide Workmen's Compensation Insurance coverage for both lay and dual-status minister employees. Consult with an insurance professional in your state to be sure.

Form I-9 - Employment Eligibility Verification

The Immigration Reform and Control Act of 1986 requires all employers to examine the applicant's documents proving identity and eligibility to work in the United States and complete Form I-9 **before hiring the applicant**. The law says that we cannot hire an alien if we know that the alien is not authorized to work in the U.S. The Form I-9 is not an IRS form, but can be obtained from the Bureau of Immigration and Customs Enforcement (ICE). Download form I-9 at their website: **http://uscis.gov/graphics/formsfee/forms/i-9.htm**

Form I-9 is not required to be filed with INS, the employer is required to keep Form I-9 for possible audit. Fines for noncompliance are from $100 to $1,000 per employee for failure to maintain the necessary paperwork. Fines for hiring illegal aliens are from $250 to $10,000 per individual illegally employed.

New Hire Reporting Requirements

Since October 1,1997, within a few business days of a new employee's date of hire (20 days in Indiana), all employers are to submit to their state unemployment department a report containing the following information: (1) the new employee's name, address and social security number; and (2) the employer's name, address and federal tax identification number. The employer may submit the report by conveying to the department a copy of the new employee's W-4 form or an alternative scannable W-4.

How To Correct Information Returns

The IRS provides Form W-2c, Form W-3c and Form 941C as the means of correcting mistakes on previously filed information returns. It is important to correct returns when you discover a mistake.

Annual Form 1096 and Forms 1099

Prepare Form 1096 and Form 1099s for payments to evangelists, musicians, and contractors whom you paid more than $600. They are required to be given to the recipients by January 31 and sent to your IRS Service Center by February 28th. You may be required to prepare and file Form 1099-INT for interest of $10 or more paid on bonds or loans from individuals. You may be required to prepare and file Form 1099-MISC for rents paid of $600 or more.

Form 1099 is not required for payments made to **corporations.**

Chart of Where to Show Transactions
For a dual-status employee, leave Form W-2, Boxes 3 and 5 blank.

Type of Transaction	*Taxable Income Box 1, W-2	Lay Employee FICA & Medicare Box 3 & 5, W-2	**Dual-Status Sch. SE Line 2	Show on Sch. C	Not to be shown anywhere	Deducted on Form 1040
INCOME						
Salary, Dual-status minister	Yes		Yes			
Soc. Security paid by employer, dual-status	Yes		Yes			
Salary, Lay employee	Yes	Yes				
Salary, Lay employee of electing church	Yes	No	***Yes			
Bonus or gift from employer	Yes	Yes	Yes			
Professional income			Yes	Yes		
Gift from relative, etc	No	No	No		Yes	
FRINGES						
Employer qualified pension- 401a,SEP,403b	No	No	No		Yes	
Premium for $50,000 term life insurance	No	No	No		Yes	
Premium for over $50,000 term life insurance	Yes	Yes	Yes			
Permanent life, employee's beneficiary	Yes	Yes	Yes			
Medical insurance paid by employer	No	No	No		Yes	
Qualified medical reimbursement plan	No	No	No		Yes	
Qualified moving reimbursement	No	No	No		Yes	
Nonqualified moving reimbursement	Yes	Yes	Yes			
Employee TSA, 403(b) lay employee	No	Yes				
Employee TSA, 403(b) dual-status	No		No			
ADJ						
Employee payments to an IRA						1040, Ln. 32
Self-employed Keogh payments						1040, Ln. 28
Unreimbursed qualified moving expenses						1040, Ln. 26
HOUSING						
Value of home provided, dual-status	No		Yes			
Parsonage Allowance, dual-status	No		Yes			
Value of home provided, lay employee (Sec.119 qualifications met)	No	No				
Value of home provided, lay employee (Sec. 119 qualifications not met)	Yes	Yes				
PROF EXP						
Auto reimbursement	No	No	No		Yes	
Employer provided auto, personal use	Yes	Yes	Yes			
Travel and professional reimbursement	No	No	No		Yes	
Expense allowance without adequate accounting to employer	Yes	Yes	Deduct			Sch. A, Ln. 20
Unreimbursed business expenses			Deduct			Sch. A, Ln. 20

*   Amounts in this column are to be shown in left-hand column of payroll sheets, line 2 of Form 941, and Box 1 of W-2.
** If a dual-status employee is exempt because he has filed Form 4361, then he is to disregard the column for Social Security and write "Exempt—Form 4361" on the self-employment line of Form 1040, Page 2.
*** Lay employees of electing church report wage on Section B, Part I, Line 5a of Sch. SE

NAME **H. James Snodgrass**

ADDRESS **2309 E. Smith Street**

CITY **South Bend** STATE **IN** ZIP **46617**

SOCIAL SECURITY NUMBER **483-12-0000**

FILING STATUS

MARRIED **X** SINGLE _____

FEDERAL–NUMBER OF EXEMPTIONS **N/A**

STATE–NUMBER OF EXEMPTIONS **N/A**

UNORDAINED ☐

ORDAINED ☒

PARSONAGE DESIGNATED $ **24,000**

EMPLOYEE'S EARNINGS RECORD

DATE TERMINATED · DATE HIRED · YEAR 2005

Payroll Period Ending	*Taxable Salary & Allowances	Parsonage	TSA	Total	Federal W/H Tax	Social Security Tax	Medicare Tax	State W/H Tax	Local W/H Tax	Net Pay	Check	Miles	Amount
FIRST QUARTER — JAN													
1	875 00	1000 00	250 00	2125 00	250 00			45 00	11 00	1569 00			
15	875 00	1000 00	250 00	2125 00	250 00			45 00	11 00	1569 00			
Monthly Total	1750 00	2000 00	500 00	4250 00	500 00			90 00	22 00	3138 00	1075	1842	874 51
FEB 1	875 00	1000 00	250 00	2125 00	250 00			45 00	11 00	1569 00			
15	875 00	1000 00	250 00	2125 00	250 00			45 00	11 00	1569 00			
Monthly Total	1750 00	2000 00	500 00	4250 00	500 00			90 00	22 00	3138 00	1080	2231	1499 90
MAR 1	875 00	1000 00	250 00	2125 00	250 00			45 00	11 00	1569 00			
15	875 00	1000 00	250 00	2125 00	250 00			45 00	11 00	1569 00			
Monthly Total	1750 00	2000 00	500 00	4250 00	500 00			90 00	22 00	3138 00	1085	2269	1328 94
Quarterly Total	5250 00	6000 00	1500 00	12750 00	1500 00			270 00	66 00	9414 00			
TOTAL TO DATE	5250 00	6000 00	1500 00	12750 00	1500 00			270 00	66 00	9414 00			
SECOND QUARTER — APR 1	875 00	1000 00	250 00	2125 00	250 00			45 00	11 00	1569 00			
15	875 00	1000 00	250 00	2125 00	250 00			45 00	11 00	1569 00			
Monthly Total	1750 00	2000 00	500 00	4250 00	500 00			90 00	22 00	3138 00	1093	1732	917 96
MAY 1	875 00	1000 00	250 00	2125 00	250 00			45 00	11 00	1569 00			
15	875 00	1000 00	250 00	2125 00	250 00			45 00	11 00	1569 00			
Monthly Total	1750 00	2000 00	500 00	4250 00	500 00			90 00	22 00	3138 00	1097	1388	673 91
JUNE 1	875 00	1000 00	250 00	2125 00	250 00			45 00	11 00	1569 00			
15	875 00	1000 00	250 00	2125 00	250 00			45 00	11 00	1569 00			
Monthly Total	1750 00	2000 00	500 00	4250 00	500 00			90 00	22 00	3138 00	1104	1673	915 53
Quarterly Total	5250 00	6000 00	1500 00	12750 00	1500 00			270 00	66 00	9414 00			
TOTAL TO DATE	10500 00	12000 00	3000 00	25500 00	3000 00			540 00	132 00	18828 00			
THIRD QUARTER — JULY 1	875 00	1000 00	250 00	2125 00	250 00			45 00	11 00	1569 00			
15	875 00	1000 00	250 00	2125 00	250 00			45 00	11 00	1569 00			
Monthly Total	1750 00	2000 00	500 00	4250 00	500 00			90 00	22 00	3138 00	1110	1558	814 81
AUG 1	875 00	1000 00	250 00	2125 00	250 00			45 00	11 00	1569 00			
15	875 00	1000 00	250 00	2125 00	250 00			45 00	11 00	1569 00			
Monthly Total	1750 00	2000 00	500 00	4250 00	500 00			90 00	22 00	3138 00	1116	2652	1345 39
SEPT 1	875 00	1000 00	250 00	2125 00	250 00			45 00	11 00	1569 00			
15	875 00	1000 00	250 00	2125 00	250 00			45 00	11 00	1569 00			
Monthly Total	1750 00	2000 00	500 00	4250 00	500 00			90 00	22 00	3138 00	1123	1227	769 88
Quarterly Total	5250 00	6000 00	1500 00	12750 00	1500 00			270 00	66 00	9414 00			
TOTAL TO DATE	15750 00	18000 00	4500 00	38250 00	4500 00			810 00	198 00	28242 00			
FOURTH QUARTER — OCT 1	875 00	1000 00	250 00	2125 00	250 00			45 00	11 00	1569 00			
15	875 00	1000 00	250 00	2125 00	250 00			45 00	11 00	1569 00			
Monthly Total	1750 00	2000 00	500 00	4250 00	500 00			90 00	22 00	3138 00	1130	1332	898 50
NOV 1	875 00	1000 00	250 00	2125 00	250 00			45 00	11 00	1569 00			
15	875 00	1000 00	250 00	2125 00	250 00			45 00	11 00	1569 00			
Monthly Total	1750 00	2000 00	500 00	4250 00	500 00			90 00	22 00	3138 00	1137	1578	982 64
DEC 1	875 00	1000 00	250 00	2125 00	250 00			45 00	11 00	1569 00			
15	875 00	1000 00	250 00	2125 00	250 00			45 00	11 00	1569 00			
Monthly Total	1750 00	2000 00	500 00	4250 00	500 00			90 00	22 00	3138 00	1143	1397	874 03
Quarterly Total	5250 00	6000 00	1500 00	12750 00	1500 00			270 00	66 00	9414 00			
TOTAL TO DATE	21000 00	24000 00	6000 00	51000 00	6000 00			1080 00	264 00	37656 00		20879	11896 00

*Amount to be shown on Form 941, Line 2 and Form W-2, Box 1. Carefully study Chapter Six in "Income Tax Guide for Ministers".

NAME ___Joseph Mop___
ADDRESS _1621 E. Jones Street_
CITY ___South Bend___ STATE _IN_ ZIP _46617_
SOCIAL SECURITY NUMBER ___403-19-0000___

FILING STATUS
MARRIED __X__ SINGLE _____
FEDERAL–NUMBER OF EXEMPTIONS _0_
STATE–NUMBER OF EXEMPTIONS __0_

UNORDAINED [X]
ORDAINED [ ]
PARSONAGE
DESIGNATED $ _____

EMPLOYEE'S EARNINGS RECORD

DATE TERMINATED   DATE HIRED   YEAR 2005

Payroll Period Ending	*Taxable Salary & Allowances	Parsonage	TSA	Total	Federal W/H Tax	Social Security Tax	Medicare Tax	State W/H Tax	Local W/H Tax	Net Pay	Reimbursement Check	Miles	Amount
FIRST QUARTER													
JAN 1	1125 00		75 00	1200 00	89 00	74 40	17 40	38 25	9 00	896 95			
JAN 15	1125 00		75 00	1200 00	89 00	74 40	17 40	38 25	9 00	896 95			
Monthly Total	2250 00		150 00	2400 00	178 00	148 80	34 80	76 50	18 00	1793 90	1076	210	141 06
FEB 1	1125 00		75 00	1200 00	89 00	74 40	17 40	38 25	9 00	896 95			
FEB 15	1125 00		75 00	1200 00	89 00	74 40	17 40	38 25	9 00	896 95			
Monthly Total	2250 00		150 00	2400 00	178 00	148 80	34 80	76 50	18 00	1793 90	1081	229	136 41
MAR 1	1125 00		75 00	1200 00	89 00	74 40	17 40	38 25	9 00	896 95			
MAR 15	1125 00		75 00	1200 00	89 00	74 40	17 40	38 25	9 00	896 95			
Monthly Total	2250 00		150 00	2400 00	178 00	148 80	34 80	76 50	18 00	1793 90	1086	189	139 77
Quarterly Total	6750 00		450 00	7200 00	534 00	446 40	104 40	229 50	54 00	5381 70			
TOTAL TO DATE	6750 00		450 00	7200 00	534 00	446 40	104 40	229 50	54 00	5381 70			
SECOND QUARTER													
APR 1	1125 00		75 00	1200 00	89 00	74 40	17 40	38 25	9 00	896 95			
APR 15	1125 00		75 00	1200 00	89 00	74 40	17 40	38 25	9 00	896 95			
Monthly Total	2250 00		150 00	2400 00	178 00	148 80	34 80	76 50	18 00	1793 90	1094	204	120 46
MAY 1	1125 00		75 00	1200 00	89 00	74 40	17 40	38 25	9 00	896 95			
MAY 15	1125 00		75 00	1200 00	89 00	74 40	17 40	38 25	9 00	896 95			
Monthly Total	2250 00		150 00	2400 00	178 00	148 80	34 80	76 50	18 00	1793 90	1098	154	141 58
JUNE 1	1125 00		75 00	1200 00	89 00	74 40	17 40	38 25	9 00	896 95			
JUNE 15	1125 00		75 00	1200 00	89 00	74 40	17 40	38 25	9 00	896 95			
Monthly Total	2250 00		150 00	2400 00	178 00	148 80	34 80	76 50	18 00	1793 90	1105	298	156 42
Quarterly Total	6750 00		450 00	7200 00	534 00	446 40	104 40	229 50	54 00	5381 70			
TOTAL TO DATE	13500 00		900 00	14400 00	1068 00	892 80	208 80	459 00	108 00	10763 40			
THIRD QUARTER													
JULY 1	1125 00		75 00	1200 00	89 00	74 40	17 40	38 25	9 00	896 95			
JULY 15	1125 00		75 00	1200 00	89 00	74 40	17 40	38 25	9 00	896 95			
Monthly Total	2250 00		150 00	2400 00	178 00	148 80	34 80	76 50	18 00	1793 90	1111	154	149 25
AUG 1	1125 00		75 00	1200 00	89 00	74 40	17 40	38 25	9 00	896 95			
AUG 15	1125 00		75 00	1200 00	89 00	74 40	17 40	38 25	9 00	896 95			
Monthly Total	2250 00		150 00	2400 00	178 00	148 80	34 80	76 50	18 00	1793 90	1117	120	94 80
SEPT 1	1125 00		75 00	1200 00	89 00	74 40	17 40	38 25	9 00	896 95			
SEPT 15	1125 00		75 00	1200 00	89 00	74 40	17 40	38 25	9 00	896 95			
Monthly Total	2250 00		150 00	2400 00	178 00	148 80	34 80	76 50	18 00	1793 90	1124	184	133 36
Quarterly Total	6750 00		450 00	7200 00	534 00	446 40	104 40	229 50	54 00	5381 70			
TOTAL TO DATE	20250 00		1350 00	21600 00	1602 00	1339 20	313 20	688 50	162 00	16145 10			
FOURTH QUARTER													
OCT 1	1125 00		75 00	1200 00	89 00	74 40	17 40	38 25	9 00	896 95			
OCT 15	1125 00		75 00	1200 00	89 00	74 40	17 40	38 25	9 00	896 95			
Monthly Total	2250 00		150 00	2400 00	178 00	148 80	34 80	76 50	18 00	1793 90	1131	145	128 50
NOV 1	1125 00		75 00	1200 00	89 00	74 40	17 40	38 25	9 00	896 95			
NOV 15	1125 00		75 00	1200 00	89 00	74 40	17 40	38 25	9 00	896 95			
Monthly Total	2250 00		150 00	2400 00	178 00	148 80	34 80	76 50	18 00	1793 90	1138	129	116 33
DEC 1	1125 00		75 00	1200 00	89 00	74 40	17 40	38 25	9 00	896 95			
DEC 15	1125 00		75 00	1200 00	89 00	74 40	17 40	38 25	9 00	896 95			
Monthly Total	2250 00		150 00	2400 00	178 00	148 80	34 80	76 50	18 00	1793 90	1144	139	110 31
Quarterly Total	6750 00		450 00	7200 00	534 00	446 40	104 40	229 50	54 00	5381 70			
TOTAL TO DATE	27000 00		1800 00	28800 00	2136 00	1785 60	417 60	918 00	216 00	21526 80		2155	1568 25

*Amount to be shown on Form 941, Line 2 and Form W-2, Box 1. Carefully study Chapter Six in "Income Tax Guide for Ministers".

Example, Nonelecting Church

Form 941

Form 941 for 2005: Employer's Quarterly Federal Tax Return
(Rev. January 2005) — Department of the Treasury — Internal Revenue Service

OMB No. 1545-0029

Employer identification number: 3 5 – 2 9 3 8 2 7 9

Name (not your trade name): Mission Community Church
Trade name (if any):
Address: 1620 E. Jones Street
Number   Street   Suite or room number
South Bend   IN   46617
City   State   ZIP code

Report for this Quarter ... (Check one.)
1: January, February, March
2: April, May, June
3: July, August, September
4: October, November, December ✓

Read the separate instructions before you fill out this form. Please type or print within the boxes.

Part 1: Answer these questions for this quarter.

1. Number of employees who received wages, tips, or other compensation for the pay period including: Mar. 12 (Quarter 1), June 12 (Quarter 2), Sept. 12 (Quarter 3), Dec. 12 (Quarter 4) ... 1   2

2. Wages, tips, and other compensation ... 2   12000 . 00

3. Total income tax withheld from wages, tips, and other compensation ... 3   2034 . 00

4. If no wages, tips, and other compensation are subject to social security or Medicare tax ... ☐ Check and go to line 6.

5. Taxable social security and Medicare wages and tips:

	Column 1		Column 2
5a Taxable social security wages	7200 . 00	× .124 =	892 . 80
5b Taxable social security tips	.	× .124 =	.
5c Taxable Medicare wages & tips	7200 . 00	× .029 =	208 . 80

5d Total social security and Medicare taxes (Column 2, lines 5a + 5b + 5c = line 5d) ... 5d   1101 . 60

6. Total taxes before adjustments (lines 3 + 5d = line 6) ... 6   3135 . 60

7. Tax adjustments (If your answer is a negative number, write it in brackets.):

7a Current quarter's fractions of cents ... 7a   .
7b Current quarter's sick pay ... 7b   .
7c Current quarter's adjustments for tips and group-term life insurance ... 7c   .
7d Current year's income tax withholding (Attach Form 941c) ... 7d   .
7e Prior quarters' social security and Medicare taxes (Attach Form 941c) ... 7e   .
7f Special additions to federal income tax (reserved use) ... 7f   .
7g Special additions to social security and Medicare (reserved use) ... 7g   .

7h Total adjustments (Combine all amounts: lines 7a through 7g.) ... 7h   .

8. Total taxes after adjustments (Combine lines 6 and 7h.) ... 8   3135 . 60

9. Advance earned income credit (EIC) payments made to employees ... 9   .

10. Total taxes after adjustment for advance EIC (lines 8 – 9 = line 10) ... 10   3135 . 60

11. Total deposits for this quarter, including overpayment applied from a prior quarter ... 11   3135 . 60

12. Balance due (lines 10 – 11 = line 12) Make checks payable to the United States Treasury ... 12   0 . 00

13. Overpayment (If line 11 is more than line 10, write the difference here.) ... ☐ Apply to next return. ☐ Send a refund.   Next ►

For Privacy Act and Paperwork Reduction Act Notice, see the back of the Payment Voucher.   Cat. No. 17001Z   Form **941** (Rev. 1-2005)

Name (not your trade name): Mission Community Church
Employer identification number: 35-2938279

Part 2: Tell us about your deposit schedule for this quarter.

If you are unsure about whether you are a monthly schedule depositor or a semiweekly schedule depositor, see Pub. 15 (Circular E), section 11.

14. Write the state abbreviation for the state where you made your deposits OR write "MU" if you made your deposits in multiple states.

15. Check one: ☐ Line 10 is less than $2,500. Go to Part 3.
☑ You were a monthly schedule depositor for the entire quarter. Fill out your tax liability for each month. Then go to Part 3.

Tax liability: Month 1   1045 . 20
Month 2   1045 . 20
Month 3   1045 . 20
Total   3135 . 60   Total must equal line 10.

☐ You were a semiweekly schedule depositor for any part of this quarter. Fill out Schedule B (Form 941); Report of Tax Liability for Semiweekly Schedule Depositors, and attach it to this form.

Form 9901   OMB No. 1545-0029

Form W-3

DO NOT STAPLE OR FOLD

a Control number: 33333   For Official Use Only ►   OMB No. 1545-0008

b Kind of Payer: 941 ☒   Military ☐   943 ☐   Hshld. emp. ☐   Medicare govt. emp. ☐   CT-1 ☐

c Total number of Forms W-2: 2   d Establishment number

e Employer identification number (EIN): 35-2938279

f Employer's name: Mission Community Church
1620 E. Jones Street
South Bend, IN 46617

g Employer's address and ZIP code
h Other EIN used this year

15 State: IN   Employer's state ID number: 35-2938279

Contact person
Email address
Telephone number ( )
Fax number ( )

1 Wages, tips, other compensation	48000.00	2 Federal income tax withheld 8136.00
3 Social security wages	28800.00	4 Social security tax withheld 1785.60
5 Medicare wages and tips	28800.00	6 Medicare tax withheld 417.60
7 Social security tips		8 Allocated tips
9 Advance EIC payments		10 Dependent care benefits
11 Nonqualified plans		12 Deferred compensation 7800.00
13 For third-party sick pay use only		
14 Income tax withheld by payer of third-party sick pay		
16 State wages, tips, etc.	48000.00	17 State income tax 1998.00
18 Local wages, tips, etc.	48000.00	19 Local income tax 480.00
		For Official Use Only

Third-party sick pay ☐

Under penalties of perjury, I declare that I have examined this return and accompanying documents, and, to the best of my knowledge and belief, they are true, correct, and complete.

Signature ►   Title ►   Date ►

Form **W-3** Transmittal of Wage and Tax Statements   **2005**

Send this entire page with the entire Copy A page of Form(s) W-2 to the Social Security Administration. Photocopies are not acceptable.

Department of the Treasury
Internal Revenue Service

Example, Nonelecting Church

a Control number 00001	22222	Void ☐	For Official Use Only ▶ OMB No. 1545-0008	

b Employer identification number (EIN) 35-2938279	1 Wages, tips, other compensation 21000.00	2 Federal income tax withheld 6000.00

c Employer's name, address, and ZIP code	3 Social security wages	4 Social security tax withheld

Mission Community Church

1620 E. Jones Street
South Bend, IN 46617

5 Medicare wages and tips	6 Medicare tax withheld
7 Social security tips	8 Allocated tips

d Employee's social security number 483-12-0000	9 Advance EIC payment	10 Dependent care benefits

e Employee's first name and initial H. James	Last name Snodgrass	11 Nonqualified plans	12a See instructions for box 12 E 6000.00

13 Statutory employee ☐ Retirement plan ☒ Third-party sick pay ☐

12b

14 Other
Ordained - Not included above $24000 Parsonage Allowance

12c

12d

2309 E. Smith Street
South Bend, IN 46617

f Employee's address and ZIP code

15 State	Employer's state ID number	16 State wages, tips, etc.	17 State income tax	18 Local wages, tips, etc.	19 Local income tax	20 Locality name
IN	35-2938279	21000.00	1080.00	21000.00	264.00	St Joseph

Form **W-2** Wage and Tax Statement **2005** Department of the Treasury—Internal Revenue Service

For Privacy Act and Paperwork Reduction Act Notice, see back of Copy D.

Cat. No. 10134D

Do Not Cut, Fold, or Staple Forms on This Page — Do Not Cut, Fold, or Staple Forms on This Page

a Control number 00002	22222	Void ☐	For Official Use Only ▶ OMB No. 1545-0008	

b Employer identification number (EIN) 35-2938279	1 Wages, tips, other compensation 27000.00	2 Federal income tax withheld 2136.00

c Employer's name, address, and ZIP code	3 Social security wages 28800.00	4 Social security tax withheld 1785.60

Mission Community Church

1620 E. Jones Street
South Bend, IN 46617

5 Medicare wages and tips 28800.00	6 Medicare tax withheld 417.60
7 Social security tips	8 Allocated tips

d Employee's social security number 409-19-0000	9 Advance EIC payment	10 Dependent care benefits

e Employee's first name and initial Joseph	Last name Mop	11 Nonqualified plans	12a See instructions for box 12 E 1800.00

13 Statutory employee ☐ Retirement plan ☒ Third-party sick pay ☐

12b

14 Other

12c

12d

1621 E. Jones Street
South Bend, IN 46617

f Employee's address and ZIP code

15 State	Employer's state ID number	16 State wages, tips, etc.	17 State income tax	18 Local wages, tips, etc.	19 Local income tax	20 Locality name
IN	35-2938279	27000.00	918.00	27000.00	216.00	St Joseph

Form **W-2** Wage and Tax Statement **2005** Department of the Treasury—Internal Revenue Service

For Privacy Act and Paperwork Reduction Act Notice, see back of Copy D.

Cat. No. 10134D

Example, Electing Church (Filed Form 8274)

Form 941

Form 941 for 2005: Employer's Quarterly Federal Tax Return

(Rev. January 2005)   Department of the Treasury — Internal Revenue Service

9901   OMB No. 1545-0029

Employer identification number: 3 5 – 2 9 3 8 2 7 9

Name (not your trade name): Mission Community Church

Trade name (if any):

Address: 1620 E. Jones Street

Number   Street   Suite or room number

South Bend   IN   46617

City   State   ZIP code

Report for this Quarter... (Check one.)
- [ ] 1: January, February, March
- [ ] 2: April, May, June
- [ ] 3: July, August, September
- [✓] 4: October, November, December

Read the separate instructions before you fill out this form. Please type or print within the boxes.

Part 1: Answer these questions for this quarter.

1	Number of employees who received wages, tips, or other compensation for the pay period including: Mar. 12 (Quarter 1), June 12 (Quarter 2), Sept. 12 (Quarter 3), Dec. 12 (Quarter 4)	1	2
2	Wages, tips, and other compensation	2	12000.00
3	Total income tax withheld from wages, tips, and other compensation	3	3051.33
4	If no wages, tips, and other compensation are subject to social security or Medicare tax . . . Check and go to line 6.		✓

5 If no wages, tips, and other compensation are subject to social security or Medicare tax . . .

5 Taxable social security and Medicare wages and tips:

	Column 1		Column 2
5a Taxable social security wages		× .124 =	
5b Taxable social security tips		× .124 =	
5c Taxable Medicare wages & tips		× .029 =	

5d	Total social security and Medicare taxes (Column 2, lines 5a + 5b + 5c = line 5d)	5d	
6	Total taxes before adjustments (lines 3 + 5d = line 6)	6	3051.33
7	Tax adjustments (If your answer is a negative number, write it in brackets.):		
7a	Current quarter's fractions of cents	7a	.
7b	Current quarter's sick pay	7b	.
7c	Current quarter's adjustments for tips and group-term life insurance	7c	.
7d	Current year's income tax withholding (Attach Form 941c)	7d	.
7e	Prior quarters' social security and Medicare taxes (Attach Form 941c)	7e	.
7f	Special additions to federal income tax (reserved use)	7f	.
7g	Special additions to social security and Medicare (reserved use)	7g	.
7h	Total adjustments (Combine all amounts: lines 7a through 7g.)	7h	3051.33
8	Total taxes after adjustments (Combine lines 6 and 7h.)	8	3051.33
9	Advance earned income credit (EIC) payments made to employees	9	.
10	Total taxes after adjustment for advance EIC (lines 8 – 9 = line 10)	10	3051.33
11	Total deposits for this quarter, including overpayment applied from a prior quarter	11	3051.33
12	Balance due (lines 10 – 11 = line 12) Make checks payable to the United States Treasury .	12	0.00
13	Overpayment (If line 11 is more than line 10, write the difference here.)		Check one [ ] Apply to next return. [ ] Send a refund. Next ▶

For Privacy Act and Paperwork Reduction Act Notice, see the back of the Payment Voucher.

Cat. No. 17001Z   Form **941** (Rev. 1-2005)

Name (not your trade name): Mission Community Church

Employer identification number: 35-2938279

Part 2: Tell us about your deposit schedule for this quarter.

If you are unsure about whether you are a monthly schedule depositor or a semiweekly schedule depositor, see Pub. 15 (Circular E), section 11.

14 Write the state abbreviation for the state where you made your deposits OR write "MU" if you made your deposits in multiple states.

15 Check one:
- [ ] Line 10 is less than $2,500. Go to Part 3.
- [✓] You were a monthly schedule depositor for the entire quarter. Fill out your tax liability for each month. Then go to Part 3.

Tax liability:		
Month 1	1017.	11
Month 2	1017.	11
Month 3	1017.	11
Total	3051.	33 Total must equal line 10.

- [ ] You were a semiweekly schedule depositor for any part of this quarter. Fill out Schedule B (Form 941), Report of Tax Liability for Semiweekly Schedule Depositors, and attach it to this form.

Form W-3

DO NOT STAPLE OR FOLD

a Control number

For Official Use Only ▶   OMB No. 1545-0008

33333

b Kind of Payer:
- 941 [X]
- Military [ ]
- 943 [ ]
- Hshld. emp. [ ]
- Medicare govt. emp. [ ]
- CT-1 [ ]
- Third-party sick pay [ ]

d Establishment number

c Total number of Forms W-2: 2

e Employer identification number (EIN): 35-2938279

f Employer's name: Mission Community Church

g Employer's address and ZIP code: 1620 E. Jones Street   South Bend, IN 46617

h Other EIN used this year

15 State: IN   Employer's state ID number: 35-2938279

Contact person

Email address

Telephone number

Fax number

Box	Description	Amount
1	Wages, tips, other compensation	48000.00
2	Federal income tax withheld	12205.32
3	Social security wages	
4	Social security tax withheld	
5	Medicare wages and tips	
6	Medicare tax withheld	
7	Social security tips	
8	Allocated tips	
9	Advance EIC payments	
10	Dependent care benefits	
11	Nonqualified plans	
12	Deferred compensation	7800.00
13	For third-party sick pay use only	
14	Income tax withheld by payer of third-party sick pay	
16	State wages, tips, etc.	48000.00
17	State income tax	1998.00
18	Local wages, tips, etc.	48000.00
19	Local income tax	480.00
	For Official Use Only	

Under penalties of perjury, I declare that I have examined this return and accompanying documents, and, to the best of my knowledge and belief, they are true, correct, and complete.

Signature ▶   Title ▶   Date ▶

Form **W-3** Transmittal of Wage and Tax Statements   2005

Department of the Treasury   Internal Revenue Service

Send this entire page with the entire Copy A page of Form(s) W-2 to the Social Security Administration. Photocopies are not acceptable.

Example, Electing Church (Filed Form 8274)

a Control number 00001	22222	Void ☐	For Official Use Only ▶ OMB No. 1545-0008	

b Employer identification number (EIN) 35-2938279	1 Wages, tips, other compensation 21000.00	2 Federal income tax withheld 6000.00

c Employer's name, address, and ZIP code	3 Social security wages	4 Social security tax withheld

Mission Community Church

1620 E. Jones Street
South Bend, IN 46617

	5 Medicare wages and tips	6 Medicare tax withheld
	7 Social security tips	8 Allocated tips

d Employee's social security number 483-12-0000	9 Advance EIC payment	10 Dependent care benefits

e Employee's first name and initial H. James	Last name Snodgrass	11 Nonqualified plans	12a See instructions for box 12 E 6000.00

13 Statutory employee ☐   Retirement plan ☒   Third-party sick pay ☐

12b

2309 E. Smith Street
South Bend, IN 46617

14 Other
Ordained - Not included above $24000 Parsonage Allowance

12c

12d

f Employee's address and ZIP code

15 State Employer's state ID number	16 State wages, tips, etc.	17 State income tax	18 Local wages, tips, etc.	19 Local income tax	20 Locality name
IN 35-2938279	21000.00	1080.00	21000.00	264.00	St Joseph

Form **W-2** Wage and Tax Statement   **2005**   Department of the Treasury—Internal Revenue Service

Copy A For Social Security Administration — Send this entire page with Form W-3 to the Social Security Administration; photocopies are **not** acceptable.   Cat. No. 10134D

For Privacy Act and Paperwork Reduction Act Notice, see back of Copy D.

Do Not Cut, Fold, or Staple Forms on This Page — Do Not Cut, Fold, or Staple Forms on This Page

a Control number 00002	22222	Void ☐	For Official Use Only ▶ OMB No. 1545-0008	

b Employer identification number (EIN) 35-2938279	1 Wages, tips, other compensation 27000.00	2 Federal income tax withheld 6205.32

c Employer's name, address, and ZIP code	3 Social security wages	4 Social security tax withheld

Mission Community Church

1620 E. Jones Street
South Bend, IN 46617

	5 Medicare wages and tips	6 Medicare tax withheld
	7 Social security tips	8 Allocated tips

d Employee's social security number 409-19-0000	9 Advance EIC payment	10 Dependent care benefits

e Employee's first name and initial Joseph	Last name Mop	11 Nonqualified plans	12a See instructions for box 12 E 1800.00

13 Statutory employee ☐   Retirement plan ☒   Third-party sick pay ☐

12b

1621 E. Jones Street
South Bend, IN 46617

14 Other
Electing church employee to pay social security on Sch SE

12c

12d

f Employee's address and ZIP code

15 State Employer's state ID number	16 State wages, tips, etc.	17 State income tax	18 Local wages, tips, etc.	19 Local income tax	20 Locality name
IN 35-2938279	27000.00	918.00	27000.00	216.00	St Joseph

Form **W-2** Wage and Tax Statement   **2005**   Department of the Treasury—Internal Revenue Service

Copy A For Social Security Administration — Send this entire page with Form W-3 to the Social Security Administration; photocopies are **not** acceptable.   Cat. No. 10134D

For Privacy Act and Paperwork Reduction Act Notice, see back of Copy D.

Note: Joseph Mop's W-2, Box 2 above includes $4,069.32 additional federal withholdings to cover self-employment tax liability that he will incur as an employee of an electing church. The Form 941 on the previous page reflects $1,017.33 ($4,069.32 x ˘) additional federal withholdings on line 3 for the fourth quarter.

## CHAPTER SEVEN

Completed Income Tax Return

A typical problem with the actual tax forms filled out seems to be the most practical way to further explain the tax law as it applies to the minister. So study the following information about Rev. Snodgrass and how it is to be shown on the tax forms.

To illustrate that **$1,036.00 difference** in tax liability resulted from Rev. Snodgrass having an accountable reimbursement plan, we have prepared his return both ways. (For States that do not utilize itemized deductions, there will be additional savings.) The proration of unreimbursed employee business expenses, according to the Dalan Case is also illustrated. His W-2 would show **$32,896** without reimbursement, and as shown in Chapter Six, **$21,000** with reimbursement.

Facts of the Problem

Rev. H. James Snodgrass and Mary T., live at 2309 E. Smith St., South Bend, Indiana 46617. Rev. Snodgrass' S.S.# is 483-12-0000; Mary's S.S.# is 483-15-0000. They have three children, Ruth, Thomas and Samuel, ages 17, 15 & 12. Children under 17 qualify for the Child Tax Credit.

Rev. Snodgrass is minister of Mission Community Church and Mrs. Snodgrass is a nurse at a local hospital. Mary's wage on her W-2 is **$40,278** with **$3,406** federal tax withheld, $2,497 social security tax, $584 medicare tax, **$1,301** State tax and **$306** Local tax withheld. Combine his salary of **$21,000/ $32,896** and her salary of **$40,278** on line 7, Form 1040.

During the year Rev. Snodgrass received **$690** professional income from weddings and funerals. In earning this income, Rev. Snodgrass spent **$114** for booklets & **$12** for Schedule C tax prep fee.

The Snodgrasses own their own home (purchased 6-10-97) and they make payments of $743 a month. Their interest was **$8,081** and principal payments were **$835**. Real estate taxes were **$1,182**. Insurance was **$340**, and repairs were **$793**. They bought a new couch & chair for **$849**, and a new TV & VCR for **$560**. Decorator items (oval rug for living room) cost **$463**. Utilities and personal phone were **$2,738**. Miscellaneous household expenses Mary kept a record of came to **$642**.

Professional expenses are as follows: Tuition for class at seminary **$345**, Office Supplies **$86**, Religious Materials **$327**, Subscriptions **$132**, Home entertainment meals **$381**. He purchased **$649** worth of books this year and also bought a fax machine for **$529**. Rev. Snodgrass was reimbursed for the depreciation factor (**$612**) for current and bonus on fax machine plus prior year purchases and chose Sec. 179 expensing for this year's purchases of books. Travel expenses are as follows: Lodging **$363**, Meals away from home **$257**, Tips for meals **$48**, Cleaning while away from home **$22**. Local transportation expenses are as follows: Parking **$11**, Tolls **$34**. The total year's reimbursement for professional and travel expenses was **$3,267** as shown on the payroll sheet.

Business auto mileage from his log book was **20,879** miles. Total miles driven for the year was **33,648**. The church reimbursed mileage allowance of **40½¢** a mile (15,345 miles) before September 1 and **48½¢** a mile (5,534 miles) during the remainder of the year for a total of **$8,899**. Actual expenses amount to less than 40½¢/48½¢ per mile for reimbursement. The return showing non-reimbursed expenses shows the actual expenses for each auto on "Worksheet for Form 2106." Without reimbursement, vehicle #1 is computed by actual method as required, and vehicle #2 is computed by optional which is slightly better. Details of their auto trade are shown on the "Auto Basis Worksheets."

Itemized deductions are as follows: Medical expenses were not greater than 7.5% of AGI. Additional State tax last spring of **$152**, Real Estate Tax is used again **$1,182**, personal property tax on the family auto of **$78**, personal property tax of **$456** on vehicle #2 must be deducted on Schedule A as taxes. He can not use auto interest of $639 on Schedule A (vehicle #1 $158 & vehicle #2 $481). Interest on home is used again **$8,081**. Personal interest of $753 can not be used. Contributions were to Mission Community Church **$5,308**, Central Bible College **$200**. Total tax return preparation fee **$165/205** less Schedule C portion - $12=**$153/193**, Nursing license **$135**, Uniforms, shoes, nylons and cost of cleaning them **$375**.

Due to the fact a minister is self-employed for social security purposes, we are able to use the business percentage of personal property tax, auto interest **$549** and business portion of tax preparation fee **$63/ 87** as a reduction of S.S. base.

Study the completed forms on the following pages to see how the Snodgrass return is prepared.

Without Accountable Reimbursement Plan

Form 1040 (2005)   Page 2

Tax and Credits	38	Amount from line 37 (adjusted gross income)	38	78,016
	39a	Check if: ☐ You were born before January 2, 1941, ☐ Blind. ☐ Spouse was born before January 2, 1941, ☐ Blind. **Total boxes checked ▶** 39a	
Standard Deduction for—	b	If your spouse itemizes on a separate return or you were a dual-status alien, see page 31 and check here ▶ 39b ☐	
• People who checked any box on line 39a or 39b or who can be claimed as a dependent, see page 31.	40	Itemized deductions (from Schedule A) or your **standard deduction** (see left margin)	40	24,723
	41	Subtract line 40 from line 38	41	53,293
	42	If line 38 is $109,475 or less, multiply $3,200 by the total number of exemptions claimed on line 6d. If line 38 is over $109,475, see the worksheet on page 33	42	16,000
	43	**Taxable income.** Subtract line 42 from line 41. If line 42 is more than line 41, enter -0-	43	37,293
• All others:	44	**Tax** (see page 33). Check if any tax is from: **a** ☐ Form(s) 8814 **b** ☐ Form 4972	44	4,861
Single or Married filing separately, $5,000	45	Alternative minimum tax (see page 35). Attach Form 6251	45	
	46	Add lines 44 and 45 ▶	46	4,861
Married filing jointly or Qualifying widow(er), $10,000	47	Foreign tax credit. Attach Form 1116 if required	47	
	48	Credit for child and dependent care expenses. Attach Form 2441	48	
	49	Credit for the elderly or the disabled. Attach Schedule R	49	
Head of household, $7,300	50	Education credits. Attach Form 8863	50	
	51	Retirement savings contributions credit. Attach Form 8880	51	
	52	Child tax credit (see page 37). Attach Form 8901 if required	52	2,000
	53	Adoption credit. Attach Form 8839	53	
	54	Credits from: **a** ☐ Form 8396 **b** ☐ Form 8859	54	
	55	Other credits. Check applicable box(es): **a** ☐ Form 3800 **b** ☐ Form 8801 **c** ☐ Specify	55	
	56	Add lines 47 through 55. These are your **total credits**	56	2,000
	57	Subtract line 56 from line 46. If line 56 is more than line 46, enter -0- ▶	57	2,861
Other Taxes	58	Self-employment tax. Attach Schedule SE	58	6,550
	59	Social security and Medicare tax on tip income not reported to employer. Attach Form 4137	59	
	60	Additional tax on IRAs, other qualified retirement plans, etc. Attach Form 5329 if required	60	
	61	Advance earned income credit payments from Form(s) W-2	61	
	62	Household employment taxes. Attach Schedule H	62	
	63	Add lines 57 through 62. This is your **total tax** ▶	63	9,411
Payments	64	Federal income tax withheld from Forms W-2 and 1099	64	9406
	65	2005 estimated tax payments and amount applied from 2004 return	65	
If you have a qualifying child, attach Schedule EIC.	66a	Earned income credit (EIC)	66a	
	b	Nontaxable combat pay election ▶	66b	
	67	Excess social security and tier 1 RRTA tax withheld (see page 54)	67	
	68	Additional child tax credit. Attach Form 8812	68	
	69	Amount paid with request for extension to file (see page 54)	69	
	70	Payments from: **a** ☐ Form 2439 **b** ☐ Form 4136 **c** ☐ Form 8885	70	
	71	Add lines 64, 65, 66a, and 67 through 70. These are your **total payments** ▶	71	9406
Refund Direct deposit? See page 54 and fill in 73b, 73c, and 73d.	72	If line 71 is more than line 63, subtract line 63 from line 71. This is the amount you **overpaid**	72	
	73a	Amount of line 72 you want **refunded to you** ▶	73a	
	▶ b	Routing number ▶ c Type: ☐ Checking ☐ Savings	
	▶ d	Account number	
Amount You Owe	74	Amount of line 72 you want **applied to your 2006 estimated tax** ▶ 74	
	75	**Amount you owe.** Subtract line 71 from line 63. For details on how to pay, see page 55 ▶	75	5
	76	Estimated tax penalty (see page 55)	76	
Third Party Designee	Do you want to allow another person to discuss this return with the IRS (see page 56)? ☐ **Yes.** Complete the following. ☐ **No**
	Designee's name ▶ Phone no. ▶ Personal identification number (PIN) ▶
Sign Here Joint return? See page 17. Keep a copy for your records.	Under penalties of perjury, I declare that I have examined this return and accompanying schedules and statements, and to the best of my knowledge and belief, they are true, correct, and complete. Declaration of preparer (other than taxpayer) is based on all information of which preparer has any knowledge.
	Your signature Date Your occupation **Minister** Daytime phone number ( )
	Spouse's signature. If a joint return, **both** must sign. Date Spouse's occupation **Nurse**
Paid Preparer's Use Only	Preparer's signature ▶ Date Check if self-employed ☐ Preparer's SSN or PTIN
	Firm's name (or yours if self-employed), address, and ZIP code ▶ EIN Phone no. ( )

Form **1040** (2005)

Form 1040 Department of the Treasury—Internal Revenue Service
U.S. Individual Income Tax Return **2005** (99) IRS Use Only—Do not write or staple in this space.

For the year Jan. 1–Dec. 31, 2005, or other tax year beginning , 2005, ending , 20   OMB No. 1545-0074

Label (See instructions on page 16.)
Your first name and initial: **H. James**   Last name: **Snodgrass**
Your social security number: **483 12 0000**

If a joint return, spouse's first name and initial: **Mary T.**   Last name: **Snodgrass**
Spouse's social security number: **483 15 0000**   ◀ You must enter your SSN(s) above.

Home address (number and street). If you have a P.O. box, see page 16.   Apt. no.
2309 E. Smith Street

City, town or post office, state, and ZIP code. If you have a foreign address, see page 16.
South Bend, IN 46617

Checking a box below will not change your tax or refund.

Presidential Election Campaign ▶ Check here if you, or your spouse if filing jointly, want $3 to go to this fund (see page 16) ▶ ☑ You ☑ Spouse

Filing Status
Check only one box.
1 ☐ Single
2 ☑ Married filing jointly (even if only one had income)
3 ☐ Married filing separately. Enter spouse's SSN above and full name here. ▶
4 ☐ Head of household (with qualifying person). (See page 17.) If the qualifying person is a child but not your dependent, enter this child's name here. ▶
5 ☐ Qualifying widow(er) with dependent child (see page 17)

Exemptions
6a ☑ **Yourself.** If someone can claim you as a dependent, **do not** check box 6a
b ☑ **Spouse**
Boxes checked on 6a and 6b: **2**

c Dependents:
(1) First name Last name	(2) Dependent's social security number	(3) Dependent's relationship to you	(4) ☐ if qualifying child for child tax credit (see page 18)
Ruth A Snodgrass	483 13 0000	Child	☑
Thomas A Snodgrass	485 14 0000	Child	☑
Samuel A Snodgrass	486 15 0000	Child	☑

If more than four dependents, see page 18.

No. of children on 6c who:
• lived with you: **3**
• did not live with you due to divorce or separation (see page 18):
Dependents on 6c not entered above:

d Total number of exemptions claimed ▶ Add numbers on lines above ▶ **5**

Income
Attach Form(s) W-2 here. Also attach Forms W-2G and 1099-R if tax was withheld.

If you did not get a W-2, see page 19.

Enclose, but do not attach, any payment. Also, please use Form 1040-V.

7	Wages, salaries, tips, etc. Attach Form(s) W-2 **Excess Parsonage Allowance** 7,517	7	80,691
8a	Taxable interest. Attach Schedule B if required	8a	
b	Tax-exempt interest. **Do not** include on line 8a	8b	
9a	Ordinary dividends. Attach Schedule B if required	9a	
b	Qualified dividends (see page 20)	9b	
10	Taxable refunds, credits, or offsets of state and local income taxes (see page 20)	10	
11	Alimony received	11	
12	Business income or (loss). Attach Schedule C or C-EZ	12	600
13	Capital gain or (loss). Attach Schedule D if required. If not required, check here ▶ ☐	13	
14	Other gains or (losses). Attach Form 4797	14	
15a	IRA distributions 15a b Taxable amount (see page 22)	15b	
16a	Pensions and annuities 16a b Taxable amount (see page 22)	16b	
17	Rental real estate, royalties, partnerships, S corporations, trusts, etc. Attach Schedule E	17	
18	Farm income or (loss). Attach Schedule F	18	
19	Unemployment compensation	19	
20a	Social security benefits 20a b Taxable amount (see page 24)	20b	
21	Other income. List type and amount (see page 24)	21	
22	Add the amounts in the far right column for lines 7 through 21. This is your **total income** ▶	22	81,291

Adjusted Gross Income

23	Educator expenses (see page 26)	23	
24	Certain business expenses of reservists, performing artists, and fee-basis government officials. Attach Form 2106 or 2106-EZ	24	
25	Health savings account deduction. Attach Form 8889	25	
26	Moving expenses. Attach Form 3903	26	
27	One-half of self-employment tax. Attach Schedule SE	27	3,275
28	Self-employed SEP, SIMPLE, and qualified plans	28	
29	Self-employed health insurance deduction (see page 30)	29	
30	Penalty on early withdrawal of savings	30	
31a	Alimony paid b Recipient's SSN ▶	31a	
32	IRA deduction (see page XX)	32	
33	Student loan interest deduction (see page XX)	33	
34	Tuition and fees deduction (see page XX)	34	
35	Domestic production activities deduction. Attach Form 8903	35	
36	Add lines 23 through 31a and 32 through 35	36	3,275
37	Subtract line 36 from line 22. This is your **adjusted gross income** ▶	37	78,016

For Disclosure, Privacy Act, and Paperwork Reduction Act Notice, see page 75.   Cat. No. 11320B   Form **1040** (2005)

Rev Snodgrass........$32,896
Mrs. Snodgrass........$40,278
Excess Parsonage........$7,517

Without Accountable Reimbursement Plan

SCHEDULE C-EZ (Form 1040)

Department of the Treasury
Internal Revenue Service

Net Profit From Business
(Sole Proprietorship)

▶ Partnerships, joint ventures, etc., must file Form 1065 or 1065-B.
▶ Attach to Form 1040 or 1041. ▶ See instructions on back.

OMB No. 1545-0074
2005
Attachment Sequence No. 09A

Name of proprietor: H. James Snodgrass
Social security number (SSN): 483 : 12 : 0000

Part I General Information

You May Use Schedule C-EZ Instead of Schedule C Only If You:

- Had business expenses of $5,000 or less.
- Use the cash method of accounting.
- Did not have an inventory at any time during the year.
- Did not have a net loss from your business.
- Had only one business as either a sole proprietor or statutory employee.

And You:

- Had no employees during the year.
- Are not required to file Form 4562, Depreciation and Amortization, for this business. See the instructions for Schedule C, line 13, on page C-4 to find out if you must file.
- Do not deduct expenses for business use of your home.
- Do not have prior year unallowed passive activity losses from this business.

A Principal business or profession, including product or service: **Honorariums**
B Enter code from pages C-7, 8, & 9 ▶ 8 1 3 0 0 0

C Business name. If no separate business name, leave blank.
D Employer ID number (EIN), if any

E Business address (including suite or room no.). Address not required if same as on Form 1040, page 1.
City, town or post office, state, and ZIP code

Part II Figure Your Net Profit

1	Gross receipts. Caution. If this income was reported to you on Form W-2 and the "Statutory employee" box on that form was checked, see Statutory Employees in the instructions for Schedule C, line 1, on page C-3 and check here ▶ □	1	5,508
2	Total expenses (see instructions). If more than $5,000, you must use Schedule C.	2	690
3	Net profit. Subtract line 2 from line 1. If less than zero, you must use Schedule C. Enter on Form 1040, line 12, and also on Schedule SE, line 2. (Statutory employees do not report this amount on Schedule SE, line 2. Estates and trusts, enter on Form 1041, line 3.)	3	90 ... 600

Part III Information on Your Vehicle. Complete this part only if you are claiming car or truck expenses on line 2.

4 When did you place your vehicle in service for business purposes? (month, day, year) ▶ / /

5 Of the total number of miles you drove your vehicle during 2005, enter the number of miles you used your vehicle for:
a Business .... b Commuting (see instructions) .... c Other ....

6 Do you (or your spouse) have another vehicle available for personal use? .... □ Yes □ No

7 Was your vehicle available for personal use during off-duty hours? .... □ Yes □ No

8a Do you have evidence to support your deduction? .... □ Yes □ No
b If "Yes," is the evidence written? .... □ Yes □ No

For Paperwork Reduction Act Notice, see Form 1040 instructions. Cat. No. 14374D Schedule C-EZ (Form 1040) 2005

SCHEDULES A&B (Form 1040)

Department of the Treasury
Internal Revenue Service (99)

Schedule A—Itemized Deductions
(Schedule B is on back)

▶ Attach to Form 1040. ▶ See Instructions for Schedules A and B (Form 1040).

OMB No. 1545-0074
2005
Attachment Sequence No. 07

Name(s) shown on Form 1040: H. James & Mary T. Snodgrass
Your social security number: 483 : 12 : 0000

Line 5 computation below:
State withholdings ($1,080 + $1,301) $2,381
Local withholdings ($264 + $306) .... $ 570
State tax paid last spring .... $ 152

Medical and Dental Expenses

Caution. Do not include expenses reimbursed or paid by others.
1	Medical and dental expenses (see page A-2)	1	3,103
2	Enter amount from Form 1040, line 38	2	
3	Multiply line 2 by 7.5% (.075)	3	
4	Subtract line 3 from line 1. If line 3 is more than line 1, enter -0-	4	4,819

Taxes You Paid (See page A-2.)

5	State and local (check only one box): a □ Income taxes, or b □ General sales taxes (see page A-3)	5	3,103
6	Real estate taxes (see page A-3)	6	1,182
7	Personal property taxes	7	534
8	Other taxes. List type and amount ▶	8	
9	Add lines 5 through 8	9	4,819

Interest You Paid (See page A-3.)

Note. Personal interest is not deductible.

10	Home mortgage interest and points reported to you on Form 1098	10	8,081
11	Home mortgage interest not reported to you on Form 1098. If paid to the person from whom you bought the home, see page A-4 and show that person's name, identifying no., and address ▶	11	
12	Points not reported to you on Form 1098. See page A-4 for special rules	12	
13	Investment interest. Attach Form 4952 if required. (See page A-4.)	13	
14	Add lines 10 through 13	14	8,081

Gifts to Charity
If you made a gift and got a benefit for it, see page A-4.

15	Gifts by cash or check. If you made any gift of $250 or more, see page A-4	15	5,508
16	Other than by cash or check. If any gift of $250 or more, see page A-4. You must attach Form 8283 if over $500	16	
17	Carryover from prior year	17	
18	Add lines 15 through 17	18	5,508

Casualty and Theft Losses

19	Casualty or theft loss(es). Attach Form 4684. (See page A-5.)	19	

Job Expenses and Most Other Miscellaneous Deductions (See page A-5.)

20	Unreimbursed employee expenses—job travel, union dues, job education, etc. Attach Form 2106 or 2106-EZ if required. (See page A-6.) ▶ Nursing Exp. 510: Form 2106 10,318 Less IRC 265 Limitation -2,953	20	7,875
21	Tax preparation fees	21	193
22	Other expenses—investment, safe deposit box, etc. List type and amount ▶	22	
23	Add lines 20 through 22	23	7,875
24	Enter amount from Form 1040, line 38	24	78,016
25	Multiply line 24 by 2% (.02)	25	1,560
26	Subtract line 25 from line 23. If line 25 is more than line 23, enter -0-	26	6,315

Other Miscellaneous Deductions

27	Other—from list on page A-6. List type and amount ▶	27	

Total Itemized Deductions

28	Is Form 1040, line 38, over $145,950 (over $72,975 if married filing separately)? □ No. Your deduction is not limited. Add the amounts in the far right column for lines 4 through 27. Also, enter this amount on Form 1040, line 40. □ Yes. Your deduction may be limited. See page A-6 for the amount to enter.	28	24,723
29	If you elect to itemize deductions even though they are less than your standard deduction, check here ▶ □		

For Paperwork Reduction Act Notice, see Form 1040 instructions. Cat. No. 11330X Schedule A (Form 1040) 2005

Without Accountable Reimbursement Plan

Form 2106 (2005)

Part II   Vehicle Expenses

Section A—General Information (You must complete this section if you are claiming vehicle expenses.)

		(a) Vehicle 1	(b) Vehicle 2
11	Enter the date the vehicle was placed in service	1/ 6 /02	3/ 10 /05
12	Total miles the vehicle was driven during 2005	9,760 miles	23,888 miles
13	Business miles included on line 12	5,320 miles	15,559 miles
14	Percent of business use. Divide line 13 by line 12	54.51 %	65.13 %
15	Average daily roundtrip commuting distance	8 miles	8 miles
16	Commuting miles included on line 12	320 miles	2,176 miles
17	Other miles. Add lines 13 and 16 and subtract the total from line 12	4,120 miles	6,153 miles
18	Do you (or your spouse) have another vehicle available for personal use?	☑ Yes ☐ No	
19	Was your vehicle available for personal use during off-duty hours?	☑ Yes ☐ No	
20	Do you have evidence to support your deduction?	☑ Yes ☐ No	
21	If "Yes," is the evidence written?	☑ Yes ☐ No	

Section B—Standard Mileage Rate (See the instructions for Part II to find out whether to complete this section or Section C.)

		(a) Vehicle 1	(b) Vehicle 2
22a	Multiply business miles driven **before** September 1, 2005 by 40.5¢ (.405)	4,060	10,025 miles before 9/1/05
b	Multiply business miles driven **after** August 31, 2005 by 48.5¢ (.485)	2,684	5,534 miles after 8/31/05
c	Add lines 22a and 22b. Enter the result here and on line 1	6,744	

Section C—Actual Expenses

		(a) Vehicle 1	(b) Vehicle 2
23	Gasoline, oil, repairs, vehicle insurance, etc.	799	799
24a	Vehicle rentals		
b	Inclusion amount (see instructions)		
c	Subtract line 24b from line 24a		
25	Value of employer-provided vehicle (applies only if 100% of annual lease value was included on Form W-2—see instructions)		
26	Add lines 23, 24c, and 25		
27	Multiply line 26 by the percentage on line 14	436	
28	Depreciation (see instructions)	484	
29	Add lines 27 and 28. Enter total here and on line 1	920	

Section D—Depreciation of Vehicles (Use this section only if you owned the vehicle and are completing Section C for the vehicle.)

54.51%

		(a) Vehicle 1	(b) Vehicle 2
30	Enter cost or other basis (see instructions)	49,923	Line G from Auto Basis Worksheet $27,213 divided by 54.51%
31	Enter section 179 deduction (see instructions)		
32	Multiply line 30 by line 14 (see instructions if you claimed the section 179 deduction or special allowance)	16,858	$49,923 x .5451 - $10,355 Special Allowance
33	Enter depreciation method and percentage (see instructions)	200 DB% .1152	
34	Multiply line 32 by the percentage on line 33 (see instructions)	971	1,942 x ½ = 971; Year of Sale Limitation
35	Add lines 31 and 34	484	
36	Enter the applicable limit explained in the line 36 instructions		
37	Multiply line 36 by the percentage on line 14	484	968 x ½ = 484; Year of Sale Limitation
38	Enter the **smaller** of line 35 or line 37. If you skipped lines 36 and 37, enter the amount from line 35. Also enter this amount on line 28 above	484	

Form **2106** (2005)

Form 2106

Department of the Treasury
Internal Revenue Service (99)

Employee Business Expenses

▶ See separate instructions.
▶ Attach to Form 1040.

OMB No. 1545-0074

2005

Attachment Sequence No. **54**

Your name: **H. James Snodgrass**   Occupation in which you incurred expenses: **Minister**   Social security number: **483 : 12 : 0000**

Part I   Employee Business Expenses and Reimbursements

Step 1   Enter Your Expenses

			Column A Other Than Meals and Entertainment	Column B Meals and Entertainment
1	Vehicle expense from line 22c or line 29. (Rural mail carriers: See instructions.) **$920 vehicle 1 + $6,744 vehicle 2**	1	7,664	
2	Parking fees, tolls, and transportation, including train, bus, etc., that **did not** involve overnight travel or commuting to and from work	2	45	
3	Travel expense while away from home overnight, including lodging, airplane, car rental, etc. **Do not** include meals and entertainment	3	385	
4	Business expenses not included on lines 1 through 3. **Do not** include meals and entertainment.	4	1,881	
5	Meals and entertainment expenses (see instructions)	5		686
6	**Total expenses.** In Column A, add lines 1 through 4 and enter the result. In Column B, enter the amount from line 5	6	9,975	686

Note: *If you were not reimbursed for any expenses in Step 1, skip line 7 and enter the amount from line 6 on line 8.*

Step 2   Enter Reimbursements Received From Your Employer for Expenses Listed in Step 1

7	Enter reimbursements received from your employer that were **not** reported to you in box 1 of Form W-2. Include any reimbursements reported under code "L" in box 12 of your Form W-2 (see instructions)	7		

Step 3   Figure Expenses To Deduct on Schedule A (Form 1040)

8	Subtract line 7 from line 6. If zero or less, enter -0-. However, if line 7 is greater than line 6 in Column A, report the excess as income on Form 1040, line 7	8	9,975	686

Note: *If both columns of line 8 are zero, you cannot deduct employee business expenses. Stop here and attach Form 2106 to your return.*

9	In Column A, enter the amount from line 8. In Column B, multiply line 8 by 50% (.50). (Employees subject to Department of Transportation (DOT) hours of service limits: Multiply meal expenses incurred while away from home on business by 70% (.70) instead of 50%. For details, see instructions.)	9	9,975	343
10	Add the amounts on line 9 of both columns and enter the total here. **Also, enter the total on Schedule A (Form 1040), line 20.** (Reservists, qualified performing artists, fee-basis state or local government officials, and individuals with disabilities: See the instructions for special rules on where to enter the total.) ▶	10	10,318	

For Paperwork Reduction Act Notice, see instructions.   Cat. No. 11700N   Form **2106** (2005)

Without Accountable Reimbursement Plan

SCHEDULE SE (Form 1040)
Department of the Treasury
Internal Revenue Service

Self-Employment Tax

► Attach to Form 1040. ► See Instructions for Schedule SE (Form 1040).

OMB No. 1545-0074
2005
Attachment Sequence No. 17

Name of person with **self-employment** income (as shown on Form 1040)
H. James Snodgrass

Social security number of person with **self-employment** income ► 483 : 12 : 0000

Who Must File Schedule SE

You must file Schedule SE if:

- You had net earnings from self-employment from **other than** church employee income (line 4 of Short Schedule SE or line 4c of Long Schedule SE) of $400 or more **or**
- You had church employee income of $108.28 or more. Income from services you performed as a minister or a member of a religious order is **not** church employee income (see page SE-1).

Note. Even if you had a loss or a small amount of income from self-employment, it may be to your benefit to file Schedule SE and use either "optional method" in Part II of Long Schedule SE (see page SE-3).

Exception. If your only self-employment income was from earnings as a minister, member of a religious order, or Christian Science practitioner **and** you filed Form 4361 and received IRS approval not to be taxed on those earnings, **do not** file Schedule SE. Instead, write "Exempt–Form 4361" on Form 1040, line 58.

May I Use Short Schedule SE or Must I Use Long Schedule SE?

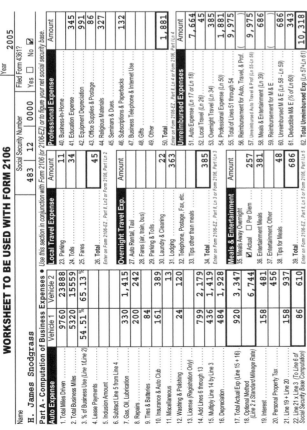

Section A—Short Schedule SE. Caution. Read above to see if you can use Short Schedule SE.

1 Net farm profit or (loss) from Schedule F, line 36, and farm partnerships, Schedule K-1 (Form 1065), box 14, code A	**1**	
2 Net profit or (loss) from Schedule C, line 31; Schedule C-EZ, line 3; Schedule K-1 (Form 1065), box 14, code A (other than farming); and Schedule K-1 (Form 1065-B), box 9. Ministers and members of religious orders, see page SE-1 for amounts to report on this line. See page SE-2 for other income to report **$45,759** from "Worksheet to Be Used with Form 2106" + $600 from Sch. C	**2**	46,359
3 Combine lines 1 and 2.	**3**	46,359
4 **Net earnings from self-employment.** Multiply line 3 by 92.35% (.9235). If less than $400, **do not** file this schedule; you do not owe self-employment tax	**4**	42,813
5 **Self-employment tax.** If the amount on line 4 is:		
• $90,000 or less, multiply line 4 by 15.3% (.153). Enter the result here and on **Form 1040, line 58.**		
• More than $90,000, multiply line 4 by 2.9% (.029). Then, add $11,160.00 to the result. Enter the total here and on **Form 1040, line 58.**	**5**	6,550
6 **Deduction for one-half of self-employment tax.** Multiply line 5 by 50% (.5). Enter the result here and on **Form 1040, line 27**	**6** 3,275	

For Paperwork Reduction Act Notice, see Form 1040 instructions. Cat. No. 11358Z   Schedule SE (Form 1040) 2005

WORKSHEET TO BE USED WITH FORM 2106

Name: **H. James Snodgrass**   Social Security Number **483 12 0000**   Year **2005**   Filed Form 4361? Yes ☐ No ☑

Part A - Computation of Business Expenses (Sec. 265)

Auto Expense	Vehicle 1	Vehicle 2
1. Total Miles Driven	9760	23888
2. Total Business Miles	5320	15559
3. % of Business Use (Line 1/Line 2)	54.51%	65.13%
4. Lease Payments		
5. Inclusion Amount		
6. Subtract Line 5 from Line 4		
7. Gas, Oil, Lubrication	330	242
8. Repairs	200	
9. Tires & Batteries	84	
10. Insurance & Auto Club	161	389
11. Miscellaneous		13
12. Washing & Polishing	24	120
13. License (Registration Only)		
14. Add Lines 6 through 13	799	2,179
15. Multiply Line 14 by Line 3	436	1,419
16. Depreciation	484	1,928
17. Total Actual Exp (Ln 15 + 16)	920	3,347
18. Optional Method (Line 2 x Standard Mileage Rate)		
19. Interest	158	481
20. Personal Property Tax		456
21. Line 19 + Line 20	158	937
22. Line 21 x Line 3 (To Line 6 of Social Security Base Computation)	86	610

Local Travel Expense

	Amount
23. Parking	11
24. Tolls	34
25. Fares	45
26. Total	

Enter on Form 2106-EZ, Part II, Ln 2 or Form 2106, Part Ln 2

Overnight Travel Exp.

	Amount
27. Auto Rental, Taxi	1,415
28. Fares (air, train, bus)	
29. Parking & Tolls	
30. Laundry & Cleaning	22
31. Miscellaneous	
32. Telephone, Postage, Fax, etc.	363
33. Tips other than meals	
34. Total	385

Enter on Form 2106-EZ, Part II, Ln 3 or Form 2106, Part Ln 3

Meals & Entertainment

	Amount
35. Meals Away Overnight ☑ Actual ☐ Per Diem	257
36. Entertainment Meals	381
37. Entertainment, Other	
38. Tips for Meals	48
39. Total	686

Enter on Form 2106-EZ, Part II, Ln 5 or Form 2106, Part Ln 5

Professional Expense

	Amount
40. Business-In-Home	
41. Education Expense	345
42. Equipment Depreciation	991
43. Office Supplies & Postage	86
44. Religious Materials	327
45. Seminars & Dues	
46. Subscriptions & Paperbacks	132
47. Business Telephone & Internet Use	
48. Gifts	
49. Other	
50. Total	1,881

Enter on Form 2106-EZ, Part II, Ln 4 or Form 2106, Part Ln 4

Unreimbursed Expenses

	Amount
51. Auto Expense (Ln 17 or Ln 18)	7,664
52. Local Travel (Ln 26)	45
53. Overnight Travel (Ln 34)	385
54. Professional Expense (Ln 50)	1,881
55. Total of Lines 51 through 54	9,975
56. Reimbursement for Auto, Travel, & Prof.	9,975
57. Unreimbursed Auto Travel & Prof (Ln 55-Ln 56)	
58. Meals & Entertainment (Ln 39)	686
59. Reimbursement for M & E	
60. Unreimbursed M & E (Ln 58 - Ln 59)	686
61. Deductible M& E (½ of Ln 60)	343
62. Total Unreimbursed Exp (Ln 57+Ln 61)	10,318

Part B - Unreimbused Expense Allocation

Use if Filing Form 2106 or Sch. C or C-EZ and claiming expense deductions

Employee Business Expenses	A. Taxable Compensation	B. Total Compensation
1. Wages from W-2	32,896	32,896
2. Unused Parsonage Allowance	7,517	
3. Parsonage Allowance Designated		24,000
4. FRV of Parsonage Provided		
5. Gross Income / Sch C or C-EZ	690	690
6. Recapture of Auto Depreciation		
7. Total for Columns A & B	41,103	57,586
8. Inclusion Percentage (Ln 7 Col. A Divided by Col. B)	71.38%	

Employee Business Expenses	Amount
9. Expense from Form 2106-EZ, Ln 6 or Form 2106, Line 10	10,318
10. Inclusion % from Ln 8	71.38%
11. Deductible Expenses to Sch A, Ln 20 (Ln 9 x Ln 10)	7,365
12. Expenses Disallowed (Ln 9 - Ln 11)	2,953

Sch C or Sch C-EZ	Amount
13. Total Expense from Sch C or C-EZ	126
14. Inclusion % from Ln 8	71.38%
15. Deductible Expense (Ln 13 x Ln 14)	90
16. Expenses Disallowed (Ln 13 - Ln 15)	36

Part C - Computation of Social Security Base

If exempt, omit

	Amount
1. Salary from W-2	32,896
2. Value of Parsonage Provided	
3. Parsonage Allowance (Part D, Ln 16)	24,000
4. Recapture of Auto Depreciation	
5. Less Business Portion of Tax Prep	(87)
6. Less Business % of Auto Int & Tax (Part A, Ln 22)	(696)
7. Less Expenses Disallowed on Sch C (Part B, Ln 16)	(36)
8. Less Unreimbursed Bus Exp (Form 2106 or Part A, Ln 62)	(10,318)
9. Total (Enter on SE)	45,759

Part D - Computation of Parsonage Allowance

If you own your home, use both Columns A & B. Otherwise, use Column B only.

	First Home			Second Home	
	Column A FRV Computation	Column B Expenses Paid by Minister		Column A FRV Computation	Column B Expenses Paid by Minister
Value of Parsonage Provided by Church					
Value of Home Owned	$ 150,000			$	
FMV of Home Owned					
1. Fair Rental Value of Home Owned	18,000				
2. Fair Rental Value of Furnishings	5,400				
3. Rent Paid					
4. Closing Costs / Downpayment					
5. Principal Payments		835			
6. Real Estate Taxes		1,182			
7. Mortgage Interest		8,081			
8. Insurance		340			
9. Repairs & Upkeep		793			
10. Furniture, Appliances, etc.		1,409			
11. Decorator Items	463	463			
12. Utilities	2,738	2,738			
13. Miscellaneous Supplies	642	642			
14. Total	27243	16,483			
15. Lesser of Line 14, Column A (if applicable) or Column B.		16,483	Pension ☐		
16. Amount Designated *(Pension not subject to Self-Employment tax)*	24,000		Pension ☐		
17. If Line 16 is greater than Ln 15, enter the difference here and as income on Form 1040, Line 7; or if amount designated is included in error on W-2, enter lesser of Line 15 or Line 16 as a deduction from Form 1040, Line 21		7,517			

Without Accountable Reimbursement Plan

Form 8824
Department of the Treasury
Internal Revenue Service

Like-Kind Exchanges
(and section 1043 conflict-of-interest sales)

▶ Attach to your tax return.

OMB No. 1545-1190

2005

Attachment Sequence No. 109

Name(s) shown on tax return: H. James & Mary T. Snodgrass

Identifying number: 483 12 0000

Part I — Information on the Like-Kind Exchange

Note: *If the property described on line 1 or line 2 is real or personal property located outside the United States, indicate the country.*

1 Description of like-kind property given up ▶ 2001 Chevy Cavalier

2 Description of like-kind property received ▶ 2004 Dodge Intrepid

3 Date like-kind property given up was originally acquired (month, day, year) . . . . **3**   1/ 6 /02

4 Date you actually transferred your property to other party (month, day, year) . . . . . **4**   3/ 10 /05

5 Date like-kind property you received was identified by written notice to another party (month, day, year). See instructions for 45-day written notice requirement . . . . **5**   3/ 10 /05

6 Date you actually received the like-kind property from other party (month, day, year). See instructions **6**   3/ 10 /05

7 Was the exchange of the property given up or received made with a related party, either directly or indirectly (such as through an intermediary)? See instructions. If "Yes," complete Part II. If "No," go to Part III . . . . ☐ Yes ☑ No

Part II — Related Party Exchange Information

8 Name of related party | Relationship to you | Related party's identifying number

Address (no., street, and apt., room, or suite no., city or town, state, and ZIP code)

9 During this tax year (and before the date that is 2 years after the last transfer of property that was part of the exchange), did the related party directly or indirectly (such as through an intermediary) sell or dispose of any part of the like-kind property received from you in the exchange? . . . . ☐ Yes ☐ No

10 During this tax year (and before the date that is 2 years after the last transfer of property that was part of the exchange), did you sell or dispose of any part of the like-kind property you received? . . . . ☐ Yes ☐ No

11 If both lines 9 and 10 are "No" and this is the year of the exchange, go to Part III. If both lines 9 and 10 are "No" and this is *not* the year of the exchange, stop here. If either line 9 or line 10 is "Yes," complete Part III and report on this year's tax return the deferred gain or (loss) from line 24 *unless* one of the exceptions on line 11 applies.

If one of the exceptions below applies to the disposition, check the applicable box:

a ☐ The disposition was after the death of either of the related parties.

b ☐ The disposition was an involuntary conversion, and the threat of conversion occurred after the exchange.

c ☐ You can establish to the satisfaction of the IRS that neither the exchange nor the disposition had tax avoidance as its principal purpose. If this box is checked, attach an explanation (see instructions).

For Paperwork Reduction Act Notice, see page 4.   Cat. No. 12311A   Form **8824** (2005)

Form 8824 (2005)   Page **2**

Name(s) shown on tax return. Do not enter name and social security number if shown on other side.

H. James & Mary T. Snodgrass

Your social security number: 483 12 0000

Part III — Realized Gain or (Loss), Recognized Gain, and Basis of Like-Kind Property Received

Caution: *If you transferred and received (a) more than one group of like-kind properties or (b) cash or other (not like-kind) property, see Reporting of multi-asset exchanges in the instructions.*

Note: *Complete lines 12 through 14 only if you gave up property that was not like-kind. Otherwise, go to line 15.*

12 Fair market value (FMV) of other property given up **12**

13 Adjusted basis of other property given up **13**

14 Gain or (loss) recognized on other property given up. Subtract line 13 from line 12. Report the gain or (loss) in the same manner as if the exchange had been a sale **14**

Caution: *If the property given up was used previously or partly as a home, see Property used as home in the instructions.*

15 Cash received, FMV of other property received, plus net liabilities assumed by other party, reduced (but not below zero) by any exchange expenses you incurred (see instructions) **15**   31,138

16 FMV of like-kind property you received **16**   31,138

17 Add lines 15 and 16 . . . . **17**

18 Adjusted basis of like-kind property you gave up, net amounts paid to other party, plus any exchange expenses **not** used on line 15 (see instructions) **18**   22,925

19 **Realized gain or (loss).** Subtract line 18 from line 17 . . . . . . **19**   8,213

20 Enter the smaller of line 15 or line 19, but not less than zero **20**   0

21 Ordinary income under recapture rules. Enter here and on Form 4797, line 16 (see instructions) . **21**

22 Subtract line 21 from line 20. If zero or less, enter -0-. If more than zero, enter here and on Schedule D or Form 4797, unless the installment method applies (see instructions) **22**   0

23 **Recognized gain.** Add lines 21 and 22 . . . . **23**   0

24 **Deferred gain or (loss).** Subtract line 23 from line 19. If a related party exchange, see instructions **24**   8,213

25 Basis of like-kind property received. Subtract line 15 from the sum of lines 18 and 23 . . . **25**   22,925

Part IV — Deferral of Gain From Section 1043 Conflict-of-Interest Sales

Note: *This part is to be used only by officers or employees of the executive branch of the Federal Government for reporting nonrecognition of gain under section 1043 on the sale of property to comply with the conflict-of-interest requirements. This part can be used only if the cost of the replacement property is more than the basis of the divested property.*

26 Enter the number from the upper right corner of your certificate of divestiture. (**Do not attach a copy of your certificate. Keep the certificate with your records.**). . . . . . ▶   ─

27 Description of divested property ▶

28 Description of replacement property ▶

29 Date divested property was sold (month, day, year) . . . . . . **29**   / /

30 Sales price of divested property (see instructions) **30**

31 Basis of divested property **31**

32 **Realized gain.** Subtract line 31 from line 30 . . . . . . **32**

33 Cost of replacement property purchased within 60 days after date of sale **33**

34 Subtract line 33 from line 30. If zero or less, enter -0- **34**

35 Ordinary income under recapture rules. Enter here and on Form 4797, line 10 (see instructions) . **35**

36 Subtract line 35 from line 34. If zero or less, enter -0-. If more than zero, enter here and on Schedule D or Form 4797 (see instructions) **36**

37 **Deferred gain.** Subtract the sum of lines 35 and 36 from line 32 . . . . **37**

38 Basis of replacement property. Subtract line 37 from line 33 . . . . . **38**

Form **8824** (2005)

Without Accountable Reimbursement Plan

Attach to Schedule or Form **Form 2106**

Description of Property	N or U	Date Acquired	Cost or Other Basis	Bus %	Business Basis	Sec 179 Exp.	Basis Before Bonus Depreciation Allowance	30%/50% Bonus Depr. Allowance	Adjusted Basis	Prior Depr.	Class Life	Method Used	Life or Rec'y Period	Year 2005	%	Year 20__	%	Year 20__	%
Total Amount of Sec. 179 Expensing, 30% or 50% Bonus Depreciation Claimed Each Year														649					
Library	N	1/01	533	100%	533		533		533	366	7	DDB½	7	48	8.93				
Library	N	1/02	400	100%	400		400	120	280	158	7	DDB½	7	35	12.49				
Library	N	1/03	366	100%	366		366	110	256	100	7	DDB½	7	45	17.49				
Equipment	N	8/11/03	538	100%	538		538	269	269	104	7	DDB½	7	47	17.49				
Library	N	1/04	496	100%	496		496	248	248	35	7	DDB½	7	61	24.49				
Library	N	1/05	649	100%	649	649	0				7	DDB½	7	0	14.29				
Fax Machine	N	7/17/05	529	100%	529		529		529		5	DDB½	5	106	20.00				
TOTAL			**3,511**											**991**					

Note: Land cannot be depreciated. Enter land value on separate line in "Cost or Other Basis" column only.

Form 4562
Department of the Treasury — Internal Revenue Service

Depreciation and Amortization
(Including Information on Listed Property)
► See separate instructions. ► Attach to your tax return.

OMB No. 1545-0172
2005
Attachment Sequence No. **67**

Name(s) shown on return: **H. James & Mary T. Snodgrass**
Business or activity to which this form relates: **Form 2106**
Identifying number: **483 12 0000**

Part I Election To Expense Certain Property Under Section 179
Note: If you have any listed property, complete Part V before you complete Part I.

1	Maximum amount. See the instructions for a higher limit for certain businesses	$105,000
2	Total cost of section 179 property placed in service (see instructions)	649
3	Threshold cost of section 179 property before reduction in limitation	$420,000
4	Reduction in limitation. Subtract line 3 from line 2. If zero or less, enter -0-	0
5	Dollar limitation for tax year. Subtract line 4 from line 1. If zero or less, enter -0-. If married filing separately, see instructions	105,000

(a) Description of property	(b) Cost (business use only)	(c) Elected cost
6 Library	649	649

7	Listed property. Enter the amount from line 29	7
8	Total elected cost of section 179 property. Add amounts in column (c), lines 6 and 7	649
9	Tentative deduction. Enter the smaller of line 5 or line 8	649
10	Carryover of disallowed deduction from line 13 of your 2004 Form 4562	0
11	Business income limitation. Enter the smaller of business income (not less than zero) or line 5 (see instructions)	81,291
12	Section 179 expense deduction. Add lines 9 and 10, but do not enter more than line 11	649
13	Carryover of disallowed deduction to 2006. Add lines 9 and 10, less line 12 ► 13	0

Note: Do not use Part II or Part III below for listed property. Instead, use Part V.

Part II Special Depreciation Allowance and Other Depreciation (Do not include listed property.) (See instructions.)

14	Special allowance for certain aircraft, certain property with a long production period, and qualified New York Liberty Zone property (other than listed property) placed in service during the tax year	
15	Property subject to section 168(f)(1) election	
16	Other depreciation (including ACRS)	

Part III MACRS Depreciation (Do not include listed property.) (See instructions.)

Section A

17	MACRS deductions for assets placed in service in tax years beginning before 2005	236
18	If you are electing to group any assets placed in service during the tax year into one or more general asset accounts, check here ► ☐	

Section B—Assets Placed in Service During 2005 Tax Year Using the General Depreciation System

(a) Classification of property	(b) Month and year placed in service	(c) Basis for depreciation (business/investment use only—see instructions)	(d) Recovery period	(e) Convention	(f) Method	(g) Depreciation deduction
19a 3-year property						
b 5-year property		529	5	HY	200DB	106
c 7-year property						
d 10-year property						
e 15-year property						
f 20-year property						
g 25-year property			25 yrs.		S/L	
h Residential rental property			27.5 yrs.	MM	S/L	
			27.5 yrs.	MM	S/L	
i Nonresidential real property			39 yrs.	MM	S/L	
				MM	S/L	

Section C—Assets Placed in Service During 2005 Tax Year Using the Alternative Depreciation System

20a Class life					S/L	
b 12-year			12 yrs.		S/L	
c 40-year			40 yrs.	MM	S/L	

Part IV Summary (see instructions)

21	Listed property. Enter amount from line 28	21
22	Total. Add amounts from line 12, lines 14 through 17, lines 19 and 20 in column (g), and line 21. Enter here and on the appropriate lines of your return. Partnerships and S corporations—see instr.	991
23	For assets shown above and placed in service during the current year, enter the portion of the basis attributable to section 263A costs 23	

For Paperwork Reduction Act Notice, see separate instructions.   Cat. No. 12906N   Form **4562** (2005)

Without Accountable Reimbursement Plan

WORKSHEET TO COMPUTE AUTO BASIS

FORMULA FOR COMPUTING GAIN OR LOSS WHEN USE IS PART BUSINESS AND PART PERSONAL:

		DESCRIPTION OF AUTO	
		DATE ACQUIRED	1/6/02
		YEAR	2002
		MAKE	Cadillac DeVille
			NEW or USED (circle one)

1. Odometer reading when traded (old car) .... 86206 Miles
2. Odometer reading when acquired (old car) .... 80 Miles
3. Total miles owned while owned (line 1 less line 2) ...... 86126 Miles
4. Business miles driven while owned (line D) .... 57286 Miles
5. Average business % while owned (line 4 divided by line 3) ... 66.51 %
6. Purchase price of old car (list price) .... $
7. Trade-in allowance towards new car or Sales price ...... $(12,000)
8. **Difference** (line 6 less line 7) .... $
9. Business portion (line 8 times line 5) .... $
10. Gain or loss on previous trade-in (if none, enter zero) .... $ _____ 0
11. Balance of lines 9 and 10 (subtract gain or add loss) ... $
12. Depreciation and expensing allowed or allowable (use worksheet below) ... $
13. Gain or loss on business portion .... $ 1,684   Gain or (Loss) (circle one)
    (Gain when line 12 is greater than line 11)
    (Loss when line 11 is greater than line 12)
14. Purchase price of new car .... $ 42,700 List price + $ 2,135 Sales Tax = $ 46,835 Total

A. Odometer reading end of year
B. Odometer reading beginning of year
C. Total miles driven during year (A minus B)
D. Business miles from log
E. Business % (D divided by C)
F. Multiply line 14 by E
G. Basis for depreciation ....
   (Balance of line 13 and F;
   Subtract gain, Add loss)

	2002 1st Year	2003 2nd Year	2004 3rd Year	2005 4th Year	5th Year	6th Year
A.	24,825	52,466	78,784	88,544		
B.	0	24,825	52,466	78,784		
C.	24,825	27,641	26,318	9,760		
D.	17,403	18,044	16,891	5,320		
E.	70.10 %	65.28 %	64.18 %	54.51 %	%	%
F.	$32,833	$30,574	$30,059	$25,529	$	$
G.	$34,517	$32,258	$31,743	$32,213	$	$

Year	Basis From (G)	(H) Expensing Sec. 179	(I) Adjusted Basis	(J) Bonus Depr. Allowance	(K) Adjusted Basis	(L) Class Life	(M) Method Used	(N) Life or RP	(O) Act Opt	(P) Depreciation Computed	(Q) Depreciation Limit	(R) Depreciation Allowed	(S) Depreciation Recapture
2002	34,517		34,517	10,355	24,162	5	DDB½	20.00	Act	15,187	5,370	5,370	
2003	32,258		32,258	10,355	21,903	5	DDB½	32.00	Act	7,009	3,199	3,199	
2004	31,743		31,743	10,355	21,388	5	DDB½	19.20	Act	4,106	1,893	1,893	
2005	27,213		27,213	10,355	16,858	5	DDB½	11.52	Act	* 971	484	484	

* Half-year convention in the year of trade or sale: $1,942 x ½ =$971

General Instructions:

Lines 1 through 11: Enter information from previous auto's worksheet if there has been a trade. Leave blank if newly acquired auto is the result of an outright purchase.

Line 12: Depreciation allowed or allowable is computed as follows:
Actual Depreciation or optional "factor" [see ¶ (P)] ... $
Plus Expensing - Sec. 179 & Special Depreciation Allowance ... $
Total to be taken to line 12 ... $

Line 13: If auto is sold, take Gain or Loss to Form 4797. If trade, complete form 8824.

(H) An election in year of purchase, reduce basis each year by amount claimed in year of purchase. Since 6-18-84, luxury auto rules severely limit the use of Code Sec. 179 expensing for autos.

(I) Adjusted basis - Line G minus Column (H).

(J) 30% or 50% of Column (I) in the year of purchase. A special bonus depreciation allowance deduction may be elected equal to 30% or 50% of the depreciable basis after any Sec.179 expensing but before figuring regular depreciation deduction under MACRS. To qualify, the auto must have been: (1) bought new; (2) bought after 9/10/01 for 30%, after 5/5/03 for 50%; (3) began using for business after 9/10/01 (30%) and 5/5/03 (50%) used it more than 50% qualified business use.

(K) Adjusted basis - Column (I) minus Column (J). (Basis used for depreciation computation.)

(L) When actual expenses are used, enter "5" for autos purchased after 12-31-86.
When optional method is used, leave blank.

(M) Indicate MACRS percentage method by using "DDB".
Indicate conventions by "½" or "¼". If 40% of purchases are after 9-30, you must use mid-quarter convention.
Indicate Straight Line method by "SL".

(N) When MACRS percentage method is chosen, enter % used.
When MACRS straight line is chosen, enter 5 years.
When optional method was chosen in 1st year and you have switched to actual, enter the life chosen according to useful life.

(O) Indicate whether depreciation computation in Column (P) is actual method "A" or optional method "O". If optional, indicate whether 7, 7½, 8, 10, 10½, 11, 11½, 12¢, 14¢, 15¢, 16¢, or 17¢ rate is used. ("O-11½" or "O-17").

(P) **COMPUTE ACTUAL DEPRECIATION AS FOLLOWS:**

MACRS percentage method: After 12-31-86 - Column (I) multiplied by:

Year	Mid-year	Mid-quarter (1st)	Mid-quarter (2nd)	Mid-quarter (3rd)	Mid-quarter (4th)
1	20%	35%	25%	15%	5%
2	32%	26%	30%	34%	38%
3	19.20%	15.60%	18%	20.40%	22.80%
4	11.52%	11.01%	11.37%	12.24%	13.68%
5	11.52%	11.01%	11.37%	11.30%	10.94%
6	5.76%	1.38%	4.26%	7.06%	9.58%

MACRS straight line method: Column (I) divided by 5 years. First year is either ½ year or mid-quarter convention.

When business use is 50% or less, only 5 year straight line can be computed for autos purchased since 6-18-84.

If Code Sec. 179 expensing has been elected, add Column (H) to actual depreciation.

Since 1-1-81, if you choose actual depreciation in year of purchase, you must continue to use actual as long as you own that car.

COMPUTE OPTIONAL DEPRECIATION FACTOR AS FOLLOWS:

1990 thru 2004: All business miles multiplied by 11¢ in 1990-91; 11½¢ in 1992-93; 12¢ in 1994-99; 14¢ in 2000; 15¢ in 2001-02; 16¢ in 2003-04.

2005: All business miles multiplied by 17¢.

If optional method is elected in the 1st year, it carries with it the election to exclude the auto from the MACRS method of depreciation.
As "non-recovery" property, depreciation is required to be computed as straight line over the useful life in any year election is changed to actual method.
As "non-recovery" property, you may choose actual or optional method each year.

(Q) Luxury auto limitations for depreciation:

Date Auto Placed in Service

	1-1-91 thru 12-31-91	1-1-92 thru 12-31-92	1-1-93 thru 12-31-93	1-1-94 thru 12-31-94	1-1-95 thru 12-31-96	1-1-97 thru 12-31-97	1-1-98 thru 12-31-98	1-1-99 thru 12-31-99	1-1-00 thru 9-10-01	9-11-01 thru 5-4-03	5-5-03 thru 12-31-03	1-1-04 thru 12-31-04	1-1-05 thru 12-31-05
1st year									30% Special Bonus Depreciation Allowance	$7,660	$10,710	$10,610	* 968
										50% Special Bonus Depreciation Allowance	$7,660		
2nd year	$2,660	$2,760	$2,860	$2,960	$3,060	$3,160	$3,060	$3,060	$3,060	$3,060	$4,900	$2,960	$2,960
3rd year	$4,300	$4,400	$4,700	$2,850	$4,900	$5,000	$5,000	$4,900	$4,900	$4,900	$4,900	$4,800	$4,800
4th-6th	$2,550	$2,650	$2,750	$1,675	$2,950	$3,050	$2,950	$2,950	$2,950	$2,950	$2,950	$2,850	$2,850
	$1,575	$1,575	$1,675		$1,775	$1,775	$1,775	$1,775	$1,775	$1,775	$1,775	$1,675	$1,675

Date Auto Placed in Service   1 / 6 / 02

Year	Amount from Table		Business %		Depr. Limit
1st	$ 7,660	X	70.10 %	= $	5,370
2nd	$ 4,900	X	65.28 %	= $	3,199
3rd	$ 2,950	X	64.18 %	= $	1,893

Year	Amount from Table		Business %		Depr. Limit
4th	$ 1,775	X	54.51 %	= $	* 968
5th		X	%	= $	
6th		X	%	= $	

* Half-year conversion: $968 x ½ = $484

of [ ] Years Owned

(R) Enter the smallest of Column (P) or (Q). In year of purchase, the smallest of Columns (H) + (J) + (P) or (Q). Also, enter this amount on Form 2106.

(S) Autos purchased after 6-18-84: Depreciation Recapture or "pay back" is to be computed if an auto was more than 50% business use in year of purchase, but drops below 50% business use in any future year when a method of accelerated depreciation was used. You must include in gross income the difference between depreciation, Code Section 179 expensing, and Special Depreciation Allowance claimed and the amount of depreciation recomputed at the 5 year straight line method. You must continue using 5 year straight line in the year of purchase.
When this happens, get another worksheet, figure the 5 year SL, and use it for the rest of the auto's life. Employees enter the income on Form 1040, line 21; Ministers also include in computation for Social Security; Self employed taxpayers on Sch. C, line 6; Farmers on Sch. F, line 10.

Without Accountable Reimbursement Plan

1/05

WORKSHEET TO COMPUTE AUTO BASIS

FORMULA FOR COMPUTING GAIN OR LOSS WHEN USE IS PART BUSINESS AND PART PERSONAL:

DESCRIPTION OF AUTO		
DATE ACQUIRED	3/10/05	
YEAR	2005	
MAKE	Lexus GS 300	
NEW or USED *(circle one)*		

1. Odometer reading when traded *(old car)* .... 88,544 Miles
2. Odometer reading when acquired *(old car)* .... 0 Miles
3. Total miles driven while owned *(line 1 less line 2)* .... 88,544 Miles
4. Business miles driven while owned *(line D)* .... 57,658 Miles
5. Average business % while owned *(line 4 divided by line 3)* .... 65.12 %
6. Purchase price of old car *(list price)* .... $ 46,835
7. Trade-in allowance towards new car or Sales price .... $(20,000)
8. **Difference** *(line 6 less line 7)* .... $ 26,835
9. Business portion *(line 8 times line 5)* .... $ 17,475
10. Gain or loss on previous trade-in *(if none, enter zero)* .... $ 1,684
11. Balance of lines 9 and 10 *(subtract gain or add loss)* .... $ 19,159
12. Depreciation and expensing allowed or allowable *(use worksheet below)* .... $ 10,946
13. Gain or loss on business portion
    (Gain when line 12 is greater than line 11)
    (Loss when line 11 is greater than line 12) .... $ 8,213 Gain or Loss *(circle one)*
14. Purchase price of new car .... $ 45,100 List price + $ 2,706 Sales Tax = $ 47,806 Total

A. Odometer reading end of year 23,888
B. Odometer reading beginning of year 0
C. Total miles driven during year *(A minus B)* 23,888
D. Business miles from log 15,559
E. Business % *(D divided by C)* .... 65.13 %
F. Multiply line 14 by E .... $ 31,138
G. Basis for depreciation .... $ 22,925
   (Balance of line 13 and F;
   Subtract gain. Add loss)

Year	Basis From (G)	(H) Expensing Sec. 179	(I) Adjusted Basis	(J) Bonus Depr. Allowance	(K) Adjusted Basis	(L) Class Life	(M) Method Used	(N) Life or RP	(O) Act Opt	(P) Depreciation Computed	(Q) Depreciation Limit	(R) Depreciation Allowed	(S) Depreciation Recapture
2005	22,925	22,925	22,925		22,925	5	SL½	10.00	Opt	2,645		2,645	

Note - Actual Depreciation would have been as follows:

| | 22,925 | 22,925 | 22,925 | | 22,925 | 5 | 65.13 % | | Act | 2293 | 1,928 | 1,928 | |
| | | | | | | | | | | | 1,928 | | 1,928 |

General Instructions:

Lines 1 through 11: Enter information from previous auto's worksheet if there has been a trade. Leave blank if newly acquired auto is the result of an outright purchase.

Line 12: Depreciation allowed or allowable is computed as follows:
Actual Depreciation or optional "factor" [see ¶ (P)] .... $ 10,946
Plus Expensing - Sec. 179 & Special Depreciation Allowance .... $
Total to be taken to line 12 .... $ 10,946

Line 13: If auto is sold, take Gain or Loss to Form 4797. If trade, complete form 8824.

(H) An election in year of purchase, reduce basis each year by amount claimed in year of purchase. Since 6-18-84, luxury auto rules severely limit the use of Code Sec. 179 expensing Column (H).

(I) Adjusted basis - Line G minus Column (H).

(J) 30% or 50% of Column (I) in the year of purchase. A special bonus depreciation allowance deduction may be elected equal to 30% or 50% of the depreciable basis after any Sec.179 expensing but before figuring regular depreciation deduction under MACRS. To qualify, the auto must have been: (1) bought new; (2) bought after 9/10/01 for 30%, after 5/5/03 for 50%; (3) began using for business after 9/10/01 (30%) and 5/5/03 (50%) used it more than 50% qualified business use.

(K) Adjusted basis - Column (I) minus Column (J). (Basis used for depreciation computation.)

(L) When actual expenses are used, enter "5" for autos purchased after 12-31-86.
When optional method is used, leave blank.

(M) Indicate MACRS percentage method by using "DDB".
Indicate conventions by "½" or "¼". If 40% of purchases are after 9-30, you must use mid-quarter convention.
Indicate Straight Line method by "SL".

(N) When MACRS straight line is chosen, enter % used.
When MACRS percentage method is chosen, enter 5 years.

(O) When optional method was chosen in 1st year and you have switched to actual, enter the life chosen according to useful life.
Indicate whether depreciation computation in Column (P) is actual method "A" or optional method "O". If optional, indicate whether 7, 7½, 8, 10, 10½, 11, 11½, 12¢, 14¢, 15¢, 16¢, or 17¢ rate is used. ("O-11½" or "O-17").

(P) **COMPUTE ACTUAL DEPRECIATION AS FOLLOWS:**

MACRS percentage method: After 12-31-86 - Column (I) multiplied by:

Year	Mid-year	Mid-quarter (1st)	Mid-quarter (2nd)	Mid-quarter (3rd)	Mid-quarter (4th)
1	20%	35%	25%	15%	5%
2	32%	26%	30%	34%	38%
3	19.20%	15.60%	18%	20.40%	22.80%
4	11.52%	11.01%	11.37%	12.24%	13.68%
5	11.52%	11.01%	11.37%	11.30%	10.94%
6	5.76%	1.38%	4.26%	7.06%	9.58%

MACRS straight line method: Column (I) divided by 5 years. First year is either ½ year or mid-quarter convention.

When business use is 50% or less, only 5 year straight line can be computed for autos purchased since 6-18-84.

If Code Sec. 179 expensing has been elected, add Column (H) to actual depreciation.

Since 1-1-81, if you choose actual depreciation in year of purchase, you must continue to use actual as long as you own that car.

COMPUTE OPTIONAL DEPRECIATION FACTOR AS FOLLOWS:

1990 thru 2004: All business miles multiplied by 11¢ in 1990-91; 11½¢ in 1992-93; 12¢ in 1994-99; 14¢ in 2000; 15¢ in 2001-02; 16¢ in 2003-04.

2005: All business miles multiplied by 17¢.

If optional method is elected in the 1st year, it carries with it the election to exclude the auto from the MACRS method of depreciation.
As "non-recovery" property, depreciation is required to be computed as straight line over the useful life in any year election is changed to actual method.
As "non-recovery" property, you may choose actual or optional method each year.

(Q) Luxury auto limitations for depreciation:

Date Auto Placed in Service

Year	1-1-91 thru 12-31-91	1-1-92 thru 12-31-92	1-1-93 thru 12-31-93	1-1-94 thru 12-31-94	1-1-95 thru 12-31-96	1-1-97 thru 12-31-97	1-1-98 thru 12-31-98	1-1-99 thru 12-31-99	1-1-00 thru 12-31-00	1-1-01 thru 9-10-01	9-11-01 thru 5-4-03	5-5-03 thru 12-31-03	1-1-04 thru 12-31-04	1-1-05 thru 12-31-05
1st year											30% Special Bonus Depreciation Allowance	$7,660	$10,610	$2,960
									50% Special Bonus Depreciation Allowance			$7,660		$2,960
2nd year	$2,660	$2,760	$2,860	$2,960	$3,060	$3,160	$3,060	$3,060	$3,060	$3,060	$3,060	$3,060	$2,960	$4,800
3rd year	$4,300	$4,400	$4,600	$4,700	$4,900	$5,000	$5,000	$5,000	$4,900	$4,900	$4,900	$4,900	$4,800	$2,850
4th-6th	$2,550	$2,650	$2,750	$2,850	$2,950	$3,050	$2,950	$2,950	$2,950	$2,950	$2,950	$2,950	$2,850	$1,675
	$1,575	$1,575	$1,675	$1,675	$1,775	$1,775	$1,775	$1,775	$1,775	$1,775	$1,775	$1,775	$1,675	

Date Auto Placed in Service   3 / 10 / 05

Year	Amount from Table		Business %		Depr. Limit	Year	Amount from Table		Business %		Depr. Limit
1st	$	2,960	X	65.13 %	= $	1,928	4th	$			% = $	
2nd	$		X		% = $		5th	$			% = $	
3rd	$		X		% = $		6th	$			% = $	

# of Years Owned

(R) Enter the smallest of Column (P) or (Q). In year of purchase, the smallest of Columns (H) + (J) + (P) or (Q). Also, enter this amount on Form 2106.

(S) Autos purchased after 6-18-84: Depreciation Recapture or "pay back" is to be computed if an auto was used more than 50% business use in year of purchase, but drops below 50% business use in any future year when a method of accelerated depreciation was used. You must include in gross income the difference between depreciation, Code Section 179 expensing, and Special Depreciation Allowance claimed and the amount of depreciation recomputed at the 5 year straight line method. You must continue using 5 year straight line even if business use rises back above 50%.
When this happens, get another worksheet, figure the 5 year SL on it and use it for the rest of the auto's life. Employees enter the income on Form 1040, line 21; Ministers also include in computation for Social Security. Self employed taxpayers on Sch. C, line 6; Farmers on Sch. F, line 10.

With Accountable Reimbursement Plan

Form 1040 (2005)   Page 2

Tax and Credits

Line	Description	Amount
38	Amount from line 37 (adjusted gross income)	66,238
39a	Check if: You were born before January 2, 1941, Blind. Spouse was born before January 2, 1941, Blind. Total boxes checked ▶ 39a	
39b	If your spouse itemizes on a separate return or you were a dual-status alien, see page 31 and check here ▶ 39b	
40	Itemized deductions (from Schedule A) or your standard deduction (see left margin)	18,408
41	Subtract line 40 from line 38	47,830
42	If line 38 is $109,475 or less, multiply $3,200 by the total number of exemptions claimed on line 6d. If line 38 is over $109,475, see the worksheet on page 33	16,000
43	Taxable income. Subtract line 42 from line 41. If line 42 is more than line 41, enter -0-	31,830
44	Tax (see page 33). Check if any tax is from: a ☐ Form(s) 8814 b ☐ Form 4972	4,044
45	Alternative minimum tax (see page 35). Attach Form 6251	
46	Add lines 44 and 45 ▶	4,044
47	Foreign tax credit. Attach Form 1116 if required	
48	Credit for child and dependent care expenses. Attach Form 2441	
49	Credit for the elderly or the disabled. Attach Schedule R	
50	Education credits. Attach Form 8863	
51	Retirement savings contributions credit. Attach Form 8880	
52	Child tax credit (see page 37). Attach Form 8901 if required	2,000
53	Adoption credit. Attach Form 8839	
54	Credits from: a ☐ Form 8396 b ☐ Form 8859	
55	Other credits. Check applicable box(es): a ☐ Form 3800 b ☐ Form 8801 c ☐ Specify	
56	Add lines 47 through 55. These are your total credits	2,000
57	Subtract line 56 from line 46. If line 56 is more than line 46, enter -0- ▶	2,044

Other Taxes

Line	Description	Amount
58	Self-employment tax. Attach Schedule SE	6,331
59	Social security and Medicare tax on tip income not reported to employer. Attach Form 4137	
60	Additional tax on IRAs, other qualified retirement plans, etc. Attach Form 5329 if required	
61	Advance earned income credit payments from Form(s) W-2	
62	Household employment taxes. Attach Schedule H	
63	Add lines 57 through 62. This is your total tax ▶	8,375

Payments

Line	Description	Amount
64	Federal income tax withheld from Forms W-2 and 1099	9,406
65	2005 estimated tax payments and amount applied from 2004 return	
66a	Earned income credit (EIC)	
66b	Nontaxable combat pay election ▶ 66b	
67	Excess social security and tier 1 RRTA tax withheld (see page 54)	
68	Additional child tax credit. Attach Form 8812	
69	Amount paid with request for extension to file (see page 54)	
70	Payments from: a ☐ Form 2439 b ☐ Form 4136 c ☐ Form 8885	
71	Add lines 64, 65, 66a, and 67 through 70. These are your total payments ▶	9,406

Refund

72	If line 71 is more than line 63, subtract line 63 from line 71. This is the amount you overpaid	1,031
73a	Amount of line 72 you want refunded to you ▶	1,031
▶b	Routing number ▶c Type: ☐ Checking ☐ Savings	
▶d	Account number	
74	Amount of line 72 you want applied to your 2006 estimated tax ▶ 74	

Amount You Owe

75	Amount you owe. Subtract line 71 from line 63. For details on how to pay, see page 55 ▶	
76	Estimated tax penalty (see page 55)	

Third Party Designee

Do you want to allow another person to discuss this return with the IRS (see page 56)? ☐ Yes. Complete the following. ☐ No

Sign Here

Under penalties of perjury, I declare that I have examined this return and accompanying schedules and statements, and to the best of my knowledge and belief, they are true, correct, and complete. Declaration of preparer (other than taxpayer) is based on all information of which preparer has any knowledge.

Your occupation: Minister
Spouse's occupation: Nurse

Paid Preparer's Use Only

Form 1040 (2005)

Form **1040** Department of the Treasury—Internal Revenue Service (99)

U.S. Individual Income Tax Return 2005 OMB No. 1545-0074 IRS Use Only—Do not write or staple in this space.

For the year Jan. 1–Dec. 31, 2005, or other tax year beginning , 2005, ending , 20

Label

Your first name and initial: H. James   Last name: Snodgrass
Your social security number: 483 12 0000

If a joint return, spouse's first name and initial: Mary T.   Last name: Snodgrass
Spouse's social security number: 483 15 0000

Home address (number and street): 2309 E. Smith Street
City, town or post office, state, and ZIP code: South Bend, IN 46617

Checking a box below will not change your tax or refund.
Presidential Election Campaign ▶ Check here if you, or your spouse if filing jointly, want $3 to go to this fund (see page 16). ▶ ☑ You ☑ Spouse

Filing Status

- 1 ☐ Single
- 2 ☑ Married filing jointly (even if only one had income)
- 3 ☐ Married filing separately. Enter spouse's SSN above and full name here. ▶
- 4 ☐ Head of household (with qualifying person). (See page 17.) If the qualifying person is a child but not your dependent, enter this child's name here. ▶
- 5 ☐ Qualifying widow(er) with dependent child (see page 17)

Exemptions

- 6a ☑ Yourself. If someone can claim you as a dependent, do not check box 6a
- b ☑ Spouse
- c Dependents:

(1) First name Last name	(2) Dependent's social security number	(3) Dependent's relationship to you	(4)✓ if qualifying child for child tax credit (see page 18)
Ruth A Snodgrass	483 13 0000	Child	☑
Thomas A Snodgrass	485 14 0000	Child	☑
Samuel A Snodgrass	486 15 0000	Child	☑

Boxes checked on 6a and 6b: 2
No. of children on 6c who: lived with you: 3
Add numbers on lines above ▶: 5

d Total number of exemptions claimed

Income

7	Wages, salaries, tips, etc. Attach Form(s) W-2 Excess Parsonage Allowance 7,517	68,795
8a	Taxable interest. Attach Schedule B if required	609
8b	Tax-exempt interest. Do not include on line 8a	
9a	Ordinary dividends. Attach Schedule B if required	
9b	Qualified dividends (see page 20)	
10	Taxable refunds, credits, or offsets of state and local income taxes (see page 20)	
11	Alimony received	
12	Business income or (loss). Attach Schedule C or C-EZ	
13	Capital gain or (loss). Attach Schedule D if required. If not required, check here ▶ ☐	
14	Other gains or (losses). Attach Form 4797	
15a	IRA distributions 15a b Taxable amount (see page 22) 15b	
16a	Pensions and annuities 16a b Taxable amount (see page 22) 16b	
17	Rental real estate, royalties, partnerships, S corporations, trusts, etc. Attach Schedule E	
18	Farm income or (loss). Attach Schedule F	
19	Unemployment compensation	
20a	Social security benefits 20a b Taxable amount (see page 24) 20b	
21	Other income. List type and amount (see page 24)	
22	Add the amounts in the far right column for lines 7 through 21. This is your total income ▶	69,404

Adjusted Gross Income

23	Educator expenses (see page 26) 23	
24	Certain business expenses of reservists, performing artists, and fee-basis government officials. Attach Form 2106 or 2106-EZ 24	
25	Health savings account deduction. Attach Form 8889 25	
26	Moving expenses. Attach Form 3903 26	
27	One-half of self-employment tax. Attach Schedule SE 27	3,166
28	Self-employed SEP, SIMPLE, and qualified plans 28	
29	Self-employed health insurance deduction (see page XX) 29	
30	Penalty on early withdrawal of savings 30	
31a	Alimony paid b Recipient's SSN ▶ 31a	
32	IRA deduction (see page XX) 32	
33	Student loan interest deduction (see page XX) 33	
34	Tuition and fees deduction (see page XX) 34	
35	Domestic production activities deduction. Attach Form 8903 35	
36	Add lines 23 through 31a and 32 through 35	3,166
37	Subtract line 36 from line 22. This is your adjusted gross income ▶	66,238

For Disclosure, Privacy Act, and Paperwork Reduction Act Notice, see page 75.   Cat. No. 11320B   Form **1040** (2005)

(Box: Rev Snodgrass.......... $21,000   Mrs. Snodgrass....... $40,278   Excess Parsonage...... $7,517)

With Accountable Reimbursement Plan

SCHEDULE A&B (Form 1040)

Schedule A—Itemized Deductions
(Schedule B is on back)

Department of the Treasury — Internal Revenue Service (99)
▶ Attach to Form 1040. ▶ See Instructions for Schedules A and B (Form 1040).

OMB No. 1545-0074 — 2005 — Attachment Sequence No. 07

Name(s) shown on Form 1040: **H. James & Mary T. Snodgrass**
Your social security number: 483 12 0000

Line 5 computation below:
State withholdings ($1,080 + $1,301) $2,381
Local withholdings ($264 + $306) .... $ 570
State tax paid last spring .... $ 152

Medical and Dental Expenses
Caution. Do not include expenses reimbursed or paid by others.
1 Medical and dental expenses (see page A-2)	1	
2 Enter amount from Form 1040, line 38	2	
3 Multiply line 2 by 7.5% (.075)	3	
4 Subtract line 3 from line 1. If line 3 is more than line 1, enter -0-	4	

Taxes You Paid (See page A-2.)
5 State and local (check only one box): a ☐ Income taxes, or b ☐ General sales taxes (see page A-2)	5	3,103
6 Real estate taxes (see page A-2)	6	1,182
7 Personal property taxes	7	534
8 Other taxes. List type and amount ▶	8	
9 Add lines 5 through 8	9	4,819

Interest You Paid (See page A-3.)
Note. Personal interest is not deductible.
10 Home mortgage interest and points reported to you on Form 1098	10	8,081
11 Home mortgage interest not reported to you on Form 1098. If paid to the person from whom you bought the home, see page A-4 and show that person's name, identifying no., and address ▶	11	
12 Points not reported to you on Form 1098. See page A-4 for special rules	12	
13 Investment interest. Attach Form 4952 if required. (See page A-4.)	13	
14 Add lines 10 through 13	14	8,081

Gifts to Charity
If you made a gift and got a benefit for it, see page A-4.
15 Gifts by cash or check. If you made any gift of $250 or more, see page A-4.	15	5,508
16 Other than by cash or check. If any gift of $250 or more, see page A-4. You must attach Form 8283 if over $500	16	
17 Carryover from prior year	17	
18 Add lines 15 through 17	18	5,508

Casualty and Theft Losses
19 Casualty or theft loss(es). Attach Form 4684. (See page A-5.)	19	

Job Expenses and Most Other Miscellaneous Deductions (See page A-5.)
20 Unreimbursed employee expenses—job travel, union dues, job education, etc. Attach Form 2106 or 2106-EZ if required. (See page A-6.) ▶ Nursing Exp. 510	20	510
21 Tax preparation fees	21	153
22 Other expenses—investment, safe deposit box, etc. List type and amount ▶	22	
23 Add lines 20 through 22	23	663
24 Enter amount from Form 1040, line 38	24	66,238
25 Multiply line 24 by 2% (.02)	25	1,325
26 Subtract line 25 from line 23. If line 25 is more than line 23, enter -0-	26	0

Other Miscellaneous Deductions
27 Other—from list on page A-6. List type and amount ▶	27	

Total Itemized Deductions
28 Is Form 1040, line 38, over $145,950 (over $72,975 if married filing separately)? ☐ No. Your deduction is not limited. Add the amounts in the far right column for lines 4 through 27. Also, enter this amount on Form 1040, line 40. ☐ Yes. Your deduction may be limited. See page A-6 for the amount to enter.	28	18,408

29 If you elect to itemize deductions even though they are less than your standard deduction, check here ▶ ☐

For Paperwork Reduction Act Notice, see Form 1040 instructions. — Cat. No. 11330X — Schedule A (Form 1040) 2005

SCHEDULE C-EZ (Form 1040)

Net Profit From Business
(Sole Proprietorship)

Department of the Treasury — Internal Revenue Service
▶ Partnerships, joint ventures, etc., must file Form 1065 or 1065-B.
▶ Attach to Form 1040 or 1041. ▶ See instructions on back.

OMB No. 1545-0074 — 2005 — Attachment Sequence No. 09A

Name of proprietor: **H. James Snodgrass**
Social security number (SSN): 483 12 0000

Part I — General Information

You May Use Schedule C-EZ Instead of Schedule C Only If You:
- Had business expenses of $5,000 or less.
- Use the cash method of accounting.
- Did not have an inventory at any time during the year.
- Did not have a net loss from your business.
- Had only one business as either a sole proprietor or statutory employee.

And You:
- Had no employees during the year.
- Are not required to file Form 4562, Depreciation and Amortization, for this business. See the instructions for Schedule C, line 13, on page C-4 to find out if you must file.
- Do not deduct expenses for business use of your home.
- Do not have prior year unallowed passive activity losses from this business.

A Principal business or profession, including product or service: **Honorariums**
B Enter code from pages C-7, 8, & 9 ▶ 8 1 3 0 0 0
C Business name. If no separate business name, leave blank.
D Employer ID number (EIN), if any
E Business address (including suite or room no.). Address not required if same as on Form 1040, page 1.
City, town or post office, state, and ZIP code

Part II — Figure Your Net Profit

1 Gross receipts. Caution. If this income was reported to you on Form W-2 and the "Statutory employee" box on that form was checked, see Statutory Employees in the instructions for Schedule C, line 1, on page C-3 and check here ☐	1	690
2 Total expenses (see instructions). If more than $5,000, you must use Schedule C. — *$126 of expense less $45 disallowed*	2	81
3 Net profit. Subtract line 2 from line 1. If less than zero, you must use Schedule C. Enter on Form 1040, line 12, and also on Schedule SE, line 2. (Statutory employees do not report this amount on Schedule SE, line 2. Estates and trusts, enter on Form 1041, line 3.)	3	609

Part III — Information on Your Vehicle. Complete this part only if you are claiming car or truck expenses on line 2.

4 When did you place your vehicle in service for business purposes? (month, day, year) ▶ / /
5 Of the total number of miles you drove your vehicle during 2005, enter the number of miles you used your vehicle for:
a Business _____ b Commuting (see instructions) _____ c Other _____
6 Do you (or your spouse) have another vehicle available for personal use? ☐ Yes ☐ No
7 Was your vehicle available for personal use during off-duty hours? ☐ Yes ☐ No
8a Do you have evidence to support your deduction? ☐ Yes ☐ No
b If "Yes," is the evidence written? ☐ Yes ☐ No

For Paperwork Reduction Act Notice, see Form 1040 instructions. — Cat. No. 14374D — Schedule C-EZ (Form 1040) 2005

With Accountable Reimbursement Plan

SCHEDULE SE (Form 1040)

Department of the Treasury Internal Revenue Service

Self-Employment Tax

▶ Attach to Form 1040. ▶ See Instructions for Schedule SE (Form 1040).

OMB No. 1545-0074   **2005**   Attachment Sequence No. 17

Name of person with self-employment income (as shown on Form 1040): **H. James Snodgrass**

Social security number of person with self-employment income ▶ 483 : 12 : 0000

Who Must File Schedule SE

You must file Schedule SE if:

- You had net earnings from self-employment from **other than** church employee income (line 4 of Short Schedule SE or line 4c of Long Schedule SE) of $400 or more **or**
- You had church employee income of $108.28 or more. Income from services you performed as a minister or a member of a religious order is **not** church employee income (see page SE-1).

Note. Even if you had a loss or a small amount of income from self-employment, it may be to your benefit to file Schedule SE and use either "optional method" in Part II of Long Schedule SE (see page SE-3).

Exception. If your only self-employment income was from earnings as a minister, member of a religious order, or Christian Science practitioner **and** you filed Form 4361 and received IRS approval not to be taxed on those earnings, **do not** file Schedule SE. Instead, write "Exempt-Form 4361" on Form 1040, line 58.

May I Use Short Schedule SE or Must I Use Long Schedule SE?

Did You Receive Wages or Tips in 2005?

Are you a minister, member of a religious order, or Christian Science practitioner who received IRS approval **not** to be taxed on earnings from these sources, **but** owe self-employment tax on other earnings? — No / Yes

Are you using one of the optional methods to figure your net earnings (see page SE-3)? — No / Yes

Did you receive church employee income reported on Form W-2? — No / Yes

Was the total of your wages and tips subject to social security or railroad retirement tax **plus** your net earnings from self-employment more than $90,000? — No / Yes

Did you receive tips subject to social security or Medicare tax that you **did not** report to your employer? — No / Yes

You May Use Short Schedule SE Below

You Must Use Long Schedule SE on page 2

Section A—Short Schedule SE. Caution. Read above to see if you can use Short Schedule SE.

1	Net farm profit or (loss) from Schedule F, line 36, and farm partnerships, Schedule K-1 (Form 1065), box 14, code A	1
2	Net profit or (loss) from Schedule C, line 31; Schedule C-EZ, line 3; Schedule K-1 (Form 1065), box 14, code A (other than farming); and Schedule K-1 (Form 1065-B), box 9. Ministers and members of religious orders, see page SE-1 for amounts to report on this line. See page SE-2 for other income to report **$44,196 from "Worksheet to Be Used with Form 2106" + $609 from Sch. C**	2 44,805
3	Combine lines 1 and 2	3 44,805
4	**Net earnings from self-employment.** Multiply line 3 by 92.35% (.9235). If less than $400, **do not** file this schedule; you do not owe self-employment tax	4 41,377
5	**Self-employment tax.** If the amount on line 4 is: • $90,000 or less, multiply line 4 by 15.3% (.153). Enter the result here and on **Form 1040, line 58.** • More than $90,000, multiply line 4 by 2.9% (.029). Then, add $11,160.00 to the result. Enter the total here and on **Form 1040, line 58.**	5 6,331
6	**Deduction for one-half of self-employment tax.** Multiply line 5 by 50% (.5). Enter the result here and on **Form 1040, line 27**	6 3,166

For Paperwork Reduction Act Notice, see Form 1040 instructions.   Cat. No. 11358Z   Schedule SE (Form 1040) 2005

WORKSHEET TO BE USED WITH FORM 2106

Name: **H. James Snodgrass**   Year 2005

Social Security Number: 483 12 0000   Filed Form 4361? Yes ☐ No ☑

Part A - Computation of Business Expenses

Use this section in conjunction with Form 2106 (or 2106-EZ) or to figure your net social security base.

Auto Expense	Vehicle 1	Vehicle 2
1. Total Miles Driven	9,760	23,888
2. Total Business Miles	5,320	15,559
3. % of Business Use (Line 1/Line 2)	54.51%	65.13%
4. Lease Payments		
5. Inclusion Amount		
6. Subtract Line 5 from Line 4		
7. Gas, Oil, Lubrication		
8. Repairs		
9. Tires & Batteries		
10. Insurance & Auto Club		
11. Miscellaneous		
12. Washing & Polishing		
13. License (Registration Only)		
14. Add Lines 6 through 13		
15. Multiply Line 14 by Line 3		
16. Depreciation		
17. Total Actual Exp (Line 15 + 16)		
18. Optional Method (Line 2 x Standard Mileage Rate)		
19. Interest	158	481
20. Personal Property Tax		456
21. Line 19 + Line 20	158	937
22. Line 21 x Line 3 (To Line 6 of Social Security Base Computation)	86	610

Local Travel Expense	Amount
23. Parking	
24. Tolls	
25. Fares	
26. Total (Enter on Form 2106-EZ, Part II, Ln 2 or Form 2106, Part Ln 2)	

Overnight Travel Exp.	Amount
27. Auto Rental, Taxi	
28. Fares (air, train, bus)	
29. Parking & Tolls	
30. Laundry & Cleaning	
31. Lodging	
32. Telephone, Postage, Fax, etc.	
33. Tips other than meals	
34. Total (Enter on Form 2106-EZ, Part II, Ln 3 or Form 2106, Part Ln 3)	

Meals & Entertainment	Amount
35. Meals Away Overnight ☐ Actual ☐ Per Diem	
36. Entertainment Meals	
37. Entertainment, Other	
38. Tips for Meals	
39. Total (Enter on Form 2106-EZ, Part II, Ln 5 or Form 2106, Part Ln 5)	

Professional Expense	Amount
40. Business-In-Home	
41. Education Expense	
42. Equipment Depreciation	
43. Office Supplies & Postage	
44. Religious Materials	
45. Seminars & Dues	
46. Subscriptions & Paperbacks	
47. Business Telephone & Internet Use	
48. Gifts	
49. Other	
50. Total (Enter on Form 2106-EZ, Part I, Ln 4 & Form 2106, Part I, Ln 4)	

Unreimbursed Expenses	Amount
51. Auto Expense (Ln 17 or Ln 18)	
52. Local Travel (Ln 26)	
53. Overnight Travel (Ln 34)	
54. Professional Expense (Ln 50)	
55. Total of Lines 51 through 54	
56. Reimbursement for Auto, Travel, & Prof.	
57. Unreimbursed Auto Travel & Prof (Ln 55 - Ln 56)	
58. Meals & Entertainment (Ln 39)	
59. Reimbursement for M & E	
60. Unreimbursed M & E (Ln 58 - Ln 59)	
61. Deductible M & E (% of Ln 60)	
62. Total Unreimbursed Exp (Ln 57 + Ln 61)	

Part B - Unreimbursed Expense Allocation (Sec. 265)

Use if filing Form 2106 or Sch. C or C-EZ and claiming expense deductions

	A. Taxable Compensation	B. Total Compensation
1. Wages from W-2	21,000	21,000
2. Unused Parsonage Allowance	7,517	
3. Parsonage Allowance Designated		24,000
4. FRV of Parsonage Provided		
5. Gross Income / Sch C or C-EZ	690	690
6. Recapture of Auto Depreciation		
7. Total for Columns A & B	29,207	45,690
8. Inclusion Percentage (Ln 7 Col. A Divided by Col. B)		63.92%

Employee Business Expenses	Amount
9. Expense from Form 2106-EZ, Ln 6 or Form 2106, Ln 10	
10. Inclusion % from Ln 8	63.92%
11. Deductible Expenses to Sch A, Ln 20 (Ln 9 x Ln 10)	
12. Expenses Disallowed (Ln 9 - Ln 11)	

Sch C or Sch C-EZ	Amount
13. Total Expense from Sch C or C-EZ	126
14. Inclusion % from Ln 8	63.92%
15. Deductible Expense (Ln 13 x Ln 14)	81
16. Expenses Disallowed (Ln 13 - Ln 15)	45

Part C - Computation of Social Security Base

If exempt, omit

	Amount
1. Salary from W-2	21,000
2. Value of Parsonage Provided	
3. Parsonage Allowance (Part D, Ln 16)	24,000
4. Recapture of Auto Depreciation	
5. Less Business Portion of Tax Prep.	(63)
6. Less Expenses Disallowed (Ln 13 x Ln 14)	(696)
7. Less Business % of Auto (Part B, Ln 16)	(45)
8. Less Unreimbursed Bus Exp (Form 2106 or Part A, Ln 62)	
9. Total (Enter on Sch SE)	44,196

Part D - Computation of Parsonage Allowance

If you own your home, use both Columns A & B. Otherwise, use Column B only.

	First Home		Second Home	
	Column A FRV Computation	Column B Expenses Paid by Minister	Column A FRV Computation	Column B Expenses Paid by Minister
Value of Parsonage Provided by Church				
FMV of Home Owned	150,000			
1. Fair Rental Value of Home Owned	18,000			
2. Fair Rental Value of Furnishings	5,400			
3. Rent Paid				
4. Closing Costs / Downpayment				
5. Principal Payments		835		
6. Real Estate Taxes		1,182		
7. Mortgage Interest		8,081		
8. Insurance		340		
9. Repairs & Upkeep		793		
10. Furniture, Appliances, etc.		1,409		
11. Decorator Items		463		463
12. Utilities		2,738		2,738
13. Miscellaneous Supplies		642		642
14. Total		27243	16,483	16,483
15. Lesser of Line 14, Column A (if applicable) or Column B				16,483
16. Amount Designated	Pension ☐	24,000	Pension ☐	24,000
17. If Line 16 is greater than Line 15, enter the difference here and as income on Form 1040, Line 7; or If amount designated is included in error on W-2, enter the lesser of Line 15 or Line 16 as a deduction on Form 1040, Line 21				7,517

☐ Prior Client
☐ New Client

CHECKLIST
Income Tax Data

Year _____

This Checklist Will Serve as a Guide in Assembling Your Tax Data and Help You to Take Advantage of All Allowable Deductions. Round off All Figures to the Nearest Even Dollar.

Taxpayer			Spouse (if joint)		
Last Name			Last Name		
First Name and Initial		Presidential Campaign?	First Name and Initial		Presidential Campaign?
Occupation	Blind?	☐ Yes ☐ No	Occupation	Blind?	☐ Yes ☐ No
Social Security Number	Birth Date		Social Security Number	Birth Date	
Indiana Only County of Residence (Jan. 1)	County of Work (Jan.1)		**Indiana Only** County of Residence (Jan. 1)	County of Work (Jan. 1)	

Address on Tax Return			Shipping Address (leave blank if the same)		
Street Address or P.O. Box			Street Address or P.O. Box		
City	State	Zip	City	State	Zip

Miscellaneous Information		
County of Residence (as of 12/31)	Township or City (as of 12/31)	School District Name (as of 12/31)

Contact Information		
Home Phone	Business Phone	Cell Phone
Fax	E-Mail	Best Time to Reach

Payment & Shipping Information (U.P.S. Requires Street Address)

CHECK HOW YOU WANT TO PAY:

☐ Send Complete Returns C.O.D.

☐ Charge to My Bank Card

☐ Send Invoice, Hold Returns Until You Receive Payment

CHECK HOW TO SEND:

☐ First Class Mail

☐ United Parcel Service

☐ American Express   ☐ Discover   ☐ MasterCard   ☐ Visa

Expiration
Month   Year

Charge this order to my Charge Account as I have indicated to be paid according to the current terms of that Account.

Signature _____

(Authorized credit card signature)

Compliments of . . .

WORTH TAX & FINANCIAL SERVICE

LOCATION:	MAIL TO:	PHONE:
Home Office	Just East of Bob Evans	P.O. Box 725	574●267●4687
Warsaw / Winona Lake, IN	3201 E. Center St.	Winona Lake, IN 46590	800●368●0363 Fax
worth1040@yahoo.com	Warsaw, IN 46582		574●267●2870 Fax

Dependents ● *Must have Social Security Number, ATIN, or ITIN*

First, Initial, Last	Date of Birth	Social Security #	Relationship	Months in Home	Full-Time Student*
					☐
					☐
					☐
					☐
					☐
					☐
					☐
					☐

* If dependent is 19 or over, check box if full-time student for at least 5 months of calendar year. See page 5 to list education expenses for either Hope Credit or Lifetime Learning Credit.

Estimated Tax Paid ● *Send copies of canceled checks*

		Federal		State		Local	
Name of State\Local							
Prior Year Credit							
1st Quarter	Amount						
	Date Paid						
2nd Quarter	Amount						
	Date Paid						
3rd Quarter	Amount						
	Date Paid						
4th Quarter	Amount						
	Date Paid						
Exten-sion	Amount						
	Date Paid						

Wages from W-2 ● *Enclose all copies of W-2 statements. If clergy, send a copy of payroll sheet.*

H/W	Employer	Wage	Fed Tax	FICA	Medicare	State	Local

IRA Distributions Received ● *Enclose all statements - 1099R & 5498*

H/W	Source & Type	Fed Tax	Amount	Value of Acc't (12/31)

Yes	No	
☐	☐	Were proceeds used for expenses as a first-time home buyer? (Did not own home for two years preceding purchase)
☐	☐	Were proceeds used to pay for higher education costs? (If yes, list on page 5)

Pension & Annuity Income Received ● *Enclose all statements - 1099R*

H/W	Source & Type	Fed Tax	Gross Amount	Taxable Amount

Interest Income ● *Enclose all 1099 statements. Indicate H for husband, W for wife, J for joint*

HWJ	Institution	Forfeiture*	Amount	HWJ	Institution	Forfeiture*	Amount
					Municipal Bond Int.		

Interest income from seller-financed mortgage for which no 1099-Int was issued:

HWJ	Name	Address	Social Security #	Amount

* Penalty on early withdrawal (Forfeiture)

Dividend Income ● *Enclose all 1099 statements and annual summaries*

HWJ	Name of Payor	Ordinary Dividends	Qualified Dividends	Total Capital Gain Distributions	Post-May 5 Capital Gain Distributions	5-year Capital Gain

Other Income

● *If income from Partnership, S-Corp.. Estate or Trust, enclose K-1*

Source (if Single enter in first "Amount" column)	Husband Amount	Wife Amount
Social Security Benefits		
Alimony Received (enclose copy of divorce decree)		
Baby Sitting (if expenses, enter on page 8, Sch C)		
Directors Fees		
Hobbies		
Jury Duty		
Odd Jobs (if expenses, enter on page 8, Sch C)		
Prizes and Awards		
Royalties (i.e. Book, Oil & Gas, etc.) Type _____		
State Refund (if itemized previous year)		
City or Local Refund (if itemized previous year)		
Tips not reported to employer		
Unemployment Compensation		
Honorariums (if expenses, enter on page 8, Sch C)		
Lottery, Gambling Sch A Losses ( )		
Other		

Itemized Deductions - Medical　　　Amount Reimbursed by Insurance $_____

Type of Expense	Amount	Type of Expense	Amount	Type of Expense	Amount
Insurance Premiums		Ambulance		Nursing Home	
Medicare Premiums		Artificial Teeth		Air Conditioner (Prescribed)	
Long-Term Care Prem		Eye Glasses		Humidifier (Prescribed)	
Prescriptions		Hearing Aid		Electricity / AC & Humidifier	
Insulin		Batteries / Hearing		Auto Travel (miles)	
Doctors		Lab Fees		Miles after 8/31/05	
Dentists		Special Shoes		Transportation	
Chiropractors		X-Rays		Lodging	
Hospitals		Supplies (Prescribed)		Other	

Taxes ● *Enclose Closing Statement for real estate purchased or sold during year*

Type of Tax	Amount	Type of Tax	Amount
Paid with State Return		Real Estate Tax #1	
Paid with Local Return		Real Estate Tax #2	
4th qtr state/local estimate (due in 1/15)		Auto Excise	
Sales Tax (not including motor vehicles)		Personal Property Tax	
Sales Tax on Motor Vehicles & Boats			

Interest Paid

Home Interest	Amount	Mortgage Interest Paid to Individual			
		Name	**Address**	**Social Security #**	**Amount**
1st Mortgage					
2nd Mortgage					
Line of Credit		**Points Paid**			
Vacation Home		New ...... ☐	**Date of Loan**	**# Years of Loan**	**Amount**
Investment Interest	**Amount**	Refinanced ☐			
				Other Interest	
			Student Loan Int.		

Contributions

Cash				Noncash (Total is $500 or Less)	
To Whom	**Amount**	**To Whom**	**Amount**	**To Whom**	**Amount**
Church		Other		Supplies	
				FMV Furniture	
Red Cross\Scouts				FMV Clothing	
Salvation Army				Other	
United Fund				**Travel**	
Missions				Mileage	
Radio Broadcasts				Lodging, Fares	
*College				Meals	
* Enter Name of College:		Date of Contribution:		Other	

Noncash Contributions (Total is More Than $500)							
Donee Organization Name/Address	Description of Items Donated	Date of Contribution	Date Acquired (m/yr)	How Acquired	Cost Basis	Fair Market Value	Method Used to Determine FMV

Note: For any items more than $5,000, additional information will be needed. Appraisal is generally required except for certain securities.

Itemized Deductions - Miscellaneous Deductions

H/W	Type of Expense	Amount	H/W	Type of Expense	Amount
	**Tax Preparation & Job Related Expenses** *(Teachers, see next section; Ministers, use page 7)*				
	Tax Preparation			Uniforms	
	Accounting Books			Cleaning of Uniforms	
	Union Dues			Small Tools	
	Professional Fees			Equipment	
	Professional Publications			Business Telephone	
	Supplies for Job			Employment Agency Fee	
	Safety Equipment			Other	
	Safety Clothing				
	Special Shoes/Nylons				
		**Teaching Expenses**			
	Supplies			Other	
	Books				
		**Job Hunting Expenses**			
	Meals			Postage, Typing	
	Lodging			Toll Calls	
	Airfare, Auto Rental			Other	
	Auto Travel (miles)				
		**Investment Expenses**			
	Publications			Escrow Fees	
	Broker Fees			Other	
	Safe Deposit Box				
		**Miles Between Two Jobs**			
	Number of days worked 2 jobs in same day			Number of miles between the two jobs sites	

Casualty or Theft

Description of Property	Date Acquired	Date of Casualty or Theft	Cost	FMV Before	FMV After	Insurance Reimbursement

Education Expenses ● Hope Credit, Lifetime Learning Credit or Job-Related Expenses

First Name of student - Husband, Wife, or dependent				
Name of School (Hope, Lifetime)				
Date(s) Tuition Paid (Hope, Lifetime)				
Type of Education - College, Vocational, Job Related, etc				
Was student enrolled at least half-time for at least one academic period in a program leading to a degree certificate, or other recognized credential? (Hope, Lifetime)	☐Yes ☐ No	☐Yes ☐ No	☐Yes ☐ No	☐Yes ☐ No
Was student in first or second year of post-secondary education? (Hope, Lifetime)	☐Yes ☐ No	☐Yes ☐ No	☐Yes ☐ No	☐Yes ☐ No
Scholarships, Grants or Amount Reimbursed by Employer				
Tuition & Fees (Hope, Lifetime, Job-related)				
Books (Hope & Lifetime - only if condition of enrollment)				
Supplies (Hope & Lifetime - only if condition of enrollment)				
	**Job Related Education Expenses**				
Auto Miles (list details under "Auto Expense", page 7)				
Lodging / Room & Board				
Meals while away from home overnight				
Were you employed while incurring expense?	☐Yes ☐ No	☐Yes ☐ No	☐Yes ☐ No	☐Yes ☐ No
Had you already met minimum requirements of your job?	☐Yes ☐ No	☐Yes ☐ No	☐Yes ☐ No	☐Yes ☐ No
Did course(s) improve job skills or required by employer or by law to keep present salary or position?	☐Yes ☐ No	☐Yes ☐ No	☐Yes ☐ No	☐Yes ☐ No
Did the course(s) lead to a new profession or business?	☐Yes ☐ No	☐Yes ☐ No	☐Yes ☐ No	☐Yes ☐ No

Clergy Information ● *Please provide copy of payroll sheet and/or breakdown of your compensation package.*

Position _____   Ordained, Licensed, or equivalent *(circle one)*

Yes	No	
☐	☐	Are you exempt from paying Social Security? *(If yes, send copy of approved Form 4361)*
☐	☐	Have you adequately accounted to your employer and been reimbursed for your professional expenses? *(If no, show details on next page)*
☐	☐	To the best of your knowledge is your W-2 prepared correctly? If no, what is incorrect?
☐	☐	Did you receive any gifts, bonuses, and allowances (other than parsonage allowance) from your employer that was not included as taxable on your W-2? If yes, what?

Amount? _____

$ _____ Parsonage Allowance officially designated in advance?

$ _____ If more than one employer during the year, amount designated with second employer?

$ _____ Amount you receive each payday? How often are you paid? _____

$ _____ Amount you receive monthly?

Parsonage Information ● *Parsonage allowance exclusion can apply to only one home at a time, the one that is your personal residence. During a transition or move, you may have incurred parsonage expenses for two homes. Separate the expenses below.*

	Home #1	Home #2	Home #3
If employer provided parsonage, what is its rental value?			
If you own, what is current fair market value of home?			
Date occupied	/ /	/ /	/ /
Location (city & state)			
Type of Expenses Paid by You	**Amount**	**Amount**	**Amount**
Rent Paid			
Principal Payments			
Taxes			
Interest			
Insurance			
Repairs and Upkeep			
Furniture / Appliances			
Decorator Items			
Utilities			
Miscellaneous Supplies and Expenses			

Moving Expenses ● *Qualified moving expenses include only the cost of moving household goods and personal effects as well as yourself and your family. Any amounts reimbursed for meals, house hunting, temporary living expenses, purchasing or selling home, etc. do not qualify and should be included as taxable on Form W-2.*

Amount Reimbursed or Paid Directly by Employer $ _____

Yes	No		
☐	☐	Was any of the amount reimbursed for nonqualifying moving expenses? If yes, how much?	$ _____
☐	☐	Was any or all of the reimbursement included on Form W-2, box 1? If yes, how much?	$ _____

_____ Distance between former residence and new job?   Date of Departure? ___ / ___ / ___

_____ Distance between former residence and former job?   Date of Arrival? ___ / ___ / ___

Expenses	Amount
Cost of moving furniture and personal effects	
Transportation of family: Auto Travel - total miles	miles
Auto miles driven after 8/31/05	miles
Fares *(air, bus, train, etc.)*	
Cost of Lodging En route	

Auto Expenses

Amount Reimbursed $_____

- If multiple business use for same auto, list mileage for each use in separate column.
- If new client, send complete history of business use of auto. Send copies of invoice and complete details of purchase and/or trade for each business auto. Even if you have always used standard mileage rate, you may have a taxable gain or deductible loss on the sale of a business auto that must be reported. If leasing, give beginning value.

Auto Information	Auto #1	Auto #2	Auto #3	Auto #4	Auto #5	Auto #6
Year						
Make						
Date of Purchase						
Purchase Price (plus sales tax)						
Odometer at Purchase						
Odometer at End of Year						
Type of Use (Clergy, Sch C, etc.)						
Total Miles for the Year						
Total Business Miles for Year						
Total Business Miles after 8/31/05						
Daily Round Trip Commuting Miles						
Commuting Miles for the Year						
Auto Lease Payments						
Garage Rent						
Gas, Oil, Lube						
Repairs						
Tires & Battery						
Insurance & Auto Club						
Miscellaneous						
Washing & Polishing						
License (Registration Only)						
Interest						
Personal Property Tax						

Yes	No	
☐	☐	Do you (or your spouse) have another vehicle available for personal use?
☐	☐	Was the vehicle available for personal use during off-duty hours?
☐	☐	Do you have written evidence to support your deduction?
☐	☐	If "Yes", is the evidence written?
☐	☐	Was the vehicle used primarily by a more than 5% owner or related person? (Sch C, E, F, only)

Travel & Professional Expenses

Amount Reimbursed $_____

Local Travel		Travel - While Away from Home Overnight		Professional Expenses	
Expense	Amount	Expense	Amount	Expense	Amount
Parking		Auto Rental / taxi / etc.		Education expenses	
Tolls		Fares (air / train / bus)		Office Supplies & Postage	
Fares		Parking & Tolls		Religious Materials	
Meals & Entertainment		Laundry & Cleaning		Seminars & Dues	
Meals/Away Overnight		Lodging		Subscriptions & Paperbacks	
# Days Away Overnight		Telephone, Postage, Fax		Business Telephone	
Entertainment, Meals		Tips (Other than meals)		Gifts	
Entertainment, Other		Other		Other	
Tips for Meals					

Equipment & Library					
Date	Description	Amount	Date	Description	Amount

Business Income & Expense: Schedule C

Principle Activity /Product or Service _____

H/W /J *(If single leave blank)* _____   Business Name & Address _____

Accounting Method: Employer Identification Number (9 digits) _ _ - _ _ _ _ _ _ _

☐ Cash   ☐ Accrual   ☐ Other   **Inventory Method:**   ☐ Cost   ☐ Lower Cost or Market   ☐ Other

If Other _____   If Other _____

	Yes	No	
	☐	☐	Did you "materially participate" in the operation of the business?
	☐	☐	Did you start or acquire the business this year?
	☐	☐	Did you cease operation of the business during the year?
	☐	☐	Were you a statutory employee with income reported on Form W-2?

Receipts

Services		Honorariums		Other:	
Sales of Merchandise		Child Care		Beginning Acc't. Receivable	
Commissions		Other:		Ending Acc't Receivable	

Cost of Goods Sold

Beginning Inventory		Cost of Labor			
Purchases		Materials & Supplies			
Less Personal Use		Freight / Receiving		Beginning Acc't Payable	
Ending Inventory		Other:		Ending Accounts Payable	

Expenses ("Auto & Truck Exp." - Show details on page 125)

Accounting		Outside Services		Travel	
Advertising		Parking & Tolls		Meals & Entertainment	
Answering Service		Pension Plans		Uniforms	
Bad Debts from Sales		Postage		Utilities	
Bank Service Charges		Printing		Wages	
Auto & Truck Exp		Rent: Machinery & Equip.		Miscellaneous:	
Commissions		Rent: Other Business Prop			
Delivery & Freight		Repairs			
Dues & Subscriptions		Security			
Employee Benefits		Supplies			
Insurance		Taxes: Real Estate			
Interest: Mortgage		Taxes: Personal Property			
Interest: Other		Taxes: Sales			
Janitorial		Taxes: FICA & Medicare			
Laundry & Cleaning		Taxes: Unemployment			
Legal & Professional		Telephone			
Office Expense		Tools			

Business-In-Home *(Enter Cost of Home, Land Value, & Impovements in "Depreciation" Below)*

Total Square Feet in Home		Rent		Heat & Light	
Sq. Feet Used for Business		Interest		Repairs *(Entire House)*	
# of Hours *(Child Care Only)*		Taxes		Repairs *(Business Portion)*	
# of Months of Bus. Activity		Insurance		Other	

Depreciation of Buildings & Equipment
(Send Depreciation Schedule for Prior Owned Items from Previous Year's Return)

Date Placed in Service	Description	Amount	Date Placed in Service	Description	Amount

Sale of Property, Stock: Schedule D

H/W/J	Description	# of Shares	Date Acquired	Date Sold	Gross Sales Price	Cost or Other Basis	Expense of Sale

Installment Sale

- *If contract began this year, send copies of contract, amortization schedule (list principal and interest), original purchase closing statement, cost of all improvements.*
- *Enter Interest on page 3, "Seller-Financed Mortgage".*

Description	Date Acquired	Date Sold	Gross Profit Percentage	Principal Received This Year	Principal Received Prior Years

Sale of Personal Residence ● *Send copies of closing statement for purchase and sale of home.*

- *If home was used as main home for 2 out of the last 5 years and gain on its sale is less than $250,000 ($500,000 jointly owned), the sale is not required to be reported on your federal return unless there was depreciation taken on home for business usage.*

Date Purchased Home ___ / ___ / ___   Date Sold Home ___ / ___ / ___

Yes No

☐ ☐ Did you own and use property as your main home for a total of at least 2 years of the 5-year period before the sale?

☐ ☐ If no, did you sell the home because of a change in health or a change in employment?

If yes, enter dates that you did use as main home: From ___ / ___ / ___   To ___ / ___ / ___

Description	Amount	Description	Amount
Original Cost		Sales Price	
Improvements:		Expense of Sale	
		Gain Postpone from Previous Sale	
		Casualty Losses Previously Allowed	
		Depreciation for Previous Business Use	

Child and Dependent Care   Employer-Provided Dependent Care Benefits $_____

● *You are required to file Sch H if amounts paid to any person working in your home is $1,300 or more in a calendar year.*

Persons or Organizations Providing the Care *(Nursery & Kindergarten school expenses may qualify).*			
Name	Address	SSN or EIN	Amount

Qualifying Person(s) for Whom Expenses Were Paid *(The total of the "Amount" column above and below should equal)*				
Name of Dependent	Age	Relationship	Social Security #	Amount

Rental Income and Expense: Schedule E

Kind & Location of Property

#1 _____

#2 _____

#3 _____

#4 _____

#5 _____

#6 _____

	#1	#2	#3	#4	#5	#6
Did you actively participate in the management of your rentals?	☐ Yes ☐ No	☐ Yes ☐ No	☐ Yes ☐ No	☐ Yes ☐ No	☐ Yes ☐ No	☐ Yes ☐ No
Did you or your family use the property for personal purposes for more than the greater of 14 days or 10% of the total days rented at fair rental value?	☐ Yes ☐ No	☐ Yes ☐ No	☐ Yes ☐ No	☐ Yes ☐ No	☐ Yes ☐ No	☐ Yes ☐ No
Date Rental Activity Began	/ /	/ /	/ /	/ /	/ /	/ /
Rents Received						

Expenses

	#1	#2	#3	#4	#5	#6
Advertising						
Association Dues						
Auto - Travel (Show details page 7)						
Cleaning and Maintenance						
Commissions						
Gardening						
Insurance						
Legal & Professional						
License & Permits						
Management Fees						
Mortgage Interest (Form 1098)						
Other Interest						
Painting & Decorating						
Pest Control						
Plumbing & Electrical						
Repairs						
Supplies						
Taxes - Real Estate						
Taxes - Other						
Telephone						
Utilities						
Wages & Salaries						
Lot Rent						
Other						

Depreciation of Building, Major Improvements, Furniture

Date	Description	Property #	Amount	Date	Description	Property #	Amount

Farm Income & Expense: Schedule F

Location and Size of Farm _____

Principal Product _____

Employer Identification Number (9 digits) __ __ - __ __ __ __ __ __ __   Accounting Method: ☐ Cash   ☐ Accrual

☐ **Yes** ☐ **No** Did you "materially participate" in the operation of this business during the year?

☐ **Yes** ☐ **No** Do you elect, or did you previously elect, to currently deduct certain preproductive period expense.

Income ● *(Do not include sales of livestock held for draft, breeding, sport, or dairy purposes. Report them in "Sales ..." section below.)*			
Sales of Livestock for Resale		Crop Insurance Proceeds	
Cost of Livestock for Resale	( )	Disaster Relief Payments	
Sales of Other Items for Resale		Custom Hire	
Cost of Other Items for Resale	( )	Federal Fuel Tax Credit	
Sales of Livestock You Raised		State Fuel Tax Credit	
Sales of Produce, Grain, Other You Raised		Other	
Patronage Dividends			
Agricultural Program Payments			
CCC Loans Reported Under Election			
CCC Loans Forfeited			

Expenses ("Car & Truck Exp." - Show details on page 125)					
Car & Truck Exp		Interest: Mortgage		Taxes: FICA & Unemployment	
Chemicals		Interest: Other		Utilities	
Conservation Exp		Labor Hired		Veterinary/Breeding/Medicine	
Custom Hire		Pension & Profit Sharing		Telephone	
Employee Benefit Programs		Rent: Vehicles/Machinery/Equip		Advertising/Accounting	
Feed Purchased		Rent: Other *(Land, Animals, Etc)*		Dues/Subscriptions	
Fertilizers & Lime		Repairs & Maintenance		Travel	
Freight & Trucking		Seeds & Plants Purchased		Meals & Entertainment	
Gasoline		Storage & Warehousing		Other	
# Gallons of Gas *(Off Road)*		Supplies			
Other Fuel & Oil		Taxes: Real Estate			
Insurance		Taxes: Personal Property			

Sales of Buildings, Machinery, Equipment, & Livestock Held for Draft, Breeding, Sport, or Dairy						
Description	Date Acquired	Date Sold	Sales Price	Cost	Depreciation Claimed	Expense of Sale

Depreciation of Buildings, Machinery, Equipment, & Livestock Held for Draft, Breeding, Sport, or Dairy *(Send Depreciation Schedule for Prior Owned Items from Previous Year's Return)*					
Date Placed in Service	Description	Amount	Date Placed in Service	Description	Amount

Retirement Contributions to IRAs, Self-Employed Plans, & Salary Reduction Plans
● *If Single, use husband column*

Type of Plan	Husband Amount	Wife Amount	Type of Plan	Husband Amount	Wife Amount
Traditional IRA			Active Participant In Employer Provided Retirement Plan?	☐ Yes ☐ No	☐ Yes ☐ No
Roth IRA			401(k) Employee Contributions		
Self-Employed SEP			403(b) Employee Contributions		
Keough			SEP Employee Contributions		
Self-Employed SIMPLE			SIMPLE Employee Contributions		
Education IRA			Other Salary Reduction Contr.		

Health Savings Accounts (HSAs) & Archer Medical Saving Accounts (MSAs)
Type of coverage under high deductible health plan? . . . . ☐ Self-Only   ☐ Family
If applicable, spouse's type of coverage under high deductible health plan? . . . . ☐ Self-Only   ☐ Family

Contributions	Amount	Distributions	Amount
Deductible Amount of Health Insurance		Total Distributions from HSA or MSA	
Employer Contributions to HSA or MSA for Year		Rollover Distributions	
Employee Contributions to HSA or MSA for Year		Total Distributions from Medicare+Choice MSA	
Number of Full Months Plan was in Place for Year		Total Unreimbursed Qualified Medical Expenses	

Alimony Paid ● *Bring Copy of Divorce Decree*
To whom _____ Social Security Number _____ Amount $_____

Reside in Foreign Country During the Year?
Name of Country_____ Date entered ____ / ____ / ____ Date Left ____ / ____ / ____

Yes No
☐   ☐   Do you consider yourself a bonafide resident of this country?
☐   ☐   If no, were you (or do you anticipate being) physically present in this country for at least 330 days during a 365 day period?

Part-Year State Breakdown ● *If you resided in more than one state during the year, breakdown income associated with each state. Interest, dividends, capital gain distributions, alimony, IRA & pension distributions are normally taxable to the state of residence when received.*

Name of State	#1	#2		State #1	State #2
Dates Resided	From: To:	From: To:	Sch C Income		
Wages			Sch C Expense		
Interest			IRA Distributions		
Dividends			Pension Distr.		
Cap Gain Dist			Sch E Income		
Alimony			Sch E Expense		
			Other		

Questions, if yes explain below
Yes No
☐   ☐   Any births, adoptions, marriages, divorce or deaths in your family during the past year?
☐   ☐   Does anyone owe you money that has become a bad debt?
☐   ☐   Have you used bartering to exchange any goods and services?
☐   ☐   Did you or your spouse receive any source of income that is not listed in this checklist?
☐   ☐   Did you sell an auto, equipment, or any property? If yes, give details.
☐   ☐   Did you receive any nontaxable income such as child support, veteran's benefits, or welfare payments?

_____

_____

Taxpayer's Statement
The Information furnished herewith is to enable you to prepare my (our) income tax return for the stated year. It is true and complete to the best of my (our) knowledge and belief, and is to be relied upon by you accordingly.

Signature _____   Date _____

Signature _____   Date _____

INDEX

Professional Tax Record Book

- *Business Mileage Diary*
- *Auto Expense*
- *Travel Expense*
- *Professional Expense*
- *Entertainment Expense*
- *Housing Expense*
- *Professional Income*
- *Monthly Summary*

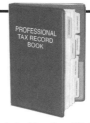

Refill Pages and Tabs without Binder

1 to 2	$17.99
3 to 14	$15.30
15 to 99	$14.40
100 or more	$10.80

Vinyl Binder with Pockets
Looseleaf — 160 Pages
6 Rings — Tab Dividers
Page Size — 3¾ X 6½

Complete Book with Binder

1 to 2	$24.99
3 to 14	$21.25
15 to 99	$19.99
100 or more	$14.99

Auto Log Book

- *Business Mileage Log and Auto Expense Only*
- *Durable Cover — 48 pages*
- *Handy Pocket Size*

1 to 2	$5.99
3 to 14	$5.10
15 to 99	$4.80
100 or more	$3.60

Minister's Compensation Package Tax & Financial Planning
with B. J. Worth

ONE HOUR AUDIO PRESENTATION of how to arrange a compensation package that provides good stewardship and how to legally lessen your tax burden and encourages financial planning for retirement.

Minister's CD or Audio Cassette

1 to 2	$10.99
3 to 14	$9.50
15 to 99	$8.80
100 or more	$6.60

Worksheet for Form 2106 for Ministers

Worksheet to Compute Auto Basis

Statement of Depreciation and Cost Recovery

1 Form	25¢
25 Forms	$3.00
50 Forms	$5.40
100 Forms	$9.00

Payroll Sheets for Employees of Non Profit Organizations

1 Sheet	50¢
25 Sheets	$6.00
50 Sheets	$10.80
100 Sheets	$18.00

Income Tax Guide for Ministers

Revised annually since 1973

1 to 2	$17.99
3 to 14	$15.30
15 to 99	$14.40
100 to 999	$10.80
1000 or more	call

Order Form • Fax, Call, Mail, or E-Mail

Fax: (800) 368-0363
Phone: (574) 267-4687
E-Mail: worth1040@yahoo.com

Name

Company or Church Name

Address

City, State, Zip

Send Order To:
Worth Tax & Financial Service
P.O. Box 725
Winona Lake, IN 46590

* Postage & Handling Schedule

$ 0 - $ 5.00	$ 2.00
$ 5.01 - $ 20.00	$ 7.00
$ 20.01 - $ 35.00	$ 8.00
$ 35.01 - $ 50.00	$ 9.00
$ 50.01 - $ 75.00	$11.00
$ 75.01 - $ 100.00	$13.00
$ 100.01 - $ 150.00	$15.00
$ 150.01 - $ 200.00	$17.00
Over $200.00	$20.00

Qty	Description	Unit Price	Total

Total	
6% Sales Tax (Indiana Only)	
*Postage & Handling	
Grand Total	

Method of Payment:
☐ Check enclosed. Make payable to: Worth Tax & Financial Service
☐ Charge to my credit card. Please enter phone number.

☐ Visa ☐ MasterCard ☐ American Express ☐ Discover

Expiration
Month   Year

Charge this order to my Charge Account as I have indicated to be paid according to current terms of that Account.

Authorized Credit Card Signature   Phone

Price Subject to Annual Change. Call for Current Prices.

CONSULTATIONS

We encourage your reading "Worth's Income Tax Law For Ministers" in its entirety. It will answer most of your questions.

We are available for consultation throughout the year and whether you are able to come to our office for an appointment or need to conduct the consultation by phone, or by letter, it is necessary for us to charge for our time. Our fee is $75.00 per hour for consultation.

We prefer phone consultations. Experience has shown us that requests for information and consultation by letter do not provide us with adequate facts. It is often necessary to call and ask for background and facts to give you the correct answer.

Up to 12 minutes -	$15.00
13 to 24 minutes -	$30.00
25 to 36 minutes -	$45.00
37 to 48 minutes -	$60.00
49 to 60 minutes -	$75.00

Please have your charge card number available or be prompt to send amount consultant requests. For brief informational calls there will be no charge.

PAYROLL SERVICE

We are available for payroll service. It is important to file all government payroll reports and to make deposits on time. Our comprehensive payroll service includes payroll check writing and the preparation of all payday, monthly, quarterly, and annual reports. If you want to write your own checks, then consider using our service for all reporting requirements. Call and ask for more information on how we can help you.

SEMINAR REGISTRATION INFORMATION

Those who attend seminars by Worth Tax & Financial Service are always enthusiastically thankful for the understandable presentation of how they can pay less tax legally. Call and ask for details on how you can sponsor a Seminar in your area.

Beverly J Worth will present seminars in person at the locations and times listed on the next page. **Registration** for this seminar is only **$109 per person** when pre-registered ($119.00 at the door.) **$20 off** seminar fee to spouse, or additional persons from same firm or organization. All seminar sessions are from 8:30 a.m. to 4:30 p.m.

* * * *

WORTH TAX & FINANCIAL SERVICE

- Specializes in tax preparation: Ministers and Payroll Reports (by mail or in person)
- Tax Consultations by phone or appointment (consultation fee based on the length of time)
- 403b's* • IRAs* • Mutual Funds* • Investments* • Lump Sum Distributions*

Jack W. and Beverly J. Worth
Registered Representatives

*Securities offered through H.D. Vest Investment Services[SM]
A non-bank subsidiary of Wells Fargo & Company, Member SIPC
6333 North State Highway 161, Fourth Floor, Irving, Texas 75038 · (972) 870-6000

WORTH TAX & FINANCIAL SERVICE • P.O. BOX 725 • WINONA LAKE, IN 46590

(574) 267-4687 • (800) 368-0363 (Fax)
E-mail: worth1040@yahoo.com

TAX SEMINARS
For Clergy and Non Profit Organizations
2006 Dates & Locations

Saturday .... Jan. 14, 2006
WARSAW, INDIANA
Holiday Inn Express
3825 Lake City Highway
(574) 268-1600
Driving Directions:
US 30 approximately
3 miles east of SR 15.

Friday .... February 17, 2006
INDIANAPOLIS, INDIANA
Holiday Inn Select - Airport
2501 South High School Road
(317) 244-6861
Driving Directions:
I-465 or I-70 to Airport Expressway
to Indianapolis International Airport.
Free 24-hour airport shuttle service.

Tuesday .... April 25, 2006
CHICAGO, ILLINOIS
Holiday Inn
860 W. Irving Park Rd. (Woodfield Area)
(630) 773-2340
Driving Directions:
I-290 west to Lake St., Exit #7. Exit Lake St. travel east to first intersection, Rohlwing Rd., north 3 stop lights to Irving Park Rd. Hotel on right.

For details, see page 142

More Seminars Coming!
Check for Dates & Locations on our website

Visit our website:
http://www.worthfinancial.com
• **Register online**
• **See all seminar details**

• **100% MONEY BACK GUARANTEE**
If you are dissatisfied with this program for any reason, a full tuition refund will be issued upon written request at the seminar.

Recommended for 8 Hours CPE credits
This seminar provides an overview of clergy taxes • No prerequisites required

Worth Tax & Financial Service is registered with the National Association of State Boards of Accountancy (NASBA) as a sponsor of continuing professional education on the National Registry of CPE Sponsors. State boards of accountancy have final authority on the acceptance of individual courses for CPE credit. Complaints regarding registered sponsors may be addressed to the National Registry of CPE Sponsors, 150 Fourth Avenue North, Suite 700, Nashville, TN 37219-2417. Web site: www.nasba.org

TAX PREPARATION BY MAIL

If you are a typical busy religious worker, you may want to let **Worth Tax & Financial Service** prepare your tax return by mail. We encourage you to take advantage of this special service. Our purpose is to be of service to you in any way possible to prevent a religious worker from being unnecessarily burdened by tax or financial problems.

WHAT YOU SHOULD SEND

1. If you are a minister - **Copy of your employer's PAYROLL RECORD**.
2. W-2s showing salaries, 1099s showing interest, dividends, etc., K-1s from partnerships, trusts, etc..
3. **COMPLETED CHECKLIST**. It is very important for you to carefully enter your income and deductions on the CHECKLIST provided in the back of this book. (**PDF version** is available on our website) Enter an expense only once. For example, if you enter your home interest under "Parsonage expense," do not enter it again under Schedule A. Keep your receipts and canceled checks.
4. Detailed auto expense for each auto. Send copies of purchase invoices and complete history of auto use. Complete questions on page 12 of CHECKLIST.
5. If you have purchased or sold real estate, send us photocopies of closing statements, contracts and 1099-Bs.
6. We have forms for federal and all states; you do not need to send your packets. If you want us to prepare **city or local** tax returns, **send** us the appropriate forms.
7. Copy of last year's tax return. If you feel your prior year's returns were not correctly prepared, it is possible to file Form 1040X and amend returns for 2002, 2003 and 2004. Corrections can result in substantial refunds or additional liability.
8. Enter your **E-mail address**, work, fax, and home phone numbers on page 1 of the CHECKLIST and tell us when it is best to reach you. If we feel we need further explanation of your data or that you did not send complete information **WE WILL CALL or E-mail. Calls must be at your expense. We will include the phone cost on the invoice for your return.**
9. Your return will be professionally prepared by a tax consultant on the computer and closely checked for accuracy and completeness.

TAX PREP FEES AND PAYMENT

Our fees are very reasonable and are based on the complexity of your return. The cost for a minister's return will average between $120.00 to $250.00. Extra State returns and/or several auto transactions creates a more complex return.

Tax preparation, consultation, and orders of books and supplies are all on a **CASH BASIS.** You may pay for our services as follows:

1. **AMERICAN EXPRESS, VISA, MASTERCARD and DISCOVER** convenience is available. Enter your number and expiration date on Page 1 of the Checklist.
2. Ask us to send invoice of fee and we will hold your return until we receive your check.
3. We can send your completed returns COD.

SHIPPING INFORMATION

Your finished return will be shipped by U.S. Priority Mail or United Parcel Service. If requesting UPS, be sure and give us a **STREET ADDRESS** as they cannot deliver to a post office box.

WORTH TAX & FINANCIAL SERVICE • P.O. BOX 725 • WINONA LAKE, IN 46590
STREET ADDRESS: 3201 E. CENTER STREET, WARSAW, IN 46582
(574) 267-4687 • (800) 368-0363 (Fax)
Alternate Fax (574) 267-2870
E-mail worth1040@yahoo.com

Visit our Web Site at http://www.worthfinancial.com